Palgrave Studies of Marketing in Emerging Economies

Series Editors
Robert E. Hinson
Durban University of Technology
University of Kigali
Kigali, Rwanda

Ogechi Adeola
Lagos Business School
Pan-Atlantic University
Lagos, Nigeria

This book series focuses on contemporary themes in marketing and marketing management research in emerging markets and developing economies. Books in the series cover the BRICS (Brazil, Russia, India, China and South Africa), MINT (Mexico, Indonesia, Nigeria and Turkey), CIVETS (Colombia, Indonesia, Vietnam, Egypt, Turkey, and South Africa); EAGLE economies (those which are expected to lead growth in the next ten years, such as Brazil, China, India, Indonesia, South Korea, Mexico, Russia, Taiwan, and Turkey) and all other African countries (classified under developing countries), taking into consideration the demographic, socio-cultural and macro-economic factors influencing consumer choices in these markets. The series synthesizes key subject areas in marketing, discuss marketing issues, processes, procedures and strategies across communities, regions and continents, and also the way digital innovation is changing the business landscape in emerging economies.

Palgrave Studies of Marketing in Emerging Economies presents a unique opportunity to examine and discuss marketing strategy and its implications in emerging economies, thereby filling a gap in current marketing literature.

All chapter submissions to the series will undergo a double blind peer review and all book proposals will undergo a single blind peer review.

More information about this series at
http://link.springer.com/series/16591

Ogechi Adeola • Robert E. Hinson
A M Sakkthivel
Editors

Marketing Communications and Brand Development in Emerging Economies Volume I

Contemporary and Future Perspectives

palgrave
macmillan

Editors
Ogechi Adeola
Lagos Business School
Pan-Atlantic University
Lagos, Nigeria

Robert E. Hinson
University of Kigali
Kigali, Rwanda

A M Sakkthivel
Skyline University College
Sharjah, United Arab Emirates

ISSN 2730-5554   ISSN 2730-5562   (electronic)
Palgrave Studies of Marketing in Emerging Economies
ISBN 978-3-030-88677-6   ISBN 978-3-030-88678-3   (eBook)
https://doi.org/10.1007/978-3-030-88678-3

© The Editor(s) (if applicable) and The Author(s), under exclusive licence to Springer Nature Switzerland AG 2022
This work is subject to copyright. All rights are solely and exclusively licensed by the Publisher, whether the whole or part of the material is concerned, specifically the rights of translation, reprinting, reuse of illustrations, recitation, broadcasting, reproduction on microfilms or in any other physical way, and transmission or information storage and retrieval, electronic adaptation, computer software, or by similar or dissimilar methodology now known or hereafter developed.
The use of general descriptive names, registered names, trademarks, service marks, etc. in this publication does not imply, even in the absence of a specific statement, that such names are exempt from the relevant protective laws and regulations and therefore free for general use.
The publisher, the authors and the editors are safe to assume that the advice and information in this book are believed to be true and accurate at the date of publication. Neither the publisher nor the authors or the editors give a warranty, expressed or implied, with respect to the material contained herein or for any errors or omissions that may have been made. The publisher remains neutral with regard to jurisdictional claims in published maps and institutional affiliations.

This Palgrave Macmillan imprint is published by the registered company Springer Nature Switzerland AG.
The registered company address is: Gewerbestrasse 11, 6330 Cham, Switzerland

Preface

Advances in technology and changes in consumer buying patterns are forcing businesses to modify their traditional marketing approach to incorporate contemporary practices that will drive customer satisfaction, meet societal expectations, and boost business performance for competitive advantage. The book, *Marketing Communications and Brand Development in Emerging Economies I*, provides insights into these important issues in a changing world, particularly in emerging economies (also referred to as emerging markets in this book). Emerging markets present opportunities for business expansion, growth, and increased profitability; however, these opportunities might remain untapped if organisations continue to adopt traditional approaches in communicating their value proposition and benefits of product and service offerings. Consumers in emerging markets have unique characteristics that companies must understand to appeal to their emotional, social, and economic needs.

One of the numerous challenges that companies encounter is effectively communicating their offerings (products and services) and value proposition to stakeholders and businesses in diverse ways. Often, firms cannot determine which marketing communication tools to apply to the life cycle of products they manage or even to the evolution of the firm. As firms increasingly strive to create brand awareness and enhance product/service visibility, identifying and applying contemporary marketing communications is of great importance. Generally, firms in emerging markets are faced with the challenge of adopting appropriate communication techniques and brand identity management strategies. Marketing communications and brand development in these markets, therefore, demand both theoretical and empirical evaluation.

Marketing perspectives in some emerging markets are predominantly based on traditional tools and techniques, while others have more advanced practices. The book offers a consideration of contextual issues to propose ways that firms can target these markets to respond to the current and future realities of marketing communications and brand development. Contributors present an interesting exploration of marketing communications and brand development in emerging markets. Authors from diverse contexts such as Brazil, India, Malaysia, Philippines, United Arab Emirates, Ghana, Kenya, Nigeria, South Africa, France, United Kingdom, USA, Peru, and Mexico have provided perspectives on the book themes. These include *Destination Brand Management, Sponsorship, Health and Personal Branding, Neuromarketing, and Digital as the future of Marketing Communications*. Conceptual and empirical insights from the themes will be of benefit to scholars and practitioners seeking an understanding of the unique context of these contemporary issues in emerging markets.

Lagos, Nigeria	Ogechi Adeola
Kigali, Rwanda	Robert E. Hinson
Sharjah, United Arab Emirates	A. M. Sakkthivel

Praise for *Marketing Communications and Brand Development in Emerging Economies Volume I*

"In a fast-changing world and business, it is not enough to have the right "lenses" to understand the past in terms of pillars for transformation, the new concept of value, and the tools that transform the competitive dynamics. In this world, it is crucial to have a vision of the future, and this is the effort of this monographic work. The book serves as a guide for companies and scholars interested in branding and marketing communication in emerging markets to find insights for strategic decisions of the next decades."
—Dr Silvio Cardinali, *Associate Professor in Marketing and Sales Management, Università Politecnica delle Marche, Italy, Vice President, Academy of Global Business Research and Practice (AGBRP)*

"I am glad that this book is coming from Emerging market countries. The future market is in emerging markets—not only because of the large population but also its ability to make impulse purchases. As nouveau rich, they buy and splash their cash. This is a boon to marketers. Moreover, building brands in these countries is a herculean task. In recent years, a few global brands have been emerging. I hope that in the future, many more international brands will compete in the global arena by adopting innovative strategies. The book brings out all these salient and crucial factors. I am confident the book will be interesting and useful not only to marketing scholars and students but also to practitioners."
—Rev. Dr. N. Casimir Raj SJ, *Founder Director of LIBA, Chennai, Director of XLRI, Jamshedpur (Rtd), India and Director of Xavier Institute of Management, Bhubaneswar (Rtd), India*

"We are at a time where technology is advancing rapidly and greatly changing the global economy. In times like this, emerging markets are at the forefront as they have the talent and innovation to come up with new ideas and products, attracting business and investors from around the globe. To create competitive brands and market these products, it is crucial not only to understand marketing communications but also to have a deep understanding of consumer behaviour

and brand development in the context of these markets. This book delineates the contemporary issues associated with these markets and positions the reader to gain insights, understand consumer demands and create a competitive strategy. I am confident that this book will be valuable to marketing professionals and business leaders or investors looking for insights to aid business decisions."
—Prof. Tayo Otubanjo, *Marketing Faculty, Lagos Business School, Pan-Atlantic University, Nigeria*

Contents

Part I Introduction ... 1

1 Marketing Communications and Brand Development: An Introduction ... 3
  Ogechi Adeola, Robert E. Hinson, and A. M. Sakkthivel

Part II Contemporary Perspectives on Marketing Communications and Brand Development: Destination Brand Management and Brand Avoidance ... 17

2 The Progress of Destination Marketing in Emerging Economies: A Focus on ASEAN ... 19
  Mohd Raziff Jamaluddin, Mohd Hafiz Mohd Hanafiah, and Daryl Ace V. Cornell

3 Nation Branding as a Strategic Approach for Emerging Economies: The Case of UAE ... 41
  Gouher Ahmed, Anas Abudaqa, C. Jayachandran, Yam Limbu, and Rashed Alzahmi

4   **Bank Brand Avoidance: Service Perspectives from Nigeria and Ghana**   59
Henry Boateng, Uchenna Uzo, Ogechi Adeola, and Robert Ebo Hinson

Part III   Contemporary Perspectives on Marketing Communications and Brand Development: Sponsorship, Health and Personal Branding   81

5   **Sponsorship: Practices and Benefits in Emerging Markets**   83
Michael M. Goldman, Gabriela Klein Netto, Shiling Lin, and Richard Wanjohi

6   **Sports Marketing Communications in South America**   103
Raúl A. Rosales and Roger G. Tito

7   **Social Media-Driven Consumer–Brand Interactions in Mexico: Healthy Food Brands Versus Indulgent Food Brands**   121
Gricel Castillo, Lorena Carrete, and Pilar Arroyo

8   **Health and Lifestyle Branding**   147
Emmanuel Silva Quaye and Leeford Edem Kojo Ameyibor

9   **Personal Branding**   181
J. N. Halm

Part IV Contemporary and Futuristic Approaches to Marketing Communications and Brand Development — 207

10 Neuromarketing: The Role of the Executive Function in Consumer Behaviour — 209
Chika Remigious Ezeugwu, Awele Achi, and Chikaodi Francisca Ezeugwu

11 Advertising in Virtual Reality: A Hierarchy of Effects Paradigm — 229
Ikeola J Bodunde and Eugene Ohu

12 The Future of Marketing: Artificial Intelligence, Virtual Reality, and Neuromarketing — 253
Ogechi Adeola, Olaniyi Evans, Jude Ndubuisi Edeh, and Isaiah Adisa

13 Leveraging Digital Marketing and Integrated Marketing Communications for Brand Building in Emerging Markets — 281
Amrita Chakraborty and Varsha Jain

Index — 307

Notes on Contributors

Anas Abudaqa is a proficient and result-oriented petroleum engineer working for ADNOC Group. Abudaqa is CIPLD Level 7, PMI-PMP and PMI-PBA certified professional. He holds MSc (Petroleum Engineering) from Heriot Watt University, UK, MBA from IMT Business School, MSc (Innovation, Leadership and Management) from University of York, UK, and his PhD (Business Management) from Universiti Sains Malaysia. His articles have appeared in reputed journals, and his research interests include HRM, organisational behaviour, leadership, organisational agility, and innovation and technology management.

Awele Achi is a PhD candidate in the Department of Strategy and Marketing at the Open University Business School, Milton Keynes, United Kingdom. Before this, Achi held a scholarly research position at Lagos Business School, Nigeria. His research interests lie in the areas of marketing strategy, innovation, entrepreneurship, and mixed methods.

Ogechi Adeola is Associate Professor of Marketing and the Head of Department of Operations, Marketing and Information Systems at the Lagos Business School, Pan-Atlantic University, Nigeria. Her multidimensional research focuses on the advancement of knowledge across the intersection of marketing, tourism, and gender studies. Her research has been published in *Annals of Tourism Research, Tourism Management, Journal of Business Research, Industrial Marketing Management,*

International Marketing Review, and *Psychology & Marketing*. Her co-authored articles won Best Paper Awards at international conferences for four consecutive years (2016–2019). Adeola's international marketing consultancy experience spans Africa, Asia, the UK, and the USA.

Isaiah Adisa is a management researcher and consultant based in Nigeria. He has co-edited book(s) with several other book chapters and journal articles in recognised outlets. He is affiliated with the Olabisi Onabanjo University, Ago-Iwoye, Ogun State, and his research interests cut across human resources management, organisational behaviour, marketing, and gender studies. Adisa's consultancy experience spans health and educational sectors.

Gouher Ahmed is a Certified PMP, with over 25 years of experience in various academic, social and business settings worldwide and consulting through North America, South Asia and Middle East. He has played a critical role in helping organizations formulate winning strategies, drive many change initiatives and improve business results. He has accumulated over 150 research publications and presented in 85 international conferences. His teaching, research and publications are focused on international business, foreign trade, emerging markets, entrepreneurship and strategic leadership. He is Professor of Strategic Leadership and International Business at the Skyline University College, UAE, and Director of Academy of Global Business Research and Practice.

Rashed Alzahmi is an assistant professor and Chair of Leadership and Organizational Agility Department at the College of Business and Economics at the UAE University. Alzahmi is SHRM Senior Certified Professional and holds a PhD in Workforce Education and Development with a specialization in HRD and OD from the Pennsylvania State University. He is a Program Ambassador for the UAE Stanford nationwide Innovation and Entrepreneurship Education Initiative. Prior to becoming a professor, Alzahmi worked in a major oil and gas company. His research areas revolve around strategic workforce planning, succession planning, human resource management strategy, work engagement, and performance management.

Leeford Ameyibor is at the marketing department of the University of Professional Studies Accra and also a doctoral candidate at the University of Witwatersrand, Wits Business School, Johannesburg South Africa. His research interest is on social marketing, public sector marketing, Macro marketing, political marketing and sports marketing.

Pilar Arroyo is a professor of the EGADE Business School of Tecnológico of Monterrey, Mexico. She holds a PhD degree in Business Administration from the Tecnológico de Monterrey. She has published articles on topics such as logistic outsourcing, supplier development, green marketing, social marketing for health care, and social entrepreneurship. Her research has been published in reputed journals such as the *Journal of Supply Chain Management, Business Process Management Journal, Teaching and Teacher Education, Management Research Review, Journal of Consumer Marketing*, and *British Food Journal*. She has also authored several books and chapters in books and participated in international conferences.

Henry Boateng is the Director of Institutional Research at D'Youville College, New York. He is also the Co-director of Western New York Data Citizens Grant. Boateng is a researcher and educator in the areas of Marketing, Knowledge Management, Branding, Scholarly Communication, Customer experience and digital marketing. He has extensive research experience in both quantitative and qualitative methods, and extensive publication.

Ikeola J. Bodunde is a researcher at the Virtual Human Computer Interaction Lab at the Lagos Business School. Her interests are in the fields of advertising, health, and organizational communication, human-computer interaction, and character development. Her first and second degrees are in Media and Communication Studies. She believes in finding and leveraging opportunities for learning and growth. She is a member of the American Psychological Association.

Lorena Carrete is a professor of the EGADE Business School of Tecnológico of Monterrey. She holds a PhD. degree in Business Administration from the University of Lyon 3, France. She is member of the research group "Consumer Behavior and Conscious Marketing". Her research interests include consumer behaviour, green marketing, social marketing, corporate social responsibility, branding, and social media. Her articles have appeared in journals such as *Journal of Business and Industrial Marketing*, *Management Research Review*, *Journal of Marketing Theory and Practice*, *Journal of Consumer Marketing*, *Qualitative Market Research: An International Journal*, and *International Journal of Environmental Research and Public Health*.

Gricel Castillo is a lecturer in the Marketing and Analysis Department of Tecnológico de Monterrey. She lectures courses on statistical thinking and statistical methods for decision making. She is a candidate to PhD degree in Marketing from the EGADE Business School. She has experience in information systems, market research, business intelligence and databases analysis. She worked in the market intelligence area at Tecnológico de Monterrey and in the finance area at PepsiCo.

Amrita Chakraborty is an FPM (Fellow Program in Management, doctoral programme) scholar at the MICA, Ahmedabad (India). Her research interests are at the intersection of marketing, consumer behaviour, digital marketing, and branding. She has 2.4 years of work experience as a Research Assistant in MICA, Ahmedabad (India), in the area of consumer behaviour, and the Indian Institute of Management, Udaipur (India), in the area of Economics. She has also been part of a one-month internship of DIRI (Digital Identity Research Initiative) project with the Indian School of Business, Hyderabad (India).

Daryl Ace V. Cornell, PhD, CGSP, is an associate professor and the Chief of the Center for Research Dissemination and Linkages of the Research Management Office of the Polytechnic University of the Philippines-Manila and a part-time faculty member in his alma mater, San Sebastian College-Recoletos. He is also appointed as an adjunct faculty member of the University College Sedaya International (UCSI) University in Sarawak, Malaysia.

Jude N. Edeh is a postdoctoral researcher at the Chair of Business as Unusual: Innovative Practices and New Business Models at the Kedge Business School Marseille, France. He received his PhD from the Faculty of Economics and Business Sciences, University of Sevilla, Spain. His research is at the intersection of innovation, global strategy, international business and digitalisation in the context of organisational transformation. His articles have appeared in several academic journals and won several academic awards.

Olaniyi Evans is a Nigerian economist and a university lecturer at Pan Atlantic University, Nigeria. He is known in academia for his work on the digital economy, financial inclusion, and tourism. He has a first class in BSc and a distinction in MSc and went on to pursue a PhD all in economics from the University of Lagos. He is the author of a substantial number of scholarly articles in top academic journals. He is the editor of *BizEcons Quarterly*.

Chika Remigious Ezeugwu is a PhD candidate funded by the LEGO-Cambridge Scholarship at the University of Cambridge. Ezeugwu's scientific interests focus on integrating neuroscience, cognition, child development, and education to improve educational practice and experience of children from a low-income context. Before joining Cambridge, Ezeugwu has worked on policy and strategy projects as a researcher at Lagos Business School, Nigeria.

Chikaodi Francisca Ezeugwu is a graduate of Marketing from Enugu State University of Science and Technology, Nigeria. Ezeugwu is interested in the integration of digital consumer behaviour, personal selling, and digital marketing for long-term competitive advantage in the marketplace.

Michael M. Goldman is an associate professor at the University of San Francisco, and Adjunct Faculty at the University of Pretoria's Gordon Institute of Business Science. His research has examined sponsorship effectiveness, brand strategy, and fan identification, which he has published in, among others, the *California Management Review*, *International Journal of Sports Marketing & Sponsorship*, *Case Research Journal*, Ivey Publishing and Emerald Publishing. Through his teaching, research, and advisory roles, Goldman assisted organisations as diverse as PepsiCo, MTN, Nedbank, World Rugby, Cricket South Africa, Business & Arts South Africa, and the United Nations Development Program.

J. N. Halm is an entrepreneur, author, speaker and business consultant specialising in Service Excellence. He has a decade of experience in Ghana's banking industry. Halm holds an MPhil in Communications from the School of Communication Studies, University of Ghana, and a BSc in Agriculture from Kwame Nkrumah University of Science and Technology. Halm is a weekly columnist with a full-page column in Ghana's leading business newsprint, *Business & Financial Times*. He is also the author of two award-winning books, *Customer Romance* and *Service Sins*. He was adjudged the Service Excellence Leader Award at the 2019 Global Brands Awards.

Mohd Hafiz Mohd Hanafiah is the Deputy Dean (Research and Industry Linkages) in the Faculty of Hotel and Tourism Management, Universiti Teknologi MARA. He also served as the board member in the Islamic Tourism Council, an agency under the Malaysia Ministry of Tourism, Arts and Culture. He has published more than 20 papers on tourism topics in *Scopus* and *Web of Science* Journal.

Robert E. Hinson is currently the Deputy Vice Chancellor – Academic at the University of Kigali with additional responsibility as Interim Vice-Chancellor of the same University. His main research interests lie in the academic areas of marketing and communications, information and technology management, service management, and social responsibility and sustainability management. He has 25 monographs/edited volumes and over 150 peer-reviewed journal papers/book chapters to his credit. He was ranked by the 2021 and 2022 Alper-Doger (AD) Scientific Index as the #1 African Marketing Scholar and leading business and management scholar in Ghana. His book collection can be accessed at www.robertebohinsonbooks.com

Varsha Jain is Professor of Integrated Marketing Communications and the Co-chairperson, Doctoral Program and research at the MICA, India, and has over 18 years of teaching and research experience. She has authored over 100 publications, including *European Journal of Marketing*, *International Journal of Information Management*, amongst others. Jain is the recipient of more than 22 national and international awards and gold medals in research and scholarship. The recent award includes the "MICA

AGK Annual Award for Excellence in Research 2020–2021". In her research career, she is a visiting guest at Emory Business School, Atlanta, and a visiting scholar and guest at the Medill School, North-western University.

Mohd Raziff Jamaluddin is a fellow researcher in Institute of Business Excellent, Universiti Teknologi MARA. Jamaluddin is the President of the Tourism Educators Association of Malaysia (TEAM) and the Editor-in-Chief for *TEAM Journal for Hospitality and Tourism*. He is an active International Resource Speaker for tourism events and destination topics with regular sharing in the webinar organised by the School of Hospitality and Tourism and Non-government Association.

C. Jayachandran is the President of the Academy of Global Business Research & Practice (AGBRP) (formerly, SGBED). He is Professor of Marketing and International Business with teaching, research and consulting interests in internationalisation of SMEs, market entry modes and marketing strategies with a focus on emerging markets. His research papers were published in a range of journals including *Economic Times, Journal of Health Care Marketing, Journal of Consumer Marketing, Journal of Services Marketing, Issues in International Business, Journal of Services Research, Economic and Political Weekly, Asian Case Research, International Journal of Business Research, International Journal of Business Innovation & Research*, among others.

Shiling Lin was born and raised in Quanzhou, China. She is completing her master's degree in Sport Management at the University of San Francisco and is also a Research Assistant at the Centre for the Development of the Sports Industry at Tsinghua University. Lin focused on leveraging brand value through sport sponsorship strategy and sponsorship activation during her career roles with the Anta Group, BDA Sport Management, and Tencent Sports. Her research interests include sport economics and sport marketing in Asian markets.

Yam Limbu is Professor of Marketing at the Montclair State University. His research interests include pharmaceutical and healthcare marketing, sales, advertising, consumer behaviour, internet marketing, and food, nutrition, and consumer health. His publications have appeared in

Industrial Marketing Management, European Journal of Marketing, Journal of Consumer Affairs, International Journal of Advertising, Journal of Business & Industrial Marketing, Health Communication, Health Education, American Journal of Health Education, British Food Journal, International Journal of Bank Marketing, Journal of Business-to-Business Marketing and *Marketing Intelligence & Planning*. He has published over 100 papers and serves as the Editor-in-Chief for the *IJBEM*. He is also the Vice-President of Academy of Global Business Research and Practice, NJ, USA.

Gabriela Klein Netto was born in Brazil and lives in the United States, where she is pursuing her master's degree in Sport Management at the University of San Francisco. With a bachelor's degree in Economics and experience in financial and administrative management, Netto is looking forward to gaining experience in the sport industry. She is part of the internship programme at Sponsor United, helping brands and properties to build authentic sponsorship relationships.

Eugene Ohu is a senior lecturer in the Department of Organisational Behaviour/Human Resource Management, Lagos Business School. His research interests are on the psychology of human-computer interactions in the workplace in order to promote individual wellbeing and organizational productivity. He is the director of the Virtual Human Computer Interactions (VHCI) Lab, where he explores the implications of immersive virtual worlds for character strengths, wellbeing, and productivity. He is a member of the American Psychological Association.

Emmanuel Silva Quaye holds a PhD in Marketing and is a postdoctoral research fellow at the University of the Witwatersrand, Wits Business School, Johannesburg. His research focuses on cross-cultural consumer behaviour, international marketing, branding, philanthropy, digital marketing, and social marketing.

Raúl A. Rosales holds a Doctor of Business Administration (DBA) from Superior School of Economics and Business Administration (ESEADE, Argentina), a master's degree in Management of Sport Organizations from Real Madrid Graduate School (Spain) and a bachelor's degree in Economic Engineering from National University of Engineering (Peru). Since 2010, Rosales is the chair of the Sport Business and Business Administration Program of the Peruvian University of Applied Sciences. During this period, he has been supporting Peruvian sport organisations in the field of management and has been a manager in the 2019 Pan American Games.

A. M. Sakkthivel is Professor of Marketing with School of Business, Skyline University College, United Arab Emirates. He holds MBA and PhD in Business Administration and possess 25 years of academic, research, industry, consulting, and training experience. He is a member of Global Academic Council, DMAT Global, UK. His research interests include online consumer behaviour, smartphone usage patterns, marketing, and branding communications. His articles have appeared in journals such as the *International Journal of Mobile Learning and Organisation, International Journal of Mobile Communications, Journal of Promotion Management*, to name a few.

Roger G. Tito has a bachelor's degree in Sports Administration and Business Administration of the Peruvian University of Applied Sciences and has studies on Digital Marketing, Sponsorship and Communication at Barça Innovation Hub. Since 2015, he has been a volunteer in social projects and sporting events such as Dakar 2018 and the Lima 2019 Pan American Games.

Uchenna Uzo is Senior Lecturer in Marketing management, Faculty director and Retail Expert in Lagos Business School. He has received awards for teaching excellence, including European Foundation for Management Development (EFMD), and Academy of International Business (AIB) best teaching case awards, among others. His research interest includes indigenous marketing practices, retail and consumer behaviour in Africa. Uzo's articles have appeared in *Strategic Entrepreneurship Journal* and *Journal of Personal Selling and Sales Management*, among others.

Richard Wanjohi is a marketing enthusiast, and sport reporter and editor, for over 15 years at Marketing Africa. He is based at Strathmore University Business School as well as the Strathmore Data Analytics Centre. He has also been a contributor and Sport Editor for Global Voices Online and has consulted on the inaugural Road to Liverpool

5-a-side football tournament, the Kenya Golf Open, and Safari Sevens. Wanjohi holds a Master of Science (Marketing) degree from University of Nairobi and a Bachelor of Commerce (Marketing) degree from the Catholic University of Eastern Africa.

List of Figures

Fig. 3.1	(**a, b**) The Anholt-GfK Nation Brands Hexagon. (Source: Hassan and Mahrous (2019, p. 4) and Alam et al. (2013, p. 3))	44
Fig. 3.2	Some examples of nation brand character. (Source: Adopted from Hassan and Mahrous (2019, p. 5))	45
Fig. 3.3	UAE logo for nation brand	47
Fig. 3.4	Sustainable efforts by UAE. (Source: Emirates Green Building Council (https://emiratesgbc.org/uae-sustainability-initiatives/))	49
Fig. 3.5	Key statistics as observed for overall healthcare system in UAE	50
Fig. 3.6	Suggested model for building NB. (Source: Hassan and Mahrous (2019, p. 8))	53
Fig. 10.1	Consumers' cognitive-behavioural processes for brand adoption in emerging markets	218
Fig. 11.1	Hierarchy of Effects models; Source: Adapted from Lavidge and Steiner	242
Fig. 13.1	Digital marketing framework for brands in emerging markets. Source: Authors	300
Fig. 13.2	Structure of digital marketing. Source: Adapted from Bleoju et al., 2016	300

List of Tables

Table 2.1	Sustainable growth	25
Table 2.2	A Classification/synthesis of topics in the research field of tourism destination marketing	28
Table 4.1	Synopsis of existing studies on the typologies of brand avoidance and redemption strategies	67
Table 12.1	Recent literature on AI in marketing	258
Table 12.2	Recent literature on VR in marketing	261
Table 12.3	Recent literature on neuromarketing	265

Part I

Introduction

1

Marketing Communications and Brand Development: An Introduction

Ogechi Adeola, Robert E. Hinson, and A. M. Sakkthivel

Introduction

Social and economic growth in emerging markets cannot be separated from the proliferation of technological innovation, rapid globalisation, and increasing market integration. Nations classified as emerging markets provide enormous socio-economic opportunities for businesses; it is

---

O. Adeola (✉)
Lagos Business School, Pan-Atlantic University, Lagos, Nigeria
e-mail: oadeola@lbs.edu.ng

R. E. Hinson
University of Kigali, Kigali, Rwanda

A. M. Sakkthivel
School of Business, Skyline University College, Sharjah, United Arab Emirates
e-mail: sakthivel@skylineuniversity.ac.ae

estimated that by 2050, emerging markets will account for 80% of global economic activities (Klein, 2008; Kaynak & Zhou, 2010; Paul, 2020). Consequently, adopting appropriate marketing strategies to communicate organisations' product and service offerings is crucial to achieving significant market share in these markets. As technology permeates all aspects of our daily lives and core processes of institutions in a society, businesses have already begun to adapt to these changes by innovating their marketing practices (Paul, 2020).

Organisations aiming to benefit from opportunities in emerging markets must be aware of key characteristics of the markets, which include the diverse culture, differences in consumers' tastes (Paul, 2020), and growing middle class with strong purchasing power. Consumers in emerging markets are heterogeneous in taste, cultural beliefs, and needs. Hence, building mutually beneficial relationships in emerging markets will require that businesses communicate offerings that fit the sociocultural and economic needs of the target audience. In other words, communication methods adopted must be fit-for-purpose to achieve set goals in emerging markets (Fill & Jamieson, 2014).

This first volume of a two-volume edited book provides insights into key concepts such as nation branding, destination marketing, brand avoidance, sports marketing communications, sponsorship, health and lifestyle branding, digital marketing, and integrated marketing communications, and also offers futuristic perspectives on neuromarketing, artificial intelligence, and virtual reality. Volume II focuses on the influences of the Covid-19 pandemic, social responsibility, and emerging technologies on marketing communications and brand development in a changing world.

The authors of the chapters recommend adopting and implementing appropriate marketing communications and brand development strategies to enhance business performance and visibility, given the increasing market competition, growing middle class with greater purchasing power, and rapid digitalisation in emerging markets. This book volume focuses on effective and contemporary marketing communications and branding tools to increase visibility, drive patronage, improve lifestyle and enhance customer experience.

Marketing Communications

Marketing communications has witnessed rapid growth due to the major shift from a production-driven economy to a customer-centric market. Marketing communications is one of the marketing mix tools, which traditionally comprises the 4Ps—*product, price, place, and promotion*—and the extended marketing elements of *people, process, and physical evidence* (7Ps) (Hinson, 2012; Lovelock & Jochen, 2016). Marketing communications, an element of the promotional aspect of the marketing mix, is defined as "all the promotional elements of the marketing mix which involve the communications between an organisation and its target audiences on all matters that affect marketing performance" (Pickton & Broderick, 2005, p.4). It represents the voice by which companies can dialogue with customers and other stakeholders about their product/service offerings and other company-related issues (Keller, 2001). Marketing communication or promotions mix comprises the range of activities/tools available to an organisation to communicate with its target audience on the features of its products and services. These marketing communication tools—*advertising, public relations, personal selling, sales promotions, and online/social media marketing*—can be utilised at individual, firm, national, and international levels (Pickton & Broderick, 2005; Shimp & Andrews, 2013).

Understanding marketing communication tools is crucial to the knowledge and applicability of marketing communications in current and future trend analyses. There is a paradigm shift from traditional means of communicating brands' offerings to technology-driven tools and platforms, which has enhanced consumer engagement in recent times (Dahiya & Gayatri, 2018; Yoga, Korry & Yulianti, 2019). Emerging markets are characterised by a younger, digitally active/savvy population (Oxford Business Group, 2021), creating innovative opportunities for organisations to reach and engage them. Therefore, organisations targeting emerging markets must begin to adopt technology-driven marketing strategies to penetrate these markets and adopt appropriate communications and branding techniques. The relevance of marketing communications and brand development in emerging markets is explored through the lens of technology and other contemporary approaches in this book.

Marketing communications and branding are interrelated concepts. Adopting and implementing appropriate marketing communications will result in enhanced brand awareness. Batra and Keller (2016) note that marketing communication options can play different roles and have different objectives in marketing and promoting a brand. For example, a symbol (for product branding), a geographical landmark (for nation branding), a Beyoncé voice (for personal branding), or a Grammy Awardee (like Nigeria's Burna Boy) would create a clear distinction between one brand identity and another. The role of marketing communications in promoting product offerings, enhancing brands and brand image, constitutes the discussion themes in this book.

Brand Development

Brand development involves the strategic actions by individuals or business enterprises to ensure that their products and services are identifiable, distinguishable from competitors, and communicate the right value proposition to the target market. This aims at creating and effectively communicating identifiable attributes of an organisation and its offerings to provide a unique differentiation of the organisation in the market.

An important aspect of brand development is to create a unique and strong brand identity that provides direction, purpose, and meaning to the brand. Brand identity is a set of associated values that the firm aspires to create and maintain as an implied promise to customers (Khedher, 2014), and it is regarded as the visible element of the brand. Just as a personal identity makes an individual unique and distinct, the brand identity of a firm, institution, or organisation is formed by unique, recognisable elements that set it apart from competing brands (Keller, 2013). Therefore, a strong brand identity is a crucial factor for the success of any branding strategy as it provides a direction and scope for an organisation over a long period (Johnson et al., 2005). Developing a good brand identity requires prioritising the core identity elements and communicating these elements to customers and potential stakeholders (Khedher, 2014).

As developing a strong brand identity is key to the success of marketing communications efforts, the branding process must be proactively managed. Effective brand development and marketing communications will ensure that all contents, communications, products, events, sub-brands, and stylistic elements are aligned to achieve visibility; communicate the value proposition; and appropriately project the image of the person, firm, and nation.

Marketing Communications and Brand Development: Emerging Trends

As firms increasingly strive to create brand awareness and enhance product/service visibility, effective management of brands in the digital age is a key concern. Firms in emerging markets are faced with the challenge of managing brand identities in an increasingly digital world and exploring innovations that enhance the communication of information about products and services. Notably, the exploration of digital-media options offers promising opportunities for marketers to explore the vast potential for marketing communications and brand development (Keller, 2016). For instance, in the COVID-19 pandemic era, some of the most common ways of communicating with customers are via digital or technological platforms; it makes reaching various customer audiences on multiple media platforms even more crucial. It could be argued that with the 2020–2022 pandemic, technological platforms have become the most common means of communication.

Technological advancements, including the proliferation of media tools such as Voice over Internet Protocol (VoIP) devices, tablets, and smartphones, have significantly increased the interaction touchpoints between consumers and brands. Marketers' communication with consumers has changed dramatically over the years, as they now manage brands and communicate product and service offerings across old, new, and emerging media platforms. Increasingly, artificial intelligence (AI), virtual reality (VR), and neuropsychological tools are impacting marketing communications and brand development, providing a more in-depth understanding of consumer experience and brand responses. Therefore, special attention must be given to emerging technologies in developing marketing communications and branding strategies.

Additionally, the growing need for communicating the values of a firm to consumers and stakeholders has become a significant area of discourse. In this COVID-19 era, most firms are deploying technological tools to communicate that beyond economic interest, they care for customers' well-being and health by showing their social and emotional values. Integrating health consciousness into marketing activities is one of the strategic methods of presenting the company as a brand interested in customers' well-being and appealing to their emotions. A business can utilise marketing communications to appeal to consumers' emotions, thereby presenting the organisation as a customer-centric brand (Finne & Grönroos, 2017).

Overall, to succeed in emerging markets, organisations must develop contemporary and futuristic approaches to marketing communications and brand development in today's increasingly complex business environment.

The Context: Emerging Markets

Emerging markets, also referred to as "emerging economies" in this book, are described as nations whose business activities have experienced rapid flux and growth. Emerging markets have a large population with a growing percentage of middle-class consumers with strong purchasing power (Wang, He & Barnes, 2017). The book takes its classification from the International Monetary Fund's broad division of the world into two economic sectors—advanced economies and emerging and developing economies—based on criteria, such as per capita income, export diversification, and degree of integration into the global financial system (Wheatley, 2015). There are many descriptions of emerging markets, and none appear to be universally accepted (Nakata & Sivakumar, 1997; Mody,

2003); however, they can be identified by attributes such as "sustained market access, progress in reaching middle-income levels, and greater global economic relevance" (Duttagupta & Pazarbasioglu, 2021, p. 5). Emerging markets often refer to low- to middle-income, rapid-growing countries with increasing participation in international economic markets (Hoskisson, Eden, Lau & Wright, 2000; Glassman, Giedion & McQueston, 2013), and they present major growth opportunities in the world economy (Arnold & Quelch, 1998). Typically, these countries have in place policies that demonstrate commitment to economic liberalisation (Arnold & Quelch, 1998; Hoskisson, Eden, Lau & Wright, 2000; Roztocki & Weistroffer, 2008), adoption of a free-market system (Hoskisson, Eden, Lau & Wright, 2000), and are continuously improving their institutions (Liu, 2021).

The importance of emerging markets to global corporations and investors is demonstrated by the proliferation of emerging market typologies, such as BRICS (Brazil, Russia, India, China, and South Africa), MINT (Mexico, Indonesia, Nigeria, and Turkey), CIVETS (Colombia, Indonesia, Vietnam, Egypt, Turkey, and South Africa); and EAGLES (Brazil, China, India, Indonesia, South Korea, Mexico, Russia, Taiwan, and Turkey) (Palgrave Series, n.d.). Other countries outside these broad groupings are also regarded as emerging markets. For instance, the United Arab Emirates (UAE) has been described as the most competitive emerging market in the Gulf Cooperation Council (GCC) (Gulf Today, 2021). The GCC comprise the Middle East countries of Bahrain, Kuwait, Oman, Qatar, Saudi Arabia, and the United Arab Emirates. African countries are classified as developing economies. The chapter authors took into consideration the demographic, socio-cultural, and macro-economic factors influencing consumer choices and the ways marketing communication and branding are changing the business landscape in these emerging markets.

There is an increasing need to understand the key role that marketing and branding principles and practices play in the drive to increase retail patronage and enhance customer service in a global business environment. Companies need to synthesise and develop marketing strategies to win in an evolving marketplace that is being rapidly shaped by digitalisation (Adeola & Evans, 2019; Adeola, Hinson & Evans, 2020; Kannan,

2017; Piercy, 2016; Ryans, More, Barclay & Deutscher, 2010). Particularly, in sub-Saharan Africa, where it is challenging to generalise marketing practices (Amankwah-Amoah, Boso & Debrah, 2018), there is a need to discuss, assess, and illuminate marketing practices on the continent. Against this background, this book presents a unique opportunity to discuss contemporary marketing practices and their implications in the unique business landscape of emerging markets, to enrich our knowledge and fill gaps in current marketing literature.

Book Thematic Areas

This volume comprises four(4) themes organised along related lines of argument for a comprehensive flow and ease of reference.

1. **Marketing Communications and Brand Development: An Introduction**

    In this first chapter, *Ogechi Adeola, Robert E. Hinson, and A. M. Sakkthivel* introduce the concept of marketing communications and brand development in emerging market contexts, providing the background to the book themes and addressing the relevance of this concept to contemporary issues in marketing.

2. **Contemporary Perspectives on Marketing Communications and Brand Development: Destination Brand Management and Brand Avoidance**

    In Chap. 2, "The Progress of Destination Marketing in Emerging Economies: A Focus on ASEAN", authors *Mohd Raziff Jamaluddin, Mohd Hafiz Mohd Hanafiah, and Daryl Ace V. Cornell* explore the concept of destination marketing, document current trends and issues and discuss the crucial role of Destination Marketing Organisations (DMOs), particularly in a post-COVID-19 era. Similarly, *Gouher Ahmed, Anas Abudaqa, C. Jayachandran, Yam Limbu, and Rashed Alzahmi,* in Chap. 3, examine "Nation Branding as a Strategic Approach for Emerging

Economies: The Case of UAE". The authors discuss the relevance, scope, and evolution of national branding in the United Arab Emirates, providing practical insights into how emerging economies can take advantage of the models of nation branding to boost tourism, trade, and investment.

Chapter 4 concludes the discussions in this section as *Henry Boateng, Uchenna Uzo, Ogechi Adeola, and Robert E. Hinson* explore "Bank Brand Avoidance: Service Perspectives from Nigeria and Ghana". The chapter investigates service experiences that inform bank customers' decisions to avoid bank brands in Ghana and Nigeria through a phenomenological approach.

3. Contemporary Perspectives on Marketing Communications and Brand Development: Sponsorship, Health, and Personal Branding

This section comprises five chapters. *Michael Goldman, Gabriela Klein Netto, Shiling Lin, and Richard Wanjohi* examine "Sponsorship: Practices and Benefits in Emerging Markets" in Chap. 5. The authors detail the strategic sponsorship activities and mechanisms that can be implemented to communicate with customers and other stakeholders. *Raúl Rosales and Roger Tito*, in Chap. 6, analyse "Sports Marketing Communications in South America". In this chapter, the authors review advances in communications through sport and present key indicators of the top international competitions in South America.

Health and lifestyle branding is the focus of *Gricel Castillo, Lorena Carrete, and Pilar Arroyo* in Chap. 7 entitled "Social Media-Driven Consumer–Brand Interactions in Mexico: Healthy Food Brands Versus Indulgent Food Brands". The authors explore how healthy and indulgent food brands influence consumer-brand interaction in Mexico. In Chap. 8: "Health and Lifestyle Branding", *Emmanuel Silva Quaye and Leeford Ameyibor* discuss the strategies that drive corporate efforts to develop and communicate branding that drives public interest in practising healthy lifestyles. In Chap. 9, *J. N. Halm* concludes the section with discussions on "Personal Branding". The author emphasises the distinct benefits of social media for individuals or organisations seeking brand management outlets.

4. **Contemporary and Futuristic Approaches to Marketing Communications and Brand Development**

Chika Remigious Ezeugwu, Awele Achi, and Chikaodi Francisca Ezeugwu, in Chap. 10, explicate the concept "Neuromarketing: The Role of Executive Function in Consumer Behaviour". The authors argue that the adoption of neuromarketing tools in emerging markets would enable organisations to understand consumers' affective, cognitive, and behavioural characteristics, as well as their mental processes for navigating through marketing stimuli. Similarly, in Chap. 11, *Ikeola J. Bodunde and Eugene Ohu* focus on "Advertising in Virtual Reality: A Hierarchy of Effects Paradigm". The authors discuss the use of virtual reality towards understanding the consumer and meeting consumers' needs in emerging markets. Applying the Hierarchy of Effects model, they suggest that VR Ads can provide a unique insight into consumers' processes of thinking, feeling, and conation towards brand affinity.

We conclude the book with two chapters. *Ogechi Adeola, Olaniyi Evans, Jude N. Edeh,* and *Isaiah Adisa* discuss "The Future of Marketing: Artificial Intelligence, Virtual Reality, and Neuromarketing", in Chap. 12. The authors examine how artificial intelligence (AI), virtual reality (VR), and neuropsychological tools are changing the way we collect, store, and analyse data linked to the marketing of products and services. By integrating various marketing literature, the authors consider the applications of these technologies to marketing in contemporary times and discuss future research directions. In Chap. 13, *Amrita Chakraborty and Varsha Jain* explore "Leveraging Digital Marketing and Integrated Marketing Communications for Brand Building in Emerging Markets". The authors assert that digital marketing, aligned with integrated marketing communications, strengthens the bond between brands and consumers in emerging markets. The authors present a digital marketing framework as a branding strategy in emerging markets.

Conclusion

The business landscape is rapidly evolving, and to win in the marketplace, businesses must understand the changing market dynamics. Digital innovation and platforms represent the new marketplace where businesses must understand how to interact with their targeted audiences, meet their needs, and enhance profitability. Emerging markets offer local and multinational businesses great opportunities to increase their market share and achieve business goals. However, the ability to comprehend contemporary and future trends in marketing communications and brand development and craft appropriate strategies will be a source of competitive advantage in emerging markets. This book elucidates how business owners and marketing managers in organisations can take advantage of the opportunities in emerging markets through innovative marketing communications and branding.

References

Adeola, O., & Evans, O. (2019). Digital tourism: Mobile phones, internet and tourism in Africa. *Tourism Recreation Research, 44*(2), 190–202.

Adeola, O., Hinson, R. E., & Evans, O. (2020). Social media in marketing communications: A synthesis of successful strategies for the digital generation. In *Digital Transformation in Business and Society* (pp. 61–81). Palgrave Macmillan.

Amankwah-Amoah, J., Boso, N., & Debrah, Y. A. (2018). Africa rising in an emerging world: An international marketing perspective. *International Marketing Review*.

Arnold, D. J., & Quelch, J. A. (1998). New strategies in emerging markets. *MIT Sloan Management Review, 40*(1), 7.

Batra, R., & Keller, K. L. (2016). Integrating marketing communications: New findings, new lessons, and new ideas. *Journal of Marketing, 80*(6), 122–145.

Duttagupta, R., & Pazarbasioglu, C. (2021). MILES to go. Finance & Development. Retrieved from https://www.elibrary.imf.org/view/journals/022/0058/002/article-A002-en.xml

Finne, A., & Grönroos, C. (2017). Communication-in-use: Customer-integrated marketing communication. *European Journal of Marketing, 51*(3), 445–463. https://doi.org/10.1108/EJM-08-2015-0553

Glassman, A., Giedion, U., & McQueston, K. (2013). Priority setting for health in emerging markets. *Journal of Comparative Effectiveness Research, 2*(3), 283–291.

Gulf Today. (February 9, 2021). UAE leads as most competitive emerging market in GCC. Retrieved July 2, 2021, from https://www.gulftoday.ae/business/2021/02/09/uae-leads-as-most-competitive-emerging-market-in-gcc.

Hinson, R. (2012). *Service marketing excellence. With a twist of corporate social responsibility*. Sedco Publishing Limited.

Hoskisson, R. E., Eden, L., Lau, C. M., & Wright, M. (2000). Strategy in emerging economies. *Academy of Management Journal, 43*(3), 249–267. https://www.ft.com/content/8a393522-39bf-11e5-bbd1-b37bc06f590c

Johnson, G., Scholes, K., & Whittington, R. (2005). *Exploring Corporate Strategy. Text and Cases* (7th ed.). Pearson Education Ltd..

Kannan, P. K. (2017). Digital marketing: A framework, review and research agenda. *International Journal of Research in Marketing, 34*(1), 22–45.

Kaynak, E., & Zhou, L. (2010). Special issue on brand equity, branding, and marketing communications in emerging markets. *Journal of Global Marketing, 23*(3), 171–176.

Keller, K. L. (2016). Unlocking the power of integrated marketing communications: How integrated is your IMC program? *Journal of Advertising, 45*(3), 286–301.

Keller, K. L. (2013). *Strategic brand management; building, measuring, and managing brand equity*. Prentice Hall.

Khedher, M. (2014). Personal branding phenomenon. *International Journal of Information, Business and Management, 6*(2), 29.

Liu, Q. (2021). Business environment in emerging market countries. *Global Journal of Emerging Market Economies, 13*(2), 239–264.

Lovelock, C., & Jochen, W. (2016). *Services marketing: People, technology, strategy* (8th ed.). World Scientific Publishing Co. Inc.

Mody, A. (2003). What is an emerging market. *Geo. J. Int'l L., 35*, 641.

Nakata, C., & Sivakumar, K. (1997). Emerging market conditions and their impact on first mover advantages: An integrative review. *International Marketing Review*

Oxford Business Group. (2021). Guide to top emerging markets for 2021- Investing in emerging markets. Retrieved from https://oxfordbusinessgroup.com/guide-top-emerging-markets-2021

Palgrave Series. (n.d.). Palgrave studies of marketing in emerging economies. Retrieved from https://www.springer.com/series/16591

Paul, J. (2020). Marketing in emerging markets: A review, theoretical synthesis and extension. *International Journal of Emerging Markets, 15*(3), 446–468. https://doi.org/10.1108/IJOEM-04-2017-0130

Pickton, D., & Broderick, A. (2005). *Integrated marketing communications*. Pearson Education UK.

Piercy, N. F. (2016). *Market-led strategic change: Transforming the process of going to market*. Routledge.

Roztocki, N., & Weistroffer, H. R. (2008). Information technology in transition economies. *Journal of Global Information Technology Management, 11*(4), 2–9. Retrieved from http://ssrn.com/abstract=1301722

Ryans, A., More, R., Barclay, D., & Deutscher, T. (2010). *Winning market leadership: Strategic market planning for technology-driven businesses*. John Wiley & Sons.

Wang, C. L., He, J., & Barnes, B. R. (2017). Brand management and consumer experience in emerging markets: Directions for future research. *International Marketing Review, 34*(4), 458–462. https://doi.org/10.1108/IMR-01-2016-0009

Wheatley, J. (2015). What is an emerging market? Financial Times, August 3. Retrieved from https://www.ft.com/content/8a393522-39bf-11e5-bbd1-b37bc06f590c

Part II

Contemporary Perspectives on Marketing Communications and Brand Development: Destination Brand Management and Brand Avoidance

2

The Progress of Destination Marketing in Emerging Economies: A Focus on ASEAN

Mohd Raziff Jamaluddin, Mohd Hafiz Mohd Hanafiah, and Daryl Ace V. Cornell

Introduction

Over the last two decades, destination planning has changed the landscape of marketing studies (Fyall et al., 2019). In contrast to the conventional thinking that a single destination should be designed as one offering, stakeholders of tourist destinations have now understood and considered the mix of different goods and services in a location. Moreover, the players in this environment have different roles that influence each other, and

---

M. R. Jamaluddin (✉) • M. H. M. Hanafiah
Faculty of Hotel and Tourism Management, Universiti Teknologi MARA, Selangor, Malaysia
e-mail: raziff@uitm.edu.my; hafizhanafiah@uitm.edu.my

D. A. V. Cornell
College of Tourism, Hospitality & Transportation Management, Polytechnic University of the Philippines, Manila, Philippines

© The Author(s), under exclusive license to Springer Nature Switzerland AG 2022
O. Adeola et al. (eds.), *Marketing Communications and Brand Development in Emerging Economies Volume I*, Palgrave Studies of Marketing in Emerging Economies, https://doi.org/10.1007/978-3-030-88678-3_2

determining the impact that each has on varying components would now require a more integrated approach to promoting the destination. Integrated marketing communication has had a significant impact on marketing research including destination marketing. For example, the marketing mix element generates a great deal of research and has become a common marketing concept in textbooks and research on emerging economies (Nekmahmud, Farkas & Hassan, 2020; Hesam et al., 2017; Maltio & Wardi, 2019; Sadq et al., 2019; Sheikhi & Pazoki, 2017). As emphasised by Amin and Priansah (2019), marketing communication remains relevant in tourism destination planning because it serves a variety of purposes for attracting customers or target audiences, including informing and demonstrating how and why a product is used, who the target market is, and where and when the product is available. However, the marketing communication landscape has also changed due to the advancement of communication process technology, as it is the case with the recent increase in internet growth and availability and destination marketers have to take advantage of technology to become more competitive.

Recently, online marketing communication has become one of the most powerful marketing strategies because of its more comprehensive coverage, allowing for greater promotional exposure to a broader audience (Krizanova et al., 2019). Online forms of marketing communication are much faster to use than traditional communication platforms since the advertiser has more networked devices to provide more information to a prospective customer at a reasonable cost. According to Gorlevskaya (2016), destination marketers must fully comprehend the sociodemographic profile, desires, attitudes, perceptions, and, most importantly, media consumption to create successful marketing communications. For example, in an emerging economy like Indonesia, Koswara et al. (2019) discovered that a "one village, one product" initiative would fail if the destination marketing organisation lacks proper marketing communication. This is due to two key issues: a lack of human resources, that is, a lack of skillset, and a lack of expertise and experience in marketing communication.

Consideration of these issues would lead to a well-planned tourist experience that will leave visitors with positive memories, resulting in a long-term and sustainable relationship between the demand and supply sides of the industry. In Asia, the Association of Southeast Asian Nations (ASEAN), the regional community comprising ten South East Asian nations, aspires to achieve political-security cooperation, economic prosperity, and sociocultural integration. The ten countries include Brunei, Cambodia, Indonesia, Laos, Malaysia, Myanmar, the Philippines, Singapore, Thailand and Vietnam. In the destination marketing aspect, the cooperation takes the form of strategic collaboration, which involves positioning and branding the region as a single destination, eliminating customer confusion, and ensuring transparency. The challenge for ASEAN as the plan unfolds is to encourage sub-regional destinations and routes to be more inclusive and visible. Through @goaseantv (a web platform that promotes travel and tourism), ASEAN promotes tourism destinations and scenic landmarks by leveraging two popular programmes, "The Eco Traveler" and "Go Fast Go Home" which are promoted across the channel (Nugroho, 2017). The partnership kicks off with the broadcast of various programmes about regional tourism products like food, culture, extreme sports, festivals, and religions. According to Nugroho (2017), most of the activities promoted in @goaseantv occur in Malaysia, and other ASEAN members have limited opportunities to promote in the platform. As a result, future programmes should consider increasing the proportion of other countries, promoted and forming a partnership with ASEAN countries' tourism networks to clearly showcase ASEAN as a ONE brand association. This chapter covers issues on competitiveness and destination marketing among emerging economies and documents the progress of destination marketing research. Next, the chapter presents a few examples focusing on marketing communication from some emerging economies in the light of the global crisis caused by COVID-19. Finally, the chapter explains how stakeholders play a part in destination marketing.

Competitiveness and Destination Marketing in Emerging Economies

Sales promotion tools remain essential in destination marketing communication to convert target audience from knowledge quest to option and purchase. Through an extensive literature search, price competitiveness is the most crucial factor for visiting. It can be presumed that knowing tourist disposable income reserved for travel is a crucial consideration for the business. ASEAN Tourism Marketing Strategy 2017–2020 was established to carry out specific initiatives under the purview of the ASEAN Tourism Marketing and Communication Working Group (MCWG) to improve the availability and reliability of market research data and analysis to enhance experience creation, packaging, pricing, distribution, and promotion (ASEAN, 2017). The flow of tourists to the destination is influenced by price competitiveness, as is vulnerability to changes in external forces (Sul et al., 2020). Destination marketing organisation relies on the country's overall economic stability, including price differentials, exchange rate fluctuations, and various tourism industry components (Dwyer et al., 2020). According to Suppiah and Selvaratnam (2020), the "2014 Visit Malaysia Year campaign" positively impacted tourism demand due to lower comparable prices; however, cross-elasticities indicate substitution effects between Malaysia and alternative destinations. Based on the study by Loganatan et al. (2019), the tax cut in Malaysia significantly affects inbound tourism because it will increase trade and stimulate its GDP. Furthermore, they advocated that fiscal policy should be more inclusive of a positive long-term effect on the tourism industry that will attract investment opportunities in mega projects. This, in turn, will create jobs and stability in the tourism industry and eventually become a unique selling proposition for the tourism industry.

Another critical issue for ASEAN is destination positioning, as it is essential to revisit how ASEAN should be positioned and promoted in its markets as a single destination to reduce the risk of market uncertainty and ensure clarification (ASEAN, 2017). The consumer should be presented with a single destination brand in which different product thematic destinations, circuits, and corridors can be introduced. According to ASEAN (2017), the most essential factor is to meet changing visitor expectations because visitors will recognise and demand constantly evolving and developing experiences like resort corridors, adventure circuits, pilgrimage circuits, and ecotourism.

The element of human interaction is one of the components that emerged in preliminary findings in the literature. The involvement of humans in tourism marketing is vital to measure the success of the overall experience. For developed tourist destinations, high-quality human resources ensure the industry has access to the right people to serve the international tourists (World Economic Forum, 2019). As proposed in the Travel and Tourism (T&T) Competitiveness Index, the high-quality human resource derived from how efficient the countries develop skills through education and training and allocate ideally to the labour market (World Economic Forum, 2019). According to Hamarneh and Jeřábek (2018), the human development index is a vital method for assessing the safety and security of the destination, with the factor of safety consisting of a collection of precautions put in place to prevent tourists and industry workers from being exposed to circumstances where they assume they are in personal danger as a result of crime, accidents, or emergencies. A study conducted in Western Europe by Nagaj and Žuromskaite (2020) suggested that to ensure that tourism continues to develop and generate income for tourist regions, all stakeholders in this sector should pay more attention to their safety and security customers. When deciding on a trip, tourists choose a tourist destination and a hotel, or more broadly, an accommodation facility, guided not only by the criterion of price, but also by the level of security in these facilities. Similarly, Malaysia has taken steps in the Tourism Blueprint post-September 11 to ensure that the tourism industry strengthens Malaysia's status as a top tourist destination by implementing strategies to ensure visitors' comfort, safety, and well-being (Ayob & Masron, 2014).

Infrastructure received considerably great attention from tourism scholars. The availability of sufficient facilities to meet visitors' needs would inevitably attract new visitors to the tourist area, making it an excellent topic for research. Jafari and Xiao (2016) mentioned that recreational facilities are an essential component of the physical infrastructure that supports overall economic and tourism growth. They suggested that tourism infrastructure is made up of hotels, other forms of infrastructure, and spas and restaurants to replace the generic description of infrastructures that include mental amenities, physical amenities, environmental amenities, and legal amenities. World Economic Forum (2019) suggested three dimensions of infrastructure used in the study for macrolevel to examine the destination's competitiveness for benchmarking purposes. Infrastructure could play a significant role in attracting conscientious tourists and promoting a more pleasant tourist experience by encouraging visitors to suggest the destination to other friends and relatives (Mikolon et al., 2015; Moscardo, 2017). However, in the current environment, the element of digital infrastructure (i.e. high-speed internet access; public and free WiFi) received overwhelming attention from the scholars in order to cater for the need of millennials that rely on information and stay connected during travels (Bozhuk et al., 2020; Kumar & Shekhar, 2020; Natocheeva et al., 2020).

For a destination, digital marketing has become an integral aspect of the global economy to advertise products or services (Natocheeva et al., 2020). Digital innovation means the destination is aware of the latest trend relevant to the tourist preference, thus digitalising the emerging technology that is quickest and most efficient in destination marketing (Natocheeva et al., 2020). Tourists plan their travel routes, choose itineraries for excursion visits, and book overnight accommodations entirely on digital, online, and social application platforms (Bozhuk et al., 2020). Hence, it is vital for promotion to maintain a positive image of the destination by disseminating content, a key message about the benefits of travel and recreation, and the destination's features that the tourists want to see, live, and experience regularly.

Tourism Malaysia's marketing and promotion strategies centred on rising tourist arrivals in the short term and maintaining a positive reputation in the long term, from the first blueprint in 1966 to 2015 (Hussin & Buchmann, 2019). It is worth noting that the grand opening of "Visit Malaysia Year 2014" coincides with the launch of a digital marketing campaign that focused on leveraging digital assets to optimise presence in the digital realm, growing and maintaining a positive relationship with fans and followers on social media, and eventually converting them into real tourists or repeat visitors (Tourism Malaysia, 2014). Tourism Malaysia uses a YouTube channel, online TV, social media, website, and an official mobile travel app as a digital marketing tool. The digital marketing strategy software was said to have received over 12.5 million views (Tourism Malaysia, 2014).

Another new idea in destination marketing that is gaining momentum in current academic discussions is "Sustainable Growth", as described by the World Travel and Tourism Council (WTTC) under "Sustainable Development Goals" (World Travel & Tourism Council, 2021). Sustainable growth focuses on eight key areas as follows (Table 2.1):

Recently, there has been an increasing body of literature on sustainable tourism in emerging markets that focuses on improving residents' quality of life by leveraging tourism's economic, social, cultural, recreational, and

Table 2.1 Sustainable growth

Key Area	Summary of description
Inclusion, Diversity & Social Impact	Due to the unpredictable nature of the environment, there is an urgent need to bond together to assist hundreds of millions of people who have lost their jobs and livelihoods and continue to assist the millions who benefit from the tourism sector by rebuilding more sustainably and responsibly. Although the industry was temporarily on hold due to the pandemic, global citizens were re-energized to solve social and environmental issues, providing a rare opportunity to harness this newfound energy to boost travel and tourism for future generations and the world.
Climate & Environment Action	There is a growing understanding of the rapid pace of climate change and its catastrophic consequences. Many destinations already feel the consequences, and the risk appears to be most significant in countries with the fastest-growing tourism industries. Given the importance of travel and tourism to the global economy, the achievement of the Sustainable Development Goals (SDGs), and the increasing need to effectively resolve climate change.
Sustainable Travel & Tourism Partners	This initiative seeks to foster extensive involvement in the tourism industry's sustainability initiatives by bringing together all Travel & Tourism companies that are involved in significant sustainability efforts under one roof, intending to increase sustainable practices in the sector, raising awareness of those practices, and tracking progress with consumers and governments.
Sustainability Reporting	This is to pave the way for globally sustained, inclusive, and sustainable economic growth by focusing on sustainable consumption and development. It has the goal of "encouraging businesses, huge and transnational companies, to adopt sustainable practices and to incorporate sustainability information into their reporting cycle." Sustainability reporting will assist market players in understanding the main principles behind reporting, providing an overview of the policies and developments that are moving this activity forward, and identifying the sector's implications and opportunities.

(*continued*)

Table 2.1 (continued)

Key Area	Summary of description
Destination Stewardship	Many destinations around the world have become victims of their success as the travel and tourism industry has grown in recent years, with words like "overcrowding," "overtourism," and "tourismphobia" dominating media headlines around the world. Tourism should benefit the communities in which it relies on while also preserving cultural and natural resources. In this sense, the WTTC brings together public and private sector stakeholders and local communities to develop tourism management strategies focused on long-term planning.
Future of Work	The travel and tourism industry employs 330 million people, about one out of every ten people on the planet, which is expected to rise. Furthermore, the travel and tourism industry has generated one out of every four new jobs globally in the last five years. The travel and tourism industry must attract, upskill, and retain skilled talent to sustain 421 million jobs by 2029. Businesses and policymakers will need to pay particular attention to talent models as the travel and tourism industry evolves and changes in the global workforce.
Illegal Wildlife Trade	The illicit wildlife trade has impacted about 7000 species of animals and plants from all over the world and generated US$20 billion annually. Since wildlife is a significant driver of travel and tourism, it is in the sector's best interests to support measures that protect it. WTTC aspires to provide the sector with a well-coordinated, high-level approach. WTTC released the Travel & Tourism Declaration on Illegal Wildlife Trade (IWT) in April 2018, committing over 100 members to actively engage in the global fight against illegal wildlife trade.
Human Trafficking	The travel and tourism industry has the ability and obligation to bring about change in the fight against human trafficking in its supply chain. As a result, at the 2019 Global Summit, WTTC unveiled its Human Trafficking Taskforce to reduce human trafficking and provide a platform for concerted action across the industry. While enhancing collaboration with the public sector and civil society, the taskforce will promote knowledge sharing and organise efforts across the private sector. Prevention, protection, intervention, and assistance will be the priority.

Source: World Travel and Tourism Council (2021)

other benefits (Sheresheva et al., 2020). The Scientific communities of research scholars, research projects, and international organisations have made sustainability a priority, premised on the United Nations' "Sustainable Development Goals", and sustainable tourism has been identified as having a potential role to play in achieving them (Martini & Buffa, 2020). Sustainable tourism marketing typically focuses on "pro-sustainability" customers who have a biospheric–altruistic value orientation, are passionate about sustainability issues, and have an interest in and positive attitude towards environmentally sustainable consumption (Vinzenz et al., 2019).

The Progress of Destination Marketing Research

It is essential to recognise that the tourism ecosystem is vast and expanding. The industry is naturally unpredictable, uncertain, dynamic, ambiguous, and disruptive, making the destination marketers confront a new set of issues and concerns (Mikulić, 2020). The difficulties that tourism scholars face in assessing and gathering critical data result from the intertwined facets of the external structures in the operating environment. Fyall and Leask (2006) introduced "15Cs Framework" that conceptualise the key issues and challenges that confront destinations. The framework is introduced as efficient means for destination marketers to synthesise several generic issues that, for their destinations, would require a highly customised management approach. The variables in the framework include (1) complexity, (2) control, (3) change, (4) crisis, (5) complacency, (6) customers, (7) culture, (8) competition, (9) commodification, (10) creativity, (11) communication, (12) channels, (13) consolidation, (14) cyberspace, and (15) collaboration. Recently, Sotiriadis (2021) elaborated on the research field of destination marketing and synthesised the relevant topics and issues. (See Table 2.2)

The marketing environment is one of the popular topics in recent years due to the unpredictable nature of occurrences (i.e., health issues, economic crises and natural disasters) in the world. The travel industry is adapting to changes in the tourism ecosystem, and it will continue to do

Table 2.2 A Classification/synthesis of topics in the research field of tourism destination marketing

Destination marketing functions: main components and activities	Topic and issues	Focus on
1. Marketing planning and market research	Marketing research Marketing environmental analysis Marketing information system Destination marketing system	Effective and efficient planning Strategic analyses, techniques, and methods Process, influencing factors, and results
2. Marketing strategies: design/elaboration of main marketing strategies	Market segmentation analysis Targeting and positioning Destination image Destination branding	Effectiveness and appropriateness of marketing choices Positioning-image-branding approach Brand development (process) and management Loyalty
3. Implementation of strategies: marketing action plans	Marketing mix Usage of tools to communicate with targeted markets Digital marketing Social media marketing	Content, media, and techniques. The 8Ps model (product, price, place/distribution, promotion, packaging, programming, partnership, and people). Assessing the appropriateness (suitable use) and effectiveness of various tools and media
4. Control and evaluation: monitoring and assessing performance	Customer feedback Performance evaluation Benchmarking Measurement of the effectiveness of marketing activities	Control methods and metrics Monitoring and assessing progress Evaluation procedures and measurements Performance measures/metrics for the action Plans and activities included in the marketing plan

Source: Sotiriadis (2021)

so as time goes on. As their priorities change, they will continue to look for the "order qualifier" (necessary attributes of a product) and "order winners" (winning attributes of a product) (Prajogo & McDermott, 2011) from the pool they have built. Furthermore, as the market becomes steeper and more complex, the market and tourism service providers are confronted with an increasing amount of data that is accessible to them across a variety of channels (Khodadadi, 2016). Because of the "online world" and accessible information, it is more difficult to obtain data that is highly relevant to the needs of a specific sector (Buhalis & Zoge, 2007). Destination marketers must also ensure that they have access to the most up-to-date and sought-after data to target tourists and businesses and sell to them accurately. To do so, they would have to be present on various platforms, especially the digital world, where most potential travellers, particularly the millennial generation, can be found.

Destination Marketing During COVID-19

The tourism industry's unpredictable and uncertain nature makes it challenging for destination marketers to prepare for inevitable changes and resource allocations that would benefit both its demand and supply. Globally, the COVID-19 pandemic has brought a lot of issues to the table and has compelled most companies to go digital due to the challenges that physical interaction poses (Fotiadis et al., 2021). In the Philippines, the state of the nation had a significant effect on the economy and an enormous impact on the tourism industry (Centeno & Marquez, 2020). Natural disasters ravaged the country in the early months, making it difficult for destination marketers to promote places of interest, and by March 2020, COVID 19 had taken over the media. With these concerns ever-present, destination marketers must formulate concrete strategies that address these issues and those that might occur in the future. To address this problem, the Philippine Department of Tourism introduced the idea of "travel bubbles" (travel corridors that permit free movement), which attract domestic tourists to locally accredited points of interest (Department of Tourism Philippines, 2020). With these contingency plans in place, the destination will adapt quickly while maintaining a favourable economic environment for all tourism stakeholders.

The website has become a standard tool for promoting a destination. The more advanced a website's architecture is, the more appealing it is to its users. Its design has evolved from posting information to a forum for various solutions geared towards customer satisfaction (Martínez-Sala et al., 2020). Destination marketers must keep up-to-date website solutions and their associated functions. There are also possibilities for borderless relationships as a result of the COVID-19 pandemic. Technology made it possible for further convergence amid increased competition from inside and outside their territories, offering destination marketers plenty of ideas to reflect on in the years ahead. As extensively reviewed by Mariani (2020), recent website variables adopted in destination marketing research included demographics of the end-user, motivation to visit the destination, information sources required, previous destination visitation experience, psychological, temporal, and spatial distance to/from the destination, identity and self-concepts, emotions, platform type, level of interactivity, media exposure, and devices used. Designation marketing organisations can utilise these variables to improve the user experience on their websites and attract more tourists.

Social networking sites such as Facebook, Twitter, MySpace vibe, Pinterest, and Instagram have risen steadily in popularity over the last decade, including Africa, a less developed continent (Dzandu et al., 2016). The social climate has changed as travellers' conversations have moved from word-of-mouth (WOM) to e-word-of-mouth (eWOM) (Gosal et al., 2020). Li et al. (2020) conducted a study on TikTok short food videos in China and analysed the effect of short food videos on destination image during COVID-19. TikTok's short videos in the form of cognitive images increased potential tourists' attention to the destination image, especially their attention to the flavour characteristics of the destination's food and the local social environment (Li et al., 2020). Furthermore, the appearance description of food in short food videos produces a noticeable impact of intention and a desire to travel together and acquire information.

The buzzwords in the travel digital space, are social networking and social media marketing, so destination marketers will need to "follow" and "subscribe" to this trend. User-generated content makes their jobs more challenging because the online world now plays a more prominent role in the decision-making of this generation (Christou & Chatzigeorgiou, 2020). To build a seamless social ecosystem for future travellers, destination marketers must remain informed with digital resources. They could use various Internet technology, such as blogging, vlogging, virtual tours, gamified content, and other social networking programmes, to maximise potential tourists' desire to travel and turn it into a reality. Javed et al. (2020) revealed that the active use of social media during travel in terms of exchanging stories, photographs, and videos influences other future visitors to travel to exotic destinations, making Web 2.0 and social media more engaging. It also opened to a new trend of following "social influencers". Hwang and Zhang (2018) described that the "influencers" could control the purchasing decisions of many followers in the virtual world. During the COVID-19 lockdown, influence arises from an influencer's personality, which includes their power, experiences, ways of thinking, leadership tendencies, profane impulses for the supporting material, or simply the followers' faith in that influencer (Hwang & Zhang, 2018; Praničević, 2020).

Digital marketing is becoming increasingly critical for destination marketing organisations (DMOs) and is being used extensively in their marketing campaigns, according to Sotiriadis (2020). DMOs will make every effort to connect with all Information communication technologies (ICTs) that use digital platforms and interactive marketing networks, such as content design, blogs, search engine marketing, optimisation, social media, smartphones, and e-mail. In their study in India, Sivakumar et al. (2020) found that social media platforms and mobile applications are preferred in the decision-making process of e-tourism services. It is well expected that the top four applications are WhatsApp, YouTube, Facebook, and Instagram. Sivakumar et al. (2020) further noted that ease of usage, security, and reliability are the essential factors determining the decision-making to use social media and mobile applications. In the post COVID-19, social media determinants were found to be centred on places of interest in image strategies; moments or events of unique tourist interest; lifestyle attributes or interests for visitors, such as biking, sailing, or gastronomy; and the use of words to connect positive feelings related to travel, according to a study conducted in the Philippines (Heras-Pedrosa et al., 2020).

In another aspect, sustainability paradigms and concepts, as examined by Sotiriadis (2021), can make a significant contribution to destination marketing. Understanding market needs, planning more sustainable offerings and experience opportunities, and finding more compelling methods of communication to influence tourists' behaviour positively are examples of how sustainability marketing can effectively utilise marketing concepts and methods. As advocated by Paunović et al. (2020), a destination's long-term success post COVID-19 is determined by its global competitiveness, as well as the ability to sustain that competitive position and be resilient in the face of unforeseen events. Future destination marketing research can use a complex mix of social, cultural, political, and economic relationships, making tourism research a transdisciplinary field of study that connects sustainability to destination marketing from a local, regional, or national perspective.

Destination Marketing and the Role of Stakeholders

In destination marketing study, the government's position was often overlooked. The government's primary role is to safeguard and boost the public interest (Dredge, 2010). It is in charge of regulating the scope and scale of tourism production. Furthermore, since the tourism industry causes numerous disputes and issues among stakeholders, it is the job of the government to mediate and function as a decision-making body. The government will project an image of being an "infrastructure and facility provider" in the early stages, but later move into a more vital position by implementing legislation and policies, strategies, and other allied services. Destination marketers may take a more organised approach to strategising how to rebrand a destination to a target market supported by government policies. The Philippines established a tourism circuit plan focusing on 21 regional clusters of the country through local government units (Alampay et al., 2018). The country has developed its own National Tourism Development Plan by working with each local government unit. Changes that could improve the social, economic, and environmental benefits are highly expected as a result of the national/local government's efforts.

Next, the destination marketing research could look at the private sector, which works closely with the government, to develop a more holistic strategy that benefits all stakeholders (Wang & Xu, 2014). Since there is rivalry among the players, government intervention would be necessary to level the playing field. Although some researchers argue that a tourism development heavily controlled by the public sector is unlikely to achieve optimal economic returns (Shone et al., 2016), the private sector will be needed to help mitigate its drawbacks. Numerous government issues can be easily solved with private-sector assistance. Strong public-private partnerships are the most important components of successful tourism business models.

Another important stakeholder in tourism, the community, also plays a critical role in sustainable tourism. The majority of community leaders and economic development experts have gradually viewed tourism as a vital industry that can boost local jobs, tax revenues, and economic diversity (Kim et al., 2013). Poverty alleviation was at the forefront of national strategies, with more opportunities for the poor to benefit from collaborations and the international community's involvement (Kişi, 2019). This is especially true in the case of the community where the destination is situated. The community sits at the centre of collaboration among the stakeholders. They are the ones who will be initially affected once a plan is approved or marketing starts. Thus, they have the right to vote in support or against a specific move from any of the stakeholders. They can withdraw support anytime, which can threaten the destination marketers' position within their community. However, if a deep connection is established within the community, the community itself can help the destination marketers promote the place and thus entail little effort from the other external stakeholders (Tosun, 2000). Therefore, a deep relationship should be established between the prime movers of the community and make them understand the benefits and drawbacks of any move that the other stakeholders may make.

Conclusion

Destination marketing has emerged as a fascinating subject in the tourism industry. With the advent of emerging technologies and the current world's unpredictability, destination marketing provides endless possibilities for future researchers to investigate the potential and assess the risks of technical advancements in the field of inbound and outbound tourism. End-users such as millennials provide a great perspective on the evolution and future of travel activity. Academic researchers should keep up with these developments and suggest a dynamic modelling methodology that can spark further debate. Increased emphasis on keeping promises made to visitors, advancement of strategic and research concepts, and an increased focus on the study of actual actions present exciting opportunities for future research. In addition, comparative studies, as suggested by the World Travel and Tourism Council, should be considered by future researchers. Various investigations of partnership in destination marketing, the role of stakeholders, and governance in destination marketing were articulated to provide suggestions for more rigorous studies in destination marketing, especially in emerging economies, as highlighted in the study. Another intriguing research area is to investigate the future of travels using a scenario approach to destination management and marketing in the context of globalisation, digitalisation, and uncertainty caused by various economic and health issues.

References

Alampay, R. B. A., Mena, M. M., & Villegas, V. H. (2018). Tourism circuit planning for subnational tourism development in the Philippines. In *Managing Asian destinations* (pp. 35–53). Springer.

Amin, M., & Priansah, P. (2019). Marketing communication strategy to improve tourism potential. *Budapest International Research and Critics Institute-Journal (BIRCI-Journal), 2*(4), 160–166.

ASEAN. (2017). *ASEAN tourism marketing strategy 2017–2020*. ASEAN Secretariat, Jakarta, INDONESIA, September 2017.

Ayob, N. M., & Masron, T. (2014). *Issues of safety and security: New challenging to Malaysia tourism industry*. SHS Web of Conferences 12, 0108 (2014).

Bozhuk, S., Pletneva, N., Maslova, T., & Evdokimov, K. (2020). *Problems of transformation in the tourism industry in the digital economy*. In SHS Web of Conferences (Vol. 73, p. 01003). EDP Sciences.

Buhalis, D., & Zoge, M. (2007). The strategic impact of the Internet on the tourism industry. *Information and Communication Technologies in Tourism, 2007*, 481–492.

Centeno, R. S., & Marquez, J. P. (2020). *How much did the tourism industry lost? Estimating earning loss of tourism in the Philippines*. arXiv preprint arXiv:2004.09952.

Christou, E., & Chatzigeorgiou, C. (2020). Adoption of social media as distribution channels in tourism marketing: A qualitative analysis of consumers' experiences. *Journal of Tourism, Heritage & Services Marketing (JTHSM), 6*(1), 25–32.

Department of Tourism Philippines. (2020). *DOT Supports Expansion of Palawan's Travel Bubble Starting Oct. 30*. Department of Tourism-Philippines. www.tourism.gov.ph/news_features/ExpansionOfPalawanTravelBubble.aspx

Dredge, D. (2010). Place change and tourism development conflict: Evaluating public interest. *Tourism Management, 31*(1), 104–112.

Dwyer, L., Forsyth, P., & Rao, P. (2020). The price competitiveness of travel and tourism: A comparison of 19 destinations. *Tourism Management, 21*, 9–22.

Dzandu, M. D., Boateng, H., Agyemang, F. G., & Quansah, F. (2016). Social media adoption among university students: The role of gender, perceived usefulness and perceived ease of use. *International Journal of Social Media and Interactive Learning Environments, 4*(2), 124–136.

Fotiadis, A., Polyzos, S., & Huan, T. C. T. (2021). The good, the bad and the ugly on COVID-19 tourism recovery. *Annals of Tourism Research, 87*, 103117.

Fyall, A., & Leask, A. (2006). Destination marketing: Future issues – Strategic challenges. *Tourism and Hospitality Research, 7*(1), 50–63.

Fyall, A., Legohérel, P., Frochot, I., & Wang, Y. (2019). *Marketing for tourism and hospitality: Collaboration, technology and experiences*. Routledge.

Gorlevskaya, L. (2016). Building effective marketing communications in tourism. *Studia Commercialia Bratislavensia, 9*(35), 252–265.

Gosal, J., Andajani, E., & Rahayu, S. (2020, January). The effect of e-WOM on travel intention, travel decision, city image, and attitude to visit a tourism city. In *17th International Symposium on Management (INSYMA 2020)* (pp. 261–265). Atlantis Press.

Hamarneh, I., & Jeřábek, P. (2018). The impact of the security situation on tourism in the countries of the former Yugoslavia. *Security & Future, 2*(3), 111–115.

Heras-Pedrosa, C. D. L., Millan-Celis, E., Iglesias-Sánchez, P. P., & Jambrino-Maldonado, C. (2020). Importance of social media in the image formation of tourist destinations from the stakeholders' perspective. *Sustainability, 12*(10), 4092.

Hesam, M., Cheraghi, M., Akbari, Z., & Rohban, S. (2017). Evaluation and prioritize of marketing mix components influence the development of rural tourism (Case study: Villages of Foman County). *Journal of Rural Research, 8*(3), 470–487.

Hussin, N. Z. I., & Buchmann, A. (2019). Understanding tourism development policies in Malaysia. *Journal of Policy Research in Tourism, Leisure and Events, 11*(2), 333–353.

Hwang, K., & Zhang, Q. (2018). Influence of parasocial relationship between digital celebrities and their followers on followers' purchase and electronic word-of-mouth intentions, and persuasion knowledge. *Computers in Human Behavior, 87*, 155–173.

Jafari, J., & Xiao, H. (Eds.). (2016). *Encyclopedia of tourism*. Springer Reference.

Javed, M., Tučková, Z., & Jibril, A. B. (2020). The role of social media on tourists' behavior: An empirical analysis of millennials from the Czech Republic. *Sustainability, 12*(18), 7735.

Khodadadi, M. (2016). Challenges and opportunities for tourism development in Iran: Perspectives of Iranian tourism suppliers. *Tourism Management Perspectives, 19*, 90–92.

Kim, K., Uysal, M., & Sirgy, M. J. (2013). How does tourism in a community impact the quality of life of community residents? *Tourism Management, 36*, 527–540.

Kişi, N. (2019). A strategic approach to sustainable tourism development using the A'WOT hybrid method: A case study of Zonguldak, Turkey. *Sustainability, 11*(4), 964.

Koswara, I., Erlandia, D. R., & Truline, P. (2019). The strategy of marketing communication in tourism industry through one village one product approach in West Java Province. *International Journal of Psychosocial Rehabilitation, 23*(2), 365–372.

Krizanova, A., Lăzăroiu, G., Gajanova, L., Kliestikova, J., Nadanyiova, M., & Moravcikova, D. (2019). The effectiveness of marketing communication and importance of its evaluation in an online environment. *Sustainability, 11*(24), 7016.

Kumar, S., & Shekhar, A. (2020). Digitalization: A strategic approach for development of tourism industry in India. *Paradigm, 24*(1), 93–108.

Li, Y., Xu, X., Song, B., & He, H. (2020). Impact of short food videos on the tourist destination image – Take Chengdu as an example. *Sustainability, 12*(17), 6739.

Loganatan, N., Ahmad, N., Mursitama, T. N., Taha, R., Mardani, A., & Streimikiene, D. (2019). The effects of exchange rate, price competitiveness indices and taxation on international tourism demand in Malaysia. *Economics & Sociology, 12*(3), 86–97.

Maltio, M., & Wardi, Y. (2019, April). The influence marketing mix, islamic tourism and satisfaction to visitor loyalty: A literature review. In *2nd Padang International Conference on Education, Economics, Business and Accounting (PICEEBA-2 2018)* (pp. 118–126). Atlantis Press.

Mariani, M. (2020). Web 2.0 and destination marketing: Current trends and future directions. *Sustainability, 12*(9), 3771.

Martínez-Sala, A. M., Monserrat-Gauchi, J., & Alemany-Martínez, D. (2020). User usable experience: A three-dimensional approach on usability in tourism websites and a model for its evaluation. *Tourism Management Perspectives, 33*, 100579.

Martini, U., & Buffa, F. (2020). Marketing for sustainable tourism. *Sustainability, 2020*(12), 1–6.

Mikolon, S., Kolberg, A., Haumann, T., & Wieseke, J. (2015). How much is too much? how perceived service complexity erodes cognitive capacity in the selling of professional services. *Journal of Service Research, 18*(4), 513–528.

Mikulić, J. (2020). Tourism in a VUCA world. *Tourism: An International Interdisciplinary Journal, 68*(2), 119–140.

Moscardo, G. (2017). Exploring mindfulness and stories in tourist experiences. *International Journal of Culture, Tourism and Hospitality Research, 11*(2), 111–124.

Nagaj, R., & Žuromskaite, B. (2020). Security measures as a factor in the competitiveness of accommodation facilities. *Journal of Risk and Financial Management, 13*(5), 99.

Natocheeva, N., Shayakhmetova, L., Bekkhozhaeva, A., Khamikhan, N., & Pshembayeva, D. (2020). Digital technologies as a driver for the development of the tourism industry. In E3S Web of Conferences (Vol. 159, p. 04002). EDP Sciences.

Nekmahmud, M., Farkas, M. F., & Hassan, A. (2020). In *Tourism marketing in Bangladesh* (pp. 11–27). Routledge.

Nugroho, A. (2017). ASEAN tourism marketing communication attribute: An exploratory research at GoASEANTV. *European Research Studies Journal, XX*(3A), 383–395.

Paunović, I., Dressler, M., Mamula Nikolić, T., & Popović Pantić, S. (2020). Developing a competitive and sustainable destination of the future: Clusters and predictors of successful national-level destination governance across destination life-cycle. *Sustainability, 12*(10), 4066.

Prajogo, D. I., & McDermott, P. (2011). Examining competitive priorities and competitive advantage in service organisations using Importance-Performance Analysis matrix. *Managing Service Quality: An International Journal, 21*, 465–483.

Praničević, D. G. (2020). Impact of influencers to the selection of certain products and services. In Proceedings of the ENTRENOVA-enterprise research innovation conference (Vol. 6, No. 1, pp. 422–429).

Sadq, Z. M., Othman, B., & Khorsheed, R. K. (2019). The impact of tourism marketing in enhancing competitive capabilities. *African Journal of Hospitality, Tourism and Leisure, 8*(5), 1–11.

Sheikhi, D., & Pazoki, M. (2017). Assessing and prioritizing the factors affecting rural tourism marketing using the marketing mix model (A case study: Jozan District, Malayer Township). *Journal of Rural Research, 8*(3), 488–501.

Sheresheva, M. Y., Polukhina, A. N., & Oborin, M. S. (2020). Marketing issues of sustainable tourism development in Russian regions. *Journal of Tourism, Heritage & Services Marketing, 6*(1), 33–38.

Shone, M. C., Simmons, D. G., & Dalziel, P. (2016). Evolving roles for local government in tourism development: A political economy perspective. *Journal of Sustainable Tourism, 24*(12), 1674–1690.

Sivakumar, V., Saranya, P. R., Leelapriyadharsini, S., & Iyappan, A. (2020). Impact of social media on e-tourism: A critical analysis of determinants of decision making. *Journal of Tourism, Hospitality & Culinary Arts, 12*(1), 92–98.

Sotiriadis, M. (2021). Tourism destination marketing: Academic knowledge. *Encyclopedia, 1*(1), 42–56.

Sul, H. K., Chi, X., & Han, H. (2020). Measurement development for tourism destination business environment and competitive advantages. *Sustainability, 12*(20), 8587.

Suppiah, R., & Selvaratnam, D. P. (2020). Tourism demand in Malaysia: A panel data analysis of 17 OECD countries. *Journal of Tourism, Hospitality & Culinary Arts, 12*(3), 52–64.

Tosun, C. (2000). Limits to community participation in the tourism development process in developing countries. *Tourism Management, 21*, 613–633.

Tourism Malaysia. (2014). *Tourism Malaysia launches integrated digital marketing programme.* https://www.tourism.gov.my/pdf/uploads/

Vinzenz, F., Priskin, J., Wirth, W., Ponnapureddy, S., & Ohnmacht, T. (2019). Marketing sustainable tourism: The role of value orientation, well-being and credibility. *Journal of Sustainable Tourism, 27*(11), 1663–1685.

Wang, C., & Xu, H. (2014). The role of local government and the private sector in China's tourism industry. *Tourism Management, 45*, 95–105.

World Economic Forum. (2019). *The travel & tourism competitiveness report 2019 travel and tourism at a tipping point.* http://www3.weforum.org

World Travel & Tourism Council. (2021). *Sustainable growth.* Sustainable Development Goals Report. https://wttc.org/Initiatives/Sustainable-Growth

3

Nation Branding as a Strategic Approach for Emerging Economies: The Case of UAE

Gouher Ahmed, Anas Abudaqa, C. Jayachandran, Yam Limbu, and Rashed Alzahmi

Introduction

The concept of nation branding covers the application of branding and marketing communication strategies and techniques to promote a nation's image (Kaur, 2020; Rojas-Méndez, 2013). Although researchers, academic stakeholders, and other public policymakers have shown their

---

G. Ahmed (✉)
School of Business, Skyline University College, University City of Sharjah, Sharjah, UAE

A. Abudaqa
School of Distance Education, Universiti Sains Malaysia, Penang, Malaysia

C. Jayachandran • Y. Limbu
Department of Marketing, School of Business, Montclair State University, Montclair, NJ, USA
e-mail: jayachandrc@mail.montclair.edu; limbuy@montclair.edu

R. Alzahmi
College of Business and Economics, UAE University, Abu Dhabi, UAE
e-mail: ralzahmi@uaeu.ac.ae

reasonable interest in the subject of nation branding (NB) (Aronczyk, 2009), it is still in the infancy stage and lacks concrete or generally accepted definition and constructs. Meanwhile, one of the growing points in the field of NB is that in the contemporary time, various nations are competing with each other to attract more international tourists, foreign investment, the flow of goods and services, and many other activities (Aronczyk, 2013; Steenkamp, 2019). For this purpose, NB includes topics like nation-related country image, country reputation, nation brand personality, and nation brand strength (He et al., 2020; Papadopoulos et al., 2016; Rojas-Méndez et al., 2019).

Many scholars have theorised concepts and definitions of NB over the past decade. For instance, NB is a sum of beliefs and impressions that people may carry about that particular place or group of places (Kotler & Gertner, 2002). Fetscherin (2010) considers that a country brand is linked with the public domain, covering multiple levels and components with the collective involvement of various stakeholders. For this reason, it comprises the whole image of a country, covering economic, social, environmental, historical, political, and a range of cultural aspects. However, NB can also be explained as an outcome of the interpenetration of the public sector and various commercial interests while communicating the national priorities among the domestic as well as international population (Pasotti, 2014). Consequently, NB helps not only towards the regeneration of capital, but also to combine various public and private resources towards creating some fiscal advantages. As such, its objective is to help and compete in successful manners for the international capital, import-export trade, skilled labour, and shifting of intellectual capital (Papadopoulos et al., 2016; Pasotti, 2014).

Theoretical Significance of Nation Branding

During the start of the last decade, Anholt (2002) argued that a country needs to significantly manage its reputation in a strategic way in order to position itself as an appealing brand. This is due to the fact that people make subjective judgements about the multiple facets of a state through its image. For this reason, a country's reputation is built on how it is perceived based on the information available about it and people's personal experiences in the country (Kang & Yang, 2010). This would further clear various arguments regarding why a nation needs to focus on its image. For example, consumers' thoughts and perceptions about any country primarily depend upon two dimensions, micro- and macro-level, where the former is dealing with the beliefs about the products/services and latter covers the country domain itself. Meanwhile, the belief aspect involves the character and competencies of both people and country.

The significance of NB can be viewed through Anholt's National Branding Model, which comprises six dimensions to cover the overall horizon of NB (Mary & Misiani, 2017; Pop et al., 2020). Anholt claims to have coined the idea of "nation branding" in 1996, and since that time to date, he has been accepted as the most prolific author on the subject, with significant efforts to institutionalise NB as an academic field (Kaneva, 2011). Furthermore, considering the significance of the NB, few indexes have been developed, which include the core components as provided by Future Brand and the Anholt-GfK nation brands index^{SM}. Such models reasonably help organisations, governments, and various businesses to understand, measure, and finally build a strong NB image and reputation. One of the most reliable models of NB is provided by the Anholt-GfK index, which measures the quality and power of each country's brand image while combining the factors like governance, exports, tourism, investment, and immigration, culture and heritage, and finally, the people itself (see Fig. 3.1a). This would justify the argument that for NB, the strategic role of all the above factors is quite significant and can help to develop long-term positive image in the mindset of the global community about a state, country, or group of states. The model also outlines various sub-factors to provide a more comprehensive view of the Nation Branding Index (NBI), as illustrated in Fig. 3.1b. Figure 3.1b indicates that the title of governance reflects the law and regulation in the economy, public opinion, and public sector in any economy, whereas the factors like culture and heritage indicate the political situation, language and history, arts and literature, and film and music as well (Alam et al., 2013). However, the term, investment and immigration has more financial implications with the presence of external investors in the form of foreign direct investment (FDI), as well as domestic internal investors.

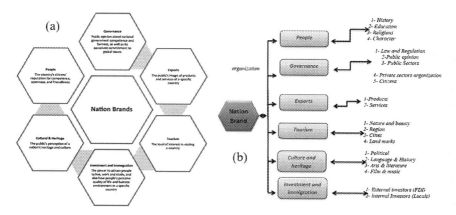

Fig. 3.1 (a, b) The Anholt-GfK Nation Brands Hexagon. (Source: Hassan and Mahrous (2019, p. 4) and Alam et al. (2013, p. 3))

In addition, the elements of NB can define and differentiate one nation brand from other nations in the mindset of larger community members. For this purpose, researchers have categorised NB into two groups: nation tangibles and nation brand intangibles (Hassan & Mahrous, 2019). Furthermore, nation brand elements can be examined while considering the perception of tourists and various other stakeholders of a country. Elements of a nation brand can play a significant role in developing the character of the brand, and for this reason, countries must choose a distinct bundle of elements which can secure the nation brand from imitation or attack from other nation brands. Figure 3.2 provides an example of some of the nation brand characters. For instance, Barbados and Dubai are reputed as some of the friendliest countries in the world as compared to Germany and Japan, which are widely known for competence.

Friendliness (Barbados, Dubai)
Exotic (Spain, Egypt)
Amazing (UAE, Mexico)
Competence (Germany, Japan)
Ruggedness (Australia, South Africa)
Sophistication (USA, France)

Fig. 3.2 Some examples of nation brand character. (Source: Adopted from Hassan and Mahrous (2019, p. 5))

Nation Branding as a Strategic Approach in UAE

Relevance, Scope, and Evolution of Nation Brand in UAE

In order to develop a positive image in the world economy, globalisation has created a lot of opportunities and complexities as well. It is believed that the world is now a single market with growing competition every single day. In fact, the recent single global market has heightened the significance of managing various strategies for different nations in order to attain the highest benefit from foreign investment, skilled labour, and many factors. However, one of the significant factors which can help any nation for building a good impression in the world is "perception". Many countries have been able to leverage perception and gain international recognition for their particular brand. These widely known reputations prove that nation brand does indeed exist, yet for research purposes, it is still challenging to study and articulate.

In addition, over the past couple of years, the level of interest from different researchers and market analysts regarding NB has been increased, specifically in the context of Asia (Anholt, 2008; Huang, 2011; Jordan, 2014; Lee, 2009; Marat, 2009). Being a part of Asian economies, United Arab Emirates (UAE) is assumed as among the most famous destinations for doing work, holidays, and a range of business-related activities due to tax-free structure and luxurious lifestyle (Ahmed, 2015a; Parcero &

Ryan, 2017). Currently, the region of UAE is widely recognised as a significant driver of various reforms in order to increase economic progress and financial development. It has won the bid for Expo 2020/21 and emerged as a market leader, not only in the Middle East, but also in North Africa. It has to put some significant efforts towards achieving the title of the top ten most valuable NB, which has motivated the researchers to examine the economy of UAE in terms of NB and its current and future outlook as well.

In 2012, UAE was recognised as the 35th most valuable NB in the world and rose to 21st in 2017. While attaining a higher level of foreign direct investment from both developed and developing economies, it has become the third strongest NB in the world, and at the most recent time of 2019, it is revealed that among the Gulf Cooperation Council (GCC) economies, UAE brands are at the top of the list. As established in 1970, UAE has promoted itself since the 1980s as a global financial gateway through the Department of Tourism and Commerce Marketing (Ahmed, 2018; Zeineddine & Nicolescu, 2018).

Since the 1990s, UAE has actively been working to build its country and its brand, allowing the country to emerge not only as a regional leader but also as a global player in the field of tourism, business, finance, innovativeness, information technology, and media (Allagui & Al-Najjar, 2018). For the development of NB, the leaders of UAE have reasonably recognised the significance of culture and national identity. Furthermore, during the last decade, UAE management has been able to portray a positive image through investment, tourism, and film industry (Saberi et al., 2018). It is no doubt a historical reality that a nation less than 50 years of age has now become an NB leader (Zeineddine, 2017).

The historical assessment of UAE has confirmed that the development of the whole image of NB is not only because of the natives, but also due to the contributions of its ethnically, lingually, and culturally diverse workforce. It is estimated that over 80 per cent of the labour force working in the UAE comprises expatriate workers, covering the titles of more than 100 ethnic groups (Ababneh & Hackett, 2019). Recent data from 2018 expressed that the share of the UAE nationals out of the total workforce as working in the region was only 7.19 per cent, which has provided enough evidence to claim that UAE depends significantly upon the expatriate skilled labourers who are constantly working to help the country in developing and maintaining a positive image (Pereira et al., 2020). Although the gigantic percentage of skilled foreign workers has made it clear that UAE depends heavily on expatriate labour, however, in the coming years, the labour gap constitutes 110,000 skilled labour by the end of 2030.

The journey towards NB by the top leadership of the UAE has not been stopped yet. During the year 2020, one of the significant steps towards the promotion of NB was observed when a logo of "seven lines" was officially launched by His Highness Shaikh Mohammed bin Rashid Al Maktoum, Vice President and Prime Minister of the UAE and Ruler of Dubai, and His Highness Shaikh Mohamed bin Zayed Al Nahyan, Crown Prince of Abu Dhabi and Deputy Supreme Commander of the UAE Armed Forces. Figure 3.3 presents the layout for the logo of NB, which covers the slogan of "Make it Happen" while covering the status of ambitions, openness, hope, achievements, and culture of possibilities as well. Additionally, the above-stated slogan also drives the country's story, thinking about its leaders while defying the impossible. Besides, the land of Emirates has been observed as a land of significant opportunities for opening doors to people across the globe while unleashing the concept of creativity, achieving full potential, and many other initiatives too.

Fig. 3.3 UAE logo for nation brand

Efforts Towards Nation Branding by UAE: A Holistic Approach

As stated earlier, the leadership of UAE is constantly working for the improvement of NB across the world through various innovative mechanisms. During a Cabinet meeting in 2010, UAE "Vision 21" was launched by H.H. Sheikh Muhammad bin Rashid Al Maktoum, Vice President and Prime Minister of the UAE and Ruler of Dubai, with the core aim to make UAE among the best countries in the world by the Golden Jubilee of the Union. For achieving this mega target and turning it into reality, six national priorities have been defined. This vision is accepted as the next stage for the journey of UAE, which will lead the country to a sustainable environment and infrastructure, world-class healthcare, a first-rate education system, competitive knowledge economy, and a safe public and fair judiciary as well. Although these key dimensions of Vision 21 are mainly aimed at improving the internal functions and systems in the country, the outcomes of these improvements will significantly and positively impact the country's global image and nation brand.

More specifically, for building a higher level of sustainable development while preserving the environment, a significant focus was made towards the higher level of air quality, preserving water resources, and contributing towards clean energy and green growth across UAE's economy. One of the common notions is that the development of a sustainable competitive position in the market must consciously incorporate environmental and social concerns. For this reason, the government of UAE, with the help of Vision 2021, is striving to diversify itself in a variety of sectors and has taken up an initiative to build a green economy for sustainable development. Under this initiative, UAE seeks to become a global hub for the new and green economy while increasing the positive image of the country and preserving the natural environment at the same time. A range of programmes has been initiated in energy, investment, agriculture, and sustainable development. Some of the key points the UAE government used to build a green NB are usage of green and renewable energy throughout the product value chain

3 Nation Branding as a Strategic Approach for Emerging… 49

- Government policies that encourage investment in the green economy for production, export, and import.
- Policies on urban planning and housing development that will increase efficiency and reduce environmental repercussions.
- Work towards better environmental outcomes such as tackling climate change, promoting organic agriculture, and protecting biodiversity.
- Rationally utilising the natural and water resources in the country.
- Putting maximum efforts towards the promotion of green technology.

UAE government's focus on creating a sustainable environment is further illustrated in Fig. 3.4 created by the Emirates Green Building Council. The figure demonstrates the country's green goals by 2050, including a 70 per cent reduction of the green footprint, a 50 per cent move to clean energy, and a 40 per cent increase in consumption efficiency. By focusing and developing some sustainable measures, the government has successfully developed a good image of their region in front of global audiences.

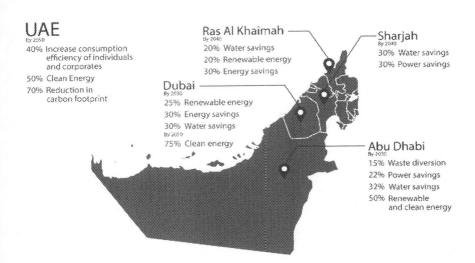

Fig. 3.4 Sustainable efforts by UAE. (Source: Emirates Green Building Council (https://emiratesgbc.org/uae-sustainability-initiatives/))

Meanwhile, like any other sector, healthcare and related facilities are to be assumed as a significant player towards building a higher level of NB in the world. The findings of USnews (2021) revealed that various approaches are followed by the developed economies to provide some outstanding health-related facilities to their citizens and to the rest of the globe. Furthermore, it is found that Canada has achieved the title of the best healthcare system in the world, followed by Denmark, Norway, the Netherlands, the United Kingdom, and Australia. Turning towards the economy of UAE, Vision 2021 has reasonably focused on the delivery of world-class healthcare. For this purpose, the government has started working with all the health authorities to improve the quality standards both in public and in private hospitals. Figure 3.5 shows some of the key output as linked with the healthcare system.

In addition, the concept of knowledge economy not only helps to generate a higher level of economic and financial output, but also creates some dramatic change for building a higher level of NB in the world. Knowledge economy refers to a system where the consumption and production are based on the intellectual capital, which considers the skills and expertise of the community members and workers in any sector

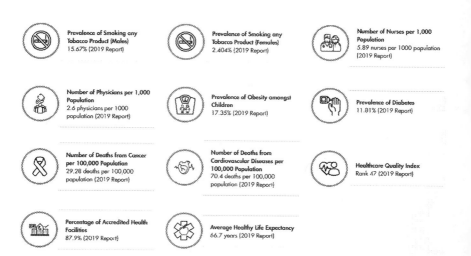

Fig. 3.5 Key statistics as observed for overall healthcare system in UAE

(Hijazi et al., 2019; Parcero & Ryan, 2017). A historical review of UAE shows a longstanding lack of development; however, the country underwent industrial development rapidly in the 1980s by establishing public sector organisations associated with oil and gas, including refineries, fertilizer plants, and aluminium smelters (Ghanem, 2001). Since the last decade, the UAE has ranked among the world's richest economies. This remarkable growth was achieved through a high dependence on expatriate workers, who make up almost 90 per cent of UAE's workforce (World Population Review, 2021), and other various localisation programmes like sector-specific jobs for UAE nationals, and general and increased localisation targets and quotas have been offered by the country in order to increase the economic and financial outcomes. Knowledge and innovation have always played a big role in the competitiveness and building of a country's image (Nurunnabi, 2017; Wang et al., 2012). It means that more focus on being a knowledge-based economy may reasonably change the current and future status of any country in the world. Observing this significant association, Parcero and Ryan (2017) have assessed the performance of UAE and Qatar in terms of their achievement for being knowledge-based economies while taking a sample of 17 benchmarking countries through the pillars of education, information and communication technologies, innovation, and finally, the factors of economy and regime. The efforts over the last three years have made it evident that UAE has earned a better ranking of 19 compared to Qatar out of 131 countries. However, still there is need for the improvement of knowledge economy in terms of quality researchers and highly talented workers.

Lastly, factors like tourism and NB are highly correlated with each other where the role of NB is observed while creating a direct perception in the mindset of the global community. Overall, in recent years, the recognition of the UAE in the global community has been very high and extremely positive, evidenced by UAE's popularity as a tourist destination. From 2018 to 2019, an increase of 5.09 per cent in the number of global visitors to the UAE was observed, which shows a dramatic increase and higher level of NB. Additionally, the top visitors came from locations such as India, the Kingdom of Saudi Arabia, United Kingdom, Oman, China, United States, Germany, Pakistan, and France (Ahmed, 2015b).

For boosting the economic dynamic of tourism, the UAE government has introduced a term under the auspices of competitive tourism, which comprises key sets of indicators such as regulatory framework, regulations, and legislation, business environment infrastructure, human resource, culture, and nature.

Strategic Lessons for Emerging Economies

As previously discussed, a remarkable achievement has been made by the leadership of the UAE towards NB and creating a significant positive image among the world community. Considering the pillars of Vision 2021, UAE does well in most of the indicators and has extended a practical guideline to various emerging economies who desire to enhance their positive image in the world. In this regard, the concept of NB is new for most emerging economies. For this reason, emerging economies must learn to manage and harness their physical and financial resources as well as their intellectual capital in ways that will showcase the country's potential and opportunities and help it gain global recognition for positive developments. As in the case of UAE, countries hoping to build a positive nation brand need a long-term strategic plan such as Vision 2021 to guide their development in sustainable environment, health, education, infrastructure, telecommunication, information technology, and competitive knowledge. More specifically, it is the obligation of the national governments to acquire and practice the title of NB to attract international skilled human capital in order to increase such stock and to boost economic competitiveness as well. This approach is similarly adopted by the government of UAE, where more than 80 per cent of the workforce comes from different regions and contributes towards the achievement of strategic objectives. Baruch et al. (2016) have further justified this concept while claiming that due to globalisation and war of talent, more than 232 million individuals are termed as "foreign" as they live and work outside their region of origin. This statement and the practical approach as adopted by UAE have provided some outstanding pathway for those economies who desire to increase their NB or country image.

Besides, other lessons for the emerging economies specify that strategic focus for building a sustainable differential advantage is needed in order to defy the regional or national stereotypes. In this regard, the NB identity can be implemented while following the key model as provided under Fig. 3.6, which comprises developing an NB board, establishing a strategic plan based on some measurable objectives, defining and articulating a cluster's brand architecture and scope, and examining the reputation of the NB among various stakeholders including policymakers, community members, business groups, and more specifically, international audiences.

Conclusion

The strategic decision-makers in any economy are more assertive towards international visibility and recognition of their country. For this reason, more commitment is required towards international marketing techniques like nation branding. To empower a country on a world map, it is a recurrent idea that NB is a core mean. Various methods and approaches are highlighted by the researchers in the field of NB, both in developed and in developing economies. However, extant literature reveals that

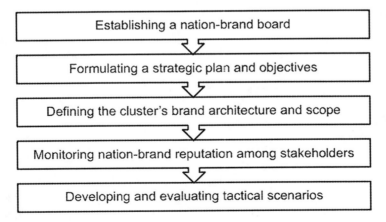

Fig. 3.6 Suggested model for building NB. (Source: Hassan and Mahrous (2019, p. 8))

those who show a higher level of resilience in the process of NB can manage to yield higher results over some longer period of time. The need for nations to actively manage their image has been widely acknowledged in the literature as it is a multifaceted term and may carry both factual and affective information. Three dimensions of NB can be viewed from the perspective of micro- and macro-dynamics for which beliefs and perceptions are fundamental to consider. This chapter provides some meaningful contributions regarding NB through past and contemporary literature and some practical approaches adopted in different economies. Furthermore, an in-depth focus is made on the economy of the UAE regarding the NB and key efforts towards it. It is determined that leadership of UAE has taken some expressive steps to promote their national identity and image recognition among global audiences. Additionally, steps towards sustainable development, environment and infrastructure, competitive knowledge economy, cohesive society and preserved identity, and gigantic growth of tourism in the region of UAE have laid out its path towards global recognition and a strong nation brand. Furthermore, practical insights for some of the emerging economies based on the key measures taken up by the government of UAE for promoting NB are also discussed.

References

Ababneh, K. I., & Hackett, R. D. (2019). The direct and indirect impacts of job characteristics on faculty organizational citizenship behavior in the United Arab Emirates (UAE). *Higher Education, 77*(1), 19–36.

Ahmed, G. (2015a). Destination 2021, Forbes Middle East Guide, August, pp. 46–47.

Ahmed, G. (2015b). "Brand UAE and its Super Brands" in the proceedings of the *5th International Research Symposium on Building and Promoting Brands in Emerging Markets*, Academy of Global Business Research and Practice, formerly (SGBED), Montclair State University, NJ, USA, Curtin University Australia & Nanjing University. December 10–11. People Republic of China.

Ahmed, G. (2018). Transforming the UAE from desert to developed economy. *Forbes Middle East*, No. 70, p. 29, April.

Alam, A., Almotairi, M., & Gaadar, K. (2013). Nation branding: An effective tool to enhance fore going direct investment (FDI) in Pakistan. *Research Journal of International Studies, 25*(25), 134–141.

Allagui, I., & Al-Najjar, A. (2018). From women empowerment to nation branding: A case study from the United Arab Emirates. *International Journal of Communication, 12*(2018), 65–85.

Anholt, S. (2002). Nation branding: A continuing theme. *Journal of Brand Management, 10*(1), 59–60.

Anholt, S. (2008). 'Nation branding' in Asia. *Place Branding and Public Diplomacy, 4*(4), 265–269.

Aronczyk, M. (2013). *Branding the nation: The global business of national identity*. Oxford University Press.

Aronczyk, M. M. (2009). How to do things with brands: Uses of national identity. *Canadian Journal of Communication, 34*(2), 291–296.

Baruch, Y., Altman, Y., & Tung, R. L. (2016). Career mobility in a global era: Advances in managing expatriation and repatriation. *Academy of Management Annals, 10*(1), 841–889.

Fetscherin, M. (2010). The determinants and measurement of a country brand: The country brand strength index. *International Marketing Review, 27*(4), 466–479.

Ghanem, S. M. (2001). Industrialization in the UAE. In I. Al-Abed & P. Hellyer (Eds.), *United Arab Emirates: A new perspective*. Trident Press Ltd.

Hassan, S., & Mahrous, A. A. (2019). Nation branding: The strategic imperative for sustainable market competitiveness. *Journal of Humanities and Applied Social Sciences, 1*(2), 146–158.

He, J., Wang, C. L., & Wu, Y. (2020). Building the connection between nation and commercial brand: An integrative review and future research directions. *International Marketing Review, 38*(1), 19–35.

Hijazi, R., Saeed, R., & Alfaki, I. (2019). Role of statisticians in building the UAE knowledge economy. *Electronic Journal of Applied Statistical Analysis, 12*(1), 303–319.

Huang, S. (2011). Nation-branding and transnational consumption: Japan-mania and the Korean wave in Taiwan. *Media, Culture Society, 33*(1), 3–18.

Jordan, P. (2014). Nation branding: A tool for nationalism? *Journal of Baltic Studies, 45*(3), 283–303.

Kaneva, N. (2011). *Nation branding: Toward an agenda for critical research, 5*(2011), 117–141.

Kang, M., & Yang, S. U. (2010). Comparing effects of country reputation and the overall corporate reputations of a country on international consumers' product attitudes and purchase intentions. *Corporate Reputation Review, 13*(1), 52–62.

Kaur, R. (2020). *Brand new nation: Capitalist dreams and nationalist designs in twenty-first-century India*. Stanford University Press.

Kotler, P., & Gertner, D. (2002). Country as brand, product, and beyond: A place marketing and brand management perspective. *Journal of Brand Management, 9*(4), 249–261.

Lee, K. M. (2009). Nation branding and sustainable competitiveness of nations. University of Twente. https://doi.org/10.3990/1.9789036528030

Marat, E. (2009). Nation branding in Central Asia: A new campaign to present ideas about the state and the nation. *Europe-Asia Studies, 61*(7), 1123–1136.

Mary, M., & Misiani, M. P. (2017). Applying Anholt's national branding model: The case of Kenya. *Business and Economics Journal, 8*, 335. https://doi.org/10.4172/2151-6219.1000335

Nurunnabi, M. (2017). Transformation from an oil-based economy to a knowledge-based economy in Saudi Arabia: The direction of Saudi vision 2030. *Journal of the Knowledge Economy, 8*(2), 536–564.

Papadopoulos, N., Hamzaoui-Essoussi, L., & El Banna, A. (2016). Nation branding for foreign direct investment: An Integrative review and directions for research and strategy. *Journal of Product Brand Management, 25*(7), 615–628.

Parcero, O. J., & Ryan, J. C. (2017). Becoming a knowledge economy: The case of Qatar, UAE, and 17 benchmark countries. *Journal of the Knowledge Economy, 8*(4), 1146–1173.

Pasotti, E. (2014). Branding the Nation: The global business of national identity, by Melissa Aronczyk. In: Taylor & Francis. *Political Communication, 31*(4), 1–3. https://doi.org/10.1080/10584609.2014.956035

Pereira, V., Neal, M., Temouri, Y., & Qureshi, W. (2020). *Human capital in the Middle East: A UAE perspective*. Springer Nature, Switzerland AG. https://doi.org/10.1007/978-3-030-42211-0

Pop, N. A., Baba, C. A., Anysz, R. N., & Tohanean, D. (2020). National branding strategy and its effects on business and tourism. *Paper presented at the Proceedings of the International Conference on Business Excellence, 14*(1), 1005–1013.

Rojas-Méndez, J. (2013). The nation brand molecule. *Journal of Product and Brand Management, 22*(7), 462–472.

Rojas-Méndez, J. I., Kannan, D., & Ruci, L. (2019). The Japan brand personality in China: is it all negative among consumers? *Branding Public Diplomacy, 15*(2), 109–123.

Saberi, D., Paris, C. M., & Marochi, B. (2018). Soft power and place branding in the United Arab Emirates: Examples of the tourism and film industries. *International Journal of Diplomacy Economy, 4*(1), 44–58.

Steenkamp, J.-B. (2019). Building strong nation brands. *International Marketing Review, 38*(1), 6–18.

USnews. (2021). Countries with the most well-developed public health care systems. https://www.usnews.com/news/best-countries/slideshows/countries-with-the-most-well-developed-public-health-care-system?slide=8

Wang, C. L., Li, D., Barnes, B. R., & Ahn, J. (2012). Country image, product image and consumer purchase intention: Evidence from an emerging economy. *International Business Review, 21*(6), 1041–1051.

World Population Review. (2021). https://worldpopulationreview.com/countries/united-arab-emirates-population

Zeineddine, C. (2017). Employing nation branding in the middle East-United Arab Emirates (UAE) and Qatar. *Management Marketing. Challenges for the Knowledge Society, 12*(2), 208–221.

Zeineddine, C., & Nicolescu, L. (2018). Nation branding and its potential for differentiation in regional politics: The case of the United Arab Emirates and Qatar. *Management Dynamics in the Knowledge Economy, 6*(1), 167–185.

4

Bank Brand Avoidance: Service Perspectives from Nigeria and Ghana

Henry Boateng, Uchenna Uzo, Ogechi Adeola, and Robert Ebo Hinson

Introduction

Brands are important for both consumers and firms. While strong brands bring financial benefits to firms and help them differentiate themselves from competing products, it also gives assurance to consumers and helps assuage the tension involved in making a purchase decision (Keller, 2001). Brands are also essential for the success of service firms (Berry, 2000). However, service branding is complicated due to its intangibility (Berry,

H. Boateng (✉)
D'Youville University, Buffalo, NY, USA
e-mail: boatengh@dyc.edu

U. Uzo • O. Adeola
Lagos Business School, Pan-Atlantic University, Lagos, Nigeria
e-mail: uuzo@lbs.edu.ng; oadeola@lbs.edu.ng

R. E. Hinson
University of Kigali, Kigali, Rwanda

© The Author(s), under exclusive license to Springer Nature Switzerland AG 2022
O. Adeola et al. (eds.), *Marketing Communications and Brand Development in Emerging Economies Volume I*, Palgrave Studies of Marketing in Emerging Economies,
https://doi.org/10.1007/978-3-030-88678-3_4

2000; Grace & O'Cass, 2005; O'loughlin & Szmigin, 2007) and the human element in service provision. Despite these, it is still critical for service providers to build strong brands since strong brands lead to favourable outcomes such as brand preference and choice (Chang & Liu, 2009; Narteh et al., 2012), brand love, brand equity, and brand loyalty (Adam et al., 2018; Ha & John, 2010; Chang & Liu, 2009; Carroll & Ahuvia, 2006).

Although the brand literature is still growing, researchers' attention has mainly focused on the positive aspects of brands, such as brand love, brand loyalty, and brand equity (Berndt et al., 2019); limited attention has been paid to negative outcomes resulting from consumer-brand interactions, such as brand avoidance and brand hate (Berndt et al., 2019). However, these negative aspects resulting from consumer-brand interactions have ramifications on the equity of the brand.

In addition, studies that have investigated negative outcomes of consumer-brand interactions, such as brand avoidance, were carried out within the context of physical products (Hellberg et al., 2016; Almqvist et al., 2016; Black & Cherrier, 2010) with a limited focus on service brands (Berndt et al., 2019; Cherrier et al., 2011; Lee et al., 2009a). However, service brands are different from physical products, and therefore, issues that will inform a consumer's decision to avoid physical product brands is different from those of service brands. Service brands are essential to the global economy; thus, it is important that more research is conducted on why consumers avoid certain service brands (Berndt et al., 2019).

Moreover, studies on brand avoidance did not focus on a specific service. The existing studies have only investigated brand avoidance in multiple service contexts (Berndt et al., 2019) or within the context of services and products (Lee et al., 2009a; Cherrier at al., 2011). Only a few have focused on the service sector, for example the mobile telecommunication sector (Hsu et al., 2019). Notably, all services are not the same. They differ in terms of the tangible and intangible components. For instance, banking services are different from telecommunication services; thus, consumers' reasons for avoiding these services are likely to differ.

Although brand avoidance is "an everyday phenomenon in the lives of consumers" (Berndt et al., 2019, p. 3), this phenomenon has not been adequately examined from a phenomenological approach. Therefore, to bridge these research gaps, we investigate service brand avoidance in the banking sector in emerging economies context. The purpose of this study is to understand why bank customers avoid some bank brands even though they could afford their service charges. Our study makes methodological contributions as well as empirical contributions, since the extant literature has rarely used a phenomenological approach to investigate service brand avoidance in the banking sector.

Context of the Study

The banking sector is one of the most competitive sectors in Ghana and Nigeria. There are many brands of banks currently operating in the banking sector of the two countries. As a merchantable space for foreign investments (Ezeoha, 2007), the focus on the African banking sector can have a remarkable influence on the overall business performance of organisations. As a highly regulated sector, banks in Nigeria and Ghana were encouraged to adopt a recapitalisation policy in 2005 and 2008, respectively. These strategies were mainly due to the inefficiencies in the banking sector birthed by a low deposit base, among others (Ezeoha, 2007; Opoku et al., 2009). Meanwhile, sparse deposit bases experienced by banks could be dependent on consumer's behaviour, that is their decision to patronise one or more bank brands and avoid others.

The thrust of this study focuses on the premise that understanding African buying behaviour is critical to business survival in most African spaces in the world. Therefore, it is pertinent to examine the service experience of customers, as well as avoidances of bank brands made as a result of these nuances in the banking sector. A unique dimension of the banking sector in Ghana and Nigeria is that many banks are handicapped in deploying state-of-the-art technology while delivering superior services to their customers (Amoako, 2012). Frequent breakdown of information technology systems, internet banking security issues, and unreliability of automated teller machines (ATMs), among others, are the challenges banks in Ghana face (Narteh, 2013). Selecting a bank brand that has superior services and satisfies customers in this regard is essential for many bank customers in these countries. Customers' choice of banks is mainly influenced by service quality and technology-related issues

(Boateng et al., 2016). For instance, bank customers in Ghana want to be treated fairly and with compassion. They also want their banking needs to be provided conveniently (Amoako, 2012). Bank choice is usually based on technology-related factors, attitudes and behaviour of bank employees, and speed in service delivery (Narteh & Owusu-Frimpong, 2011). Therefore, it is reasonable to explore the reasons for brand aversion among African consumers using bank brands. We chose Nigeria and Ghana as the study context because Nigeria is the largest economy in sub-Saharan Africa and has a competitive banking sector. Similarly, Ghana also has a competitive banking sector.

Brand Avoidance: A Review of Literature

Generally, the focal point of consumer studies is on consumer behaviours and attitudes. It spurs the thought as to why people choose to buy or consume a product or service. However, brand avoidance, otherwise known as anti-consumption or brand aversion, is concerned with consumers' reasons for avoiding a product or service of a brand; an insightful understanding of consumers' judgement demands a thorough study of both facets (Lee et al., 2009b).

Brand avoidance is a situation whereby "consumers deliberately choose to keep away from or reject a brand" (Lee et al., 2009a, p. 422). A major feature that characterises the brand avoidance phenomenon is when customers are financially capable of purchasing a brand that is also readily available but still chooses to avoid the said brand (Lee et al., 2009a; Knittel et al., 2016; Johansson et al., 2016). Therefore, for the purpose of this study, brand avoidance will be conceived as a conscious phenomenon whereby consumers avert certain bank brands despite affordability and availability.

The objective of this study is to examine the reasons behind brand avoidance in the absence of spatial and financial barriers.

The next section, therefore, examines the reasons behind brand aversion. It explicates the four forms of brand avoidance identified by Lee et al. (2009a, 2009b), namely experiential, identity, moral and deficit-value brand avoidance, as well as Knittel et al. (2016) advertising avoidance. Myriads of studies have examined brand avoidance praxis in various sectors of the economy. In the following section, we also clarify the gaps in the literature.

Major Forms of Brand Avoidance

Experiential Brand Avoidance

According to Lee et al. (2009a), experiential brand avoidance surfaces when a consumer is unable to admit the previous experience she or he had with a particular product or service. Put differently, when consumers avoid brands based on past negative encounters with the brand(s), a prolonged negative perception of the brands could develop. This perception is birthed from a consumer experience that constitutes the basis of experiential brand avoidance (Kim et al., 2013). Berndt et al. (2019) noted that core service failure and service failure encounters contribute to service brand avoidance. For example, they noted that people had avoided some brands in the mobile phone network sector due to unreliable networks. Similarly, Hsu et al. (2019) found that service failure severity spurs anger among consumers who experience them, and consequently, these consumers avoid the service providers involved.

Identity Brand Avoidance

Identity brand avoidance is a form of anti-consumption stemming from the glaring collision between the image a brand portrays and the consumer's identity (Lee et al., 2009a; Lee et al., 2009b; Kim et al., 2013). Therefore, incongruent symbolic viewpoints of a brand could lead to the avoidance of the brand. The incongruence implies that a consumer could rebuff a brand that antagonises his or her self-concept (Knittel et al., 2016). Findings also advance that the aversion of a brand could be related to the political axiom of individuals. For instance, an individual who opposes public health policymakers is more likely to avoid consumption of the public health services since she or he detests the policy formulator(s)

(Kaplan & Kaplan, 2011). In tandem with Kaplan and Kaplan's position, Cherrier et al., (2011) also stated that the act of brand avoidance is subjectively adopted based on self-concepts, individualities, and ordinary circumstances for sustainability purposes. Hoffmann (2011) further found that consumers could avoid a brand due to ethnocentric reasons, which is purchasing only domestic products to support the economy of their home country rather than buying a foreign-made product that contributes little or nothing to its host economy.

Moral Brand Avoidance

This is the form of courteous brand avoidance that emerges from the inconsistencies amongst a consumer's ethical and ideological beliefs, and the features of a brand (Hellberg et al., 2016; Kim et al., 2013; Lee et al., 2012; Strandvik et al., 2013). In other words, the decision one takes with thoughts beyond one's interest, but rather with societal aspect in mind, and therefore avoiding certain brands, as a result, is moral (Lee et al., 2009b). Therefore, while the need for ethical consumption increases, so does the avoidance of certain products due to moral concerns (see, e.g., Bridges et al., 2018). Black and Cherrier (2010) also submitted that anti-consumption for sustainability could encourage the act of avoiding the consumption of a particular product. However, the nexus between the needs of the individual and the demands for environmental preservation perhaps determines anti-consumption practices for sustainability.

Kaplan and Kaplan (2011) noted that moral incompatibility with public service gives rise to brand avoidance. Put differently, the duo argued that the public might deliberately boycott the consumption of a health facility because they perceive the treatment to be catastrophic or incongruent to ideological and moral values. Additionally, people could refrain from consuming a healthcare service when they believe that the threat is fabricated and the treatment is excessive. Brand avoidance also occurs when there is irresponsible behaviour in the environment in which the brand operates (Hoffmann, 2011).

Deficit-Value Brand Avoidance

This occurs when consumers desist from the consumption of certain brands due to their cost, which they perceive as incongruous with the level of value and quality of the product (Lee et al., 2009a; Lee et al., 2012). Within the confines of consumer research, dissatisfaction could occur when the value offered by a particular product or service is below its cost. When this happens, consumers are likely offered a diminished value of their financial expenditure (Kim et al., 2013).

Advert Brand Avoidance

Knittel et al. (2016) argued that advert brand avoidance occurs among millennials that are not only technologically savvy but highly educated, thus not anxious to attempt the consumption of novel products and services. Authors have argued that the strands of advertising that could encourage brand avoidance among consumers include the advertisement content, celebrity used for endorsement purpose, and the music in the advert session, as well as the response to the ad (Knittel et al., 2016), collaborations, channels, trustworthiness, frequency, and timing (Almqvist et al., 2016). Notably, the nature of a product or service's advertisement could influence consumers' purchasing behaviour (Knittel et al., 2016).

Alternative Forms of Brand Avoidance

There are also alternative forms of brand avoidance. For instance, Kaplan and Kaplan (2011) argued that consumers are likely to avoid a health service when they perceive that natural alternatives would suit a particular ailment rather than the use of drugs. This situation signifies that a consumer could fail to patronise a specific brand due to the perceived efficacy of a close substitute. This form of avoidance is called *need-based brand avoidance*.

Hoffmann (2011) also noted that the proximity of a particular product or service could influence a buyer's behaviour. In practical terms, a consumer will deliberately avoid a brand when space is distant. However, buyers consume brands that are closer to them distance-wise. This form of avoidance is called *spatial brand avoidance*. While the other types of avoidance are as a result of a direct encounter with the consumer, Hellberg et al. (2016) noted that there is a third-party phenomenon that could encourage brand avoidance. Specifically, negative comments about a product or service could induce the buyer or potential buyer to avoid the said brand. This type of avoidance is *called negative word-of-mouth (WoM) brand avoidance.*

Organisations that suffer product or service brand avoidance create action plans in (re)gaining their customers. These action plans are regarded as redemption strategies in this chapter. Dursun and Kabadayi (2013), via their experimental study, opined that the anti-consumer of a particular brand does not tend to alter their consumption attitude even when they are exposed to positive messages about a brand unless the brand-related positive message is strong. Hutter and Hoffmann (2013) confirmed that consumers are more willing to participate in activities for organisations that conduct ecological-friendly businesses and boycott the products or services of those whose actions are detrimental to the environment within which they operate.

As shown in Table 4.1, one could deduce that most previous studies have focused mainly on Lee et al.'s typologies of brand avoidance as well as Knittel et al.'s advert avoidance. However, less attention has been given to need-based avoidance, spatial avoidance, and negative WoM avoidance. Also, several available studies on brand avoidance have focused on random products and services, fashion, biotechnology, cosmetics and sportswear industries, manufacturing, public health and education sectors, and non-governmental and frozen foods organisations. However, attention is yet to be given to the examination of brand avoidance and redemption models, especially in the African banking sector. This study will, therefore, call for a modification in the existing brand avoidance model through the examination of the banking sector in Africa.

Table 4.1 Synopsis of existing studies on the typologies of brand avoidance and redemption strategies

Reasons for brand avoidance			
S/N	Avoidance type	Study sectors	Authors/Year
1	Experiential brand avoidance	Random products and services	Lee et al. (2009a)
		Fashion industry	Kim et al. (2013)
		Services	Berndt et al. (2019)
2	Identity brand avoidance	Random products and services	Lee et al. (2009a); Lee et al. (2009b)
		Random products and services	Cherrier et al. (2011)
		Manufacturing sector	Hoffmann (2011)
		Public health sector	Kaplan and Kaplan (2011)
		Biotechnology industry	Lee et al. (2012)
		Fashion industry	Kim et al. (2013)
		Random products and services	Knittel et al. (2016)
3	Moral brand avoidance	Random products	Black and Cherrier (2010)
		Manufacturing sector	Hoffmann (2011)
		Public health sector	Kaplan and Kaplan (2011)
		Biotechnology industry	Lee et al. (2012)
		Fashion industry	Kim et al. (2013)
		Non-governmental organisations	Strandvik et al. (2013)
		Cosmetics industry	Hellberg et al. (2016)
4	Deficit-value avoidance	Fashion industry	Kim et al. (2013)
		Random products and services	Lee et al. (2009a)
		Biotechnology industry	Lee et al. (2012)
5	Advert avoidance	Sportswear industry	Almqvist et al. (2016)
		Random products and services	Knittel et al. (2016)
6	Need-based avoidance	Public health sector	Kaplan and Kaplan (2011)
7	Spatial avoidance	Manufacturing sector	Hoffmann (2011)
8	Negative WoM avoidance	Cosmetics industry	Hellberg et al. (2016)

Source: Authors' Compilation

Methodology

This study employed a phenomenological approach to understanding bank brand avoidance in two emerging markets in sub-Saharan Africa. According to Creswell (2007), "phenomenology describes the meanings of several individuals of their lived experience of a concept or a phenomenon" (p. 57). Similarly, van Manen (1990) asserted that phenomenological research involves studying "the way that a person experiences or understands his or her world as real or meaningful" (p. 183). From the definitions, phenomenology deals with lived experience and a phenomenon. Since "brand avoidance is an everyday phenomenon in the lives of consumers" (Berndt et al., 2019, p. 3), we believe that we can understand bank brand avoidance using phenomenology since banking services are experienced, and brand avoidance is a phenomenon. This approach is appropriate not only because the extant studies have utilised this approach but also because this approach allows the participants to share the "lived experience" informing their decisions to avoid a bank brand. This approach also helps us to have first-hand knowledge of the experiences leading to participants' decisions to avoid a bank brand. The basic goal is to arrive at a description of participants' experience with the bank brands, leading to their decisions to avoid the brands.

We conducted semi-structured interviews with 30 participants: 17 from Ghana and 13 from Nigeria. These participants were purposefully selected based on the following criterion: they could afford the charges of bank brands but actively choose not to bank with them and instead avoid these bank brands.

One of the authors from Nigeria interviewed Nigerian participants in Nigeria, while the Ghanaian counterparts conducted that of the Ghanaian participants. The decision to use interviews for this study is in accordance with van Manen (1990), who postulated that an interview is a suitable data collection method for phenomenology research. Since many people own bank accounts, it was easy to identify bank customers and approach them for participation in the study. A short questionnaire was self-administered to the bank customers we identified. We asked them to confirm if they have a bank account. We also asked them if there are any bank brands that they could afford to use their services but actively choose not to use their banking services. Those who confirmed that they have a bank account, and that they actively choose not to use the banking services of some banks even though they could afford to, were interviewed.

During the interviews, we asked participants to share their experiences, leading to their decision not to do business with the bank brands they mentioned. We further asked them questions regarding the criteria they use to select their current bank brand and why they are still using their services. These questions helped to have detailed information about the participants' experiences and the context informing their decisions to avoid the banks.

The participants' ages range from 18 to 54 years. Many of the interviews took a maximum of 35 minutes. We recorded all the interviews and transcribed them afterwards for analysis. We also made notes during the interviews, which were also analysed. We used thematic analysis techniques to analyse the data. This was to enable us to identify the key service issues that informed the participants' decision to avoid certain bank brands. This approach also enabled us to be logical about the interviews we conducted (see Malhotra, 2012). We have identified the bank brands the participants mentioned during the interview and instead we have used pseudonyms such as *Abank, Bbank, and Zbank*. Similarly, we have used pseudonyms to represent the participants of the study. This was to ensure confidentiality.

To ensure the trustworthiness of the study, we followed Creswell (2007) and Guba (1981). We had a prolonged engagement with the participants on bank brand avoidance during the interviews. We have quoted their words verbatim from the interviews to support our claims. We also applied member checking, where the researchers cross-checked the coding and extracts used to support the findings. Finally, we ensured that the analysis was free from bias by using the exact words of the participants to support our findings.

Presentation of Findings

Delivering superior services is key for customers' continued usage of services. Bank customers, for instance, require that banks provide prompt and individualised services. They also require banks to keep to their promises. However, many banks in emerging economies do not meet these expectations (Amoako, 2012). Service failure is widespread in the banking sector in emerging economies. Customers who experience service failure avoid repeat business transactions with such a service provider. We found from this study that the participants avoid some bank brands due to service failure issues which relate to lack of empathy, delays and complex procedures, and technology. The next section presents a detailed discussion of these identified issues.

Brand Avoidance Resulting from Lack of Empathy

Service customers expect their service providers to provide individualised service and show concern in a peculiar situation. However, from the interviews, some banks do not recognise the need to sympathise with their customers and provide such individualised service. This has led some of the participants of the study to avoid certain banks. Some participants cited instances where their service providers have shown no empathy informing their decisions to avoid using the services of the bank:

> *I had to pay some clients of mine at the Tema harbor and the amount involved was a bit huge, and so I rushed to the Bbank Tema branch, and they calmly told me that due to the amount involved they can't give me that amount and that I should rather go to my branch (which is at Accra high street) to do that transaction. Because of time unavailability [given] me by my clients, that option [was] bad for me, and so I had to [resort] to calling friends who sent me cash through other electronic mediums. It was really the worse encounter ever. (CD7)*

This participant expected the bank to show concern in this instance and allow him to withdraw the amount. By not allowing the customer to withdraw the money and directing him to the branch where he opened the bank account, the bank did not show sympathy for the customer's urgent need. Similarly, another participant intimated a lack of empathy as the reason why she has avoided a bank:

> *I remember going to the banking hall to withdraw some cash and apparently their system was down; for more than 30mins we sat in the banking hall, and none of their staff members seemed to even care about us. We were actually ignored .... If I can say that. I felt very agitated and decided not to bank with them again!* (CD16)

From this extract, it can be observed that the service provider showed no empathy to the client. This customer needed sympathy and did not get it from the service provider, even though the bank failed by delivering prompt services to this customer. From the extract, it can be inferred that the customer's decision to avoid the bank is due to a lack of empathy from the bank. It can also be inferred from the extract that delays in service delivery may lead to brand avoidance.

Brand Avoidance Resulting from Delays and Complex Procedures

Many customers want services to be delivered promptly and without going through any complex procedures. Bank customers, in this case, do not want to wait for a long time in queues or go through a complicated process to access a service. Some of the participants informed us during the interview that they have avoided some banks because of long waiting times and the complex processes they had to go through to open a bank account. The following are some extracts from the interviews which support this view:

> *I went with my dad to Kbank to cash out my school fees. We waited for hours because of the slow nature of attending to customers. As for Abank, I went there to cash a cheque of #5000, and they had their systems down for more than 5hours. Eventually, they resulted in delivering services to customers manually. As you would expect, the process was laborious and made me sick. I even lost the joy of having money in my pocket when I later stepped out of the bank after about 6 hours.* (CD1)

Similarly, another participant said the following:

Actually, I am a Bbank customer. Xbank was the first bank account I had, but using the bank's services is almost like you are punishing yourself. Walking into Xbank branch, things are never done on time, I think with the exception of the Airport, Opeibea branch where things are fast. There is always a long queue, you never leave there early, they have many customers, so if you need any request, it takes forever before you are sorted. (CD6)

From the extracts, it can be concluded that two participants have avoided the respective banks due to delays in service delivery. That is long waiting in queues and sluggishness on the part of a service provider in a way inform a customer's decision to avoid a bank brand. The complexity of service delivery, which is associated with delays, is also evident from the first extract (CD1). We find another support for how complexity in service delivery leads to bank brand avoidance. One of the participants had this to say:

Their processes are very complicated when opening a current account, even though I had an account with them already, I had to bring my offer letter, water bill, light bill and I didn't see the need for that. (CD9)

From this extract, it is observed that the customer wanted to go through a simple procedure since she is already a customer of the bank. This participant wanted the bank to use her existing records to open the current account instead of repeating a procedure she has gone through already to establish her identity. Thus, redundancy in the service delivery process leads to bank service brand avoidance.

Brand Avoidance Resulting from Service Failure Relating to Technology

We also observed from the analysis that some of the participants had avoided some banks due to service failure resulting from technology-related issues such as insecurity, slow internet, and malfunctioning Automated Teller Machines (ATMs). There were instances where some of

4 Bank Brand Avoidance: Service Perspectives from Nigeria...

the participants needed access to the service but could not due to technology failure. For instance, one participant narrated how he had avoided a bank because he could not withdraw money from the bank's ATM:

2015 Xmas was not enjoyable due to technology. Couldn't withdraw cash from a PPBank ATM, with a PPBank card and nothing was done till after the Xmas break. (CD3)

Another participant also shared a similar story:

I went to the ATM to withdraw cash, I entered the amount and received a debit alert, but the machine did not dispense. The ATM deducted money without actually dispensing, and it took the bank ages to process my complaint and refund my money. (CD19)

In these two instances, both participants had issues with ATMs. The banks involved were not responsive, and they delayed in resolving the participants' complaints and recovering the failed services. Other participants shared their experiences with the banks' ATMs, and websites informed their decisions to avoid the banks. The issues relate to ATM malfunctioning and slow loading of the banks' websites. This was what the participant said:

Their ATM and internet service is poor, which means you have to enter the banking hall for withdrawal. Poor internet banking—their internet platform is not easy to access. (CD20)

Similarly, another participant had this to say:

Their internet banking platform is not secured, I received several emails from fraudsters asking me to log in with my details. (CD24)

From the extracts, it can be observed that the participants do require not only internet banking but a fast and secure internet banking website. The participants also wanted easy access to the internet banking website. However, the banks failed to provide these services, leading to the decision to avoid the banks' brands.

Discussion of Findings and Conclusion

The purpose of this study was to understand the customer service experience that informs their decisions to avoid bank brands. The participants of the study were customers of banks in Ghana and Nigeria, whose service experience with some banks has led them to avoid those banks. The findings of the study show that the participants' decisions to avoid those bank brands resulted from a lack of empathy, delays, and complex procedures in service delivery and service failure relating to technology. Some participants of the study shared their experiences where the banks did not show any concern when they needed individualised services. For instance, a customer wanted to withdraw a huge sum from another branch of his bank; however, the branch did not allow this transaction. They would rather send him to his original branch to perform the transaction. By this decision, the bank has inconvenienced the customer in addition to showing no concern to the peculiar needs of the customer. As noted by Lee et al. (2009a), when consumers encounter negative experiences with a product or a service, those consumers avoid the brand. It is not surprising, therefore, that participants indicated that they had avoided some bank brands due to the negative service experience they had with those bank brands.

As indicated earlier, delays and complex procedures in service delivery emerged as one of the major reasons why the participants have avoided some bank brands. These participants wanted their required services to be delivered at a greater speed and without complexity. However, from the findings, some of the procedures that the participants had to go through were redundant and or had prolonged process times, leading participants to decide not to use the services of these banks. Also, unlike customers in developed economies, most bank customers in developing economies still prefer to conduct their banking transactions in the banking hall. This creates a situation where the banking halls are usually packed and with long queues. Some of the banks also have sluggish employees, and this compounds the delays. We are not surprised by these findings since, according to Narteh and Owusu-Frimpong (2011), speed in service delivery is one of the many factors that bank customers consider when selecting a bank brand.

Additionally, Narteh and Owusu-Frimpong (2011) found in their study that many bank customers in Ghana select their banks based on technology-related factors. These same factors are the reason why some participants of this study have decided not to use the services of some banks. We found in our study that service failure relating to technology such as insecurity, slow internet, and malfunctioning Automated Teller Machines (ATMs) is one of the reasons why some participants of this study decided to avoid some bank brands. Some of the participants, for example, shared their experience of where they had received emails from fraudsters requesting their personal account details. According to them, this situation shows that the brands' internet banking is not secured; thus, their decision not to use their full service.

From these results, we have learnt that negative service experience in the banking sector is a major factor for bank brand avoidance. We have also learnt from these findings that service experiences that lead to brand avoidance in the banking sector are human and technology related, and procedural in nature.

Implications and Recommendations

The findings of this study have implications for theory and practice. From a theoretical perspective, the findings imply that brand avoidance resulting from service experience can be conceptualised from three perspectives: human relations, technology related, and process and procedures. Brand avoidance resulting from human relations involves a lack of empathy, bank employees showing no concern to customers' needs, and their unwillingness to provide individualised services to bank customers. The findings also suggest that speed in service delivery and simple and convenient processes and procedures can avoid brand avoidance in the banking sector. Technology-related service experience resulting in brand avoidance includes insecurity, slow internet, and malfunctioning Automated Teller Machines (ATMs). We concluded that bank brand avoidance resulting from service experiences is multi-faceted, as we have shown in the study.

From a practical perspective, the study implies the need for banks to train their employees on how best to relate to their customers. Specific emphasis should be on training employees to be able to identify themselves with customers and their peculiar situations. They should be flexible in dealing with their customers in order not to inconvenience them. Again, bank managers should provide their employees with time-saving tools and train them on the pertinent issues they need to focus on while rendering services to customers. Additionally, they should encourage their employees, especially the tellers, to consistently practise with the banking software to improve mastery.

Management should track the employees' speed in service delivery in real time. Managers can also improve speed in service delivery by investing in state-of-the-art technology. They should provide more modern ATMs at strategic locations. This will reduce the number of customers who go to the banking halls to perform their transactions. Management must also invest in system security. They should make sure that they protect their customers' banking details from third parties. We also recommend that management should redesign the service delivery process and procedures to make it simpler. Any redundancy in their existing systems should be eliminated.

Limitations and Recommendations for Future Studies

Our study used a qualitative approach, where we interviewed 30 people from Ghana and Nigeria. As a result, we are unable to generalise the findings to the entire banking sector. Thus, we recommend that future studies consider using a quantitative approach where these findings can be tested on many respondents. The hospitality sector is one of the most vibrant industries in the service sector but has left customers with many negative service experiences. Future studies may, therefore, use our approach to investigate service experience, which results in brand avoidance in the hospitality sector.

References

Adam, D. R., Ofori, K. S., Okoe, A. F., & Boateng, H. (2018). Effects of structural and bonding-based attachment on brand loyalty. *African Journal of Economic and Management Studies, 9*(3), 305–318.

Almqvist, T., Forsberg, M., & Holmström, A. (2016). *Brand avoidance: A study focusing on marketing communication within the sportswear industry in Sweden.* Being a Bachelor thesis submitted at International Business School, Jonkoping University.

Amoako, G. K. (2012). Improving customer service in the banking industry-case of Ghana Commercial Bank (GCB)-Ghana. *International Business Research, 5*(4), 134–148.

Berndt, A., Petzer, D. J., & Mostert, P. (2019). Brand avoidance – A services perspective. *European Business Review*, (just-accepted), 00-00.

Berry, L. L. (2000). Cultivating service brand equity. *Journal of the Academy of marketing Science, 28*(1), 128–137.

Black, I., & R, & Cherrier, H. (2010). Anti-consumption as part of living a sustainable lifestyle: Daily practices, contextual motivations and subjective values. *Journal of Consumer Behaviour, 9*, 437–453.

Boateng, H., Adam, D. R., Okoe, A. F., & Anning-Dorson, T. (2016). Assessing the determinants of internet banking adoption intentions: A social cognitive theory perspective. *Computers in Human Behavior, 65*, 468–478.

Bridges, E., Schramm, M., & Roy, A. (2018). Consumer choices among service brands offering ethical attributes. *The Service Industries Journal*, 1–23.

Carroll, B. A., & Ahuvia, A. C. (2006). Some antecedents and outcomes of brand love. *Marketing letters, 17*(2), 79–89.

Chang, H. H., & Liu, Y. M. (2009). The impact of brand equity on brand preference and purchase intentions in the service industries. *The Service Industries Journal, 29*(12), 1687–1706.

Cherrier, H., Black, I. R., & Lee, M. (2011). Intentional non-consumption for sustainability: Consumer resistance and/or anti-consumption?. *European Journal of Marketing, 45*(11/12), 1757–1767.

Creswell, J. (2007). *Qualitative inquiry & research design: Choosing among five approaches* (2nd ed.). Sage.

Dursun, I., & Kabadayi, E. (2013). Resistance to persuasion in an anti consumption context: Biased assimilation of positive product information. *Journal of Consumer Behaviour, 12*, 93–101.

Ezeoha, A. (2007). Structural effects of banking industry consolidation in Nigeria: A review. *Journal of Banking Regulation, 8*, 159–176.

Grace, D., & O'Cass, A. (2005). Service branding: consumer verdicts on service brands. *Journal of Retailing and Consumer Services, 12*(2), 125–139.

Guba, E. G. (1981). Criteria for assessing the trustworthiness of naturalistic inquiries. *Ectj, 29*(2), 75–91.

Ha, H. Y., & John, J. (2010). Role of customer orientation in an integrative model of brand loyalty in services. *The Service Industries Journal, 30*(7), 1025–1046.

Hellberg, A., Melander, J., & Vong, A. (2016). *Why do consumers avoid certain brands?* Bachelor thesis submitted at International Business School, Jonkoping University.

Hoffmann, S. (2011). Anti-consumption as a means to Save Jobs. *European Journal of Marketing, 45*(11/12), 1702–1714.

Hsu, L. C., Wang, K. Y., Chih, W. H., & Lin, W. C. (2019). Modeling revenge and avoidance in the mobile service industry: Moderation role of technology anxiety. *The Service Industries Journal, 39*(1), 1–24.

Hutter, K., & Hoffmann, S. (2013). Carrotmob and anti-consumption: Same motives but different willingness to make sacrifices? *Journal of Macromarketing, 33*(3), 217–231.

Johansson, W., Nikolov, N. A., & Pehrsson, J. (2016). Identity brand avoidance: Understanding the interdependencies and main drivers of brand avoidance (dissertation). Retrieved August 18, 2021, from https://www.diva-portal.org/smash/get/diva2:932803/FULLTEXT01.pdf

Kaplan, M. D., & Kaplan, Y. C. (2011). Anti-consumption of public services: Vaccine(not)ion for Swine Flu. *Management Research Review, 34*(3), 353–363.

Keller, K. L. (2001). Building customer-based brand equity. *Marketing Management, 10*(2), 14–19.

Kim, H., Choo, H., & Yoon, N. (2013). The motivational drivers of fast fashion avoidance. *Journal of Fashion Marketing and Management: An International Journal, 17*(2), 243–260.

Knittel, Z., Beurer, K., & Berndt, A. (2016). Brand avoidance among generation Y consumers. *Qualitative Market Research: An International Journal, 19*(1), 27–43.

Lee, M., Conroy, D., & Motion, J. (2009a). "Brand avoidance: A negative promises perspective", in McGill, A.L. & Shavitt, S. (Eds). *Advances in Consumer Research, 36*, 421–429.

Lee, M., Fernandez, K. V., & Hyman, M. (2009b). Anti-consumption: An overview and research agenda. *Journal of Business Research, 62*(2), 145–147.

Lee, M., Conroy, D., & Motion, J. (2012). Brand avoidance, genetic modification, and brandlessness. *Australasian Marketing Journal, 20*, 297–302.

Malhotra, N. K. (2012). *Marketing research: An applied approach.* Harlow, Pearson.

Narteh, B. (2013). Service quality in automated teller machines: An empirical investigation. *Managing Service Quality: An International Journal, 23*(1), 62–89.

Narteh, B., Odoom, R., Braimah, M., & Buame, S. (2012). Key drivers of automobile brand choice in sub-Saharan Africa: The case of Ghana. *Journal of Product & Brand Management, 21*(7), 516–528.

Narteh, B., & Owusu-Frimpong, N. (2011). An analysis of students' knowledge and choice criteria in retail bank selection in Sub-Saharan Africa: The case of Ghana. *International Journal of Bank Marketing, 29*(5), 373–397.

O'loughlin, D., & Szmigin, I. (2007). Services branding: Revealing the rhetoric within retail banking. *The Service Industries Journal, 27*(4), 435–452.

Opoku, R., & A, Atuobi-Yiadom, H., Chong, C., S, & Abratt, R. (2009). The impact of internal marketing on the perception of service quality in retail banking: A Ghanaian case. *Journal of Financial Services Marketing, 13*(4), 317–329.

Strandvik, T., Rindell, A., & Wilén, K. (2013). Ethical consumers' brand avoidance. *Journal of Product & Brand Management, 22*(7), 484–490.

van Manen, M. (1990). *Researching lived experience: Human science for an action sensitive pedagogy.* State University of New York Press.

Part III

Contemporary Perspectives on Marketing Communications and Brand Development: Sponsorship, Health and Personal Branding

5

Sponsorship: Practices and Benefits in Emerging Markets

Michael M. Goldman, Gabriela Klein Netto, Shiling Lin, and Richard Wanjohi

Introduction

BBVA Argentina, a part of the Spanish banking giant Banco Bilbao Vizcaya Argentaria (BBVA), operates as a full-service bank in the Latin American country. To generate growth and acquire new customers, the company has used sponsorship of sport, music, art, and entertainment, as part of their marketing communications. The bank has had a strategic

---

M. M. Goldman (✉)
University of San Francisco, San Francisco, CA, USA

University of Pretoria, Pretoria, South Africa
e-mail: mmgoldman@usfca.edu

G. Klein Netto • S. Lin
University of San Francisco, San Francisco, CA, USA
e-mail: gkleinnetto@dons.usfca.edu; slin65@dons.usfca.edu

R. Wanjohi
Strathmore Business School, Nairobi, Kenya

© The Author(s), under exclusive license to Springer Nature Switzerland AG 2022
O. Adeola et al. (eds.), *Marketing Communications and Brand Development in Emerging Economies Volume I*, Palgrave Studies of Marketing in Emerging Economies,
https://doi.org/10.1007/978-3-030-88678-3_5

sponsorship with Boca Juniors, River Plate, and Talleres, three of Argentina's most prominent football teams. The co-branded credit cards for fans of the teams provide access to early ticket and shirt sales, discounts on merchandise and apparel purchases, and invitations to events, the teams' training sessions, or the club museums. BBVA Argentina has sponsored performances by Katy Perry, Ed Sheeran, U2, Sting, and other artists to competitively position the brand relative to its competitors. To strengthen the bank's relationship with its existing customers, BBVA Argentina has sponsored and provided access to Cirque du Soleil's Septimo Dia show. The company's sponsorship portfolio also includes supporting art performances and classes at the Teatro Colon in Buenos Aires and the "San Isidro Jazz y Mas" festival.

BBVA Argentina exemplifies a brand's strategic use of sponsorship in an emerging market context. This chapter discusses the theoretical foundations of sponsorship, and recent research about the benefits and risks of using this marketing communications tool.

What Is Sponsorship?

Sponsorship has been defined by IEG, a global sponsorship valuation and measurement agency, as "a cash or in-kind fee paid to a property (typically in sports, arts, entertainment, or causes) in return for access to the exploitable commercial potential of that property" (Cornwall & Kwon, 2020, p. 607-608). This expression echoes Meenaghan's academic definition of sponsorship as "the provision of assistance either financial or in-kind to an activity or commercial organisation for the purpose of achieving commercial objectives" (Meenaghan, 1983, p. 9). In this way, the central concept underlying sponsorship is exchange theory, which refers to two parties exchanging goods that each party values equally (Crompton, 2014). Sponsorships, therefore, involve the mutual benefit of both parties and mutual exchange (McCarville & Copeland, 1994). This differentiates sponsorships from philanthropic acts, donations, or acts of charity, where the party offering a resource is unlikely to receive or expect any benefit in return. These sponsorships are seen as integrated market-oriented activities where the sponsorship investment needs to

5 Sponsorship: Practices and Benefits in Emerging Markets

exceed the event value and the return on investment can be calculated based on the investment required and brand value obtained (Jensen & Cobbs, 2014). A sponsoring brand can be viewed as a public and visible marketing alliance or partnership with the property's brand, which can include an individual (such as an artist or athlete), organisation (such as a music group, sport team, or art gallery), or event (such as a music festival or sport tournament) (Farrelly et al., 2005).

Sponsors typically spend as much on activating their sponsorships as they do on their initial rights fees. Activation refers to marketing activities directly linked to a sponsorship, which aim to increase the awareness, engagement, trial, purchase, and advocacy a sponsor sets out to achieve through the sponsorship (Cornwell, 2014). In practice, a company needs to activate its sponsorship with additional components of the marketing communications mix to achieve its business objectives. For example, Tusker Malt Lager in East Africa purchased the naming rights to Tusker Project Fame, a reality TV singing competition show for contestants from Burundi, Kenya, South Sudan, Tanzania, and Uganda. To reach younger beer drinkers, Tusker activated their sponsorship by creating official viewing bars that screened the TV show, provided training and branded materials to retailers, and ran promotions and mobile contests for the target segment. Bill Chipps from IEG expressed an often-mentioned way of thinking about sponsorship rights and activations in the industry:

> It's what we call buying a toy without batteries. Smart sponsors are not just signing the sponsorship and walking away from it, hoping they get all this return on investment. When you buy a sponsorship, you get the typical benefits - it might be tickets for hospitality, signage, that kind of thing. That's all fine and dandy, but to really get the biggest bang for their buck, a marketer needs to allocate additional dollars to activate the sponsorship and bring it to life. (Chudgar, 2011, para. 38)

Sponsorship rights are the contracted commercial exploitable assets that typically form part of the sponsorship package that the sponsor buys from the sponsored property. A generic inventory of these assets include naming and signage rights, category exclusivity, licensing and merchandise rights, physical and digital activation rights, content rights, and ticket and hospitality rights (Skildum-Reid & Grey, 2014). For example, an analysis of the media value generated by sponsors of the inaugural Overwatch League, a global franchised esports league, indicated that video boards, LED screens, full-screen graphics, and digital billboards were the most valuable media assets (Nielsen, 2019). Recent data from the Association of National Advertisers in the United States suggests that an increasing number of sponsors are looking for both shorter-term sales-related financial returns and longer-term brand-building returns from sponsorship investments, indicating a maturing of the industry beyond just media equivalency and brand awareness, attitudes, and preference results (Association of National Advertisers, 2018). In this way, the traditional focus on mere brand exposure from media impressions of the sponsor's logo, calculated via a comparable paid media rate card, is increasingly seen as insufficient. Day (2009) argued that sponsorships should be "based on facts and figures rather than gut feeling, then there needs to be rigorous evaluation in place. Successful sponsorships will all have put in place pre- and post-research and measurement criteria, so that their activities can be scientifically assessed and analysed".

Global spend on sponsorships by brands was estimated at almost $66 billion in 2018. These sponsorships were mostly spent on sports, with the balance made up of sponsorship of other entertainment, social causes, arts, festivals, fairs, and annual events, associations, and membership organisations. Approximately 64% of this spend was focused on North America and Europe, with another 25% focused on the Asia Pacific region, and less than 12% of the spend focused on Africa, Central America, and South America (Guttmann, 2019). The cancellation or postponement of numerous sports and entertainment events in 2020 and 2021, due to the spread of the COVID-19 pandemic, negatively impacted sponsorship spend. Many sponsors received "makegood" sponsorship collateral and case rebates, although less than half of sponsorship decision-makers surveyed in 2020 believed that the lost sponsorship value could be made up (IEG, 2020).

How Sponsorship Works

Sponsorship has been referred to as an "indirect marketing approach", along with product placement and influencer marketing (Cornwell, 2008). In this way, sponsorship is a communication platform, or "a meeting place when using hospitality, as thematic inspiration for advertising and as a starting point for engagement in social media" (Cornwell, 2020, p. 71-72). Research has provided an increasingly clear view of the mechanics involved in sponsorship communication.

The first mechanism involved in a customer's processing of sponsorship is repeated exposure, which has been shown to increase liking and preference. Similarly, low-level processing or background branding is a mechanism that can influence attitudes and behaviours. Alternatively, a prominent sponsorship can serve as a signal of category leadership or financial resources. In this way, Turkcell's sponsorship of the Zorlu Performing Arts Center in Istanbul, Turkey, provides the telecommunications brand with repeated and prominent exposure to thousands of concert and festival attendees each year. Another processing mechanism is fit or congruency, which has a positive relationship with the achievement of sponsorship objectives. Woisetschlager, Eiting, Haselhoff, and Michaelis (2010) defined sponsorship fit as the "perceived match of attributes between sponsoring firms and sponsored objects" (p. 170). Gwinner (2014) discussed seven types of fit between an athlete, event or team, and the sponsoring brand. These include similarity of usage, size, audience, geography, attitude, image, and time. Sponsorship fit has been shown to reduce the risk of dissolution (Jensen & Cornwell, 2017), while perceived authenticity of the sponsor-sponsee relationship is important in judging the compatibility of the brand partnership (Charlton & Cornwell, 2019). For example, Chinese skincare brand Thanmelin, which targets older women in smaller cities, sponsored the popular Chinese reality TV show *Sisters Who Make Waves* about women over 30 vying for a spot on an all-female pop group. The TV show contestants were seen using Thanmelin products, which contributed to the brand's increased national profile in China and the increased customer demand.

In an effective sponsorship, the brand image of the property is transferred to the sponsoring brand through the mechanism of an image transfer process, which can also work in reverse (Charbonneau & Garland, 2010; Gwinner, 2014). For example, if the brand image of the Indian Premier League (IPL) is pan-Indian, ambitious, and the ultimate leveller, then fans of the tournament may transfer these perceptions to its sponsors, including Vivo, the Chinese smartphone manufacturer. These brand associations would benefit Vivo in their attempts to compete in the Indian mobile market. However, Vivo's negative Chinese brand image, as a result of the China-India border dispute, saw strong public sentiments expressed in India, leading to the Board of Control for Cricket in India (BCCI) suspending its IPL title sponsorship deal with Vivo. Companies, therefore, invest in sponsorship with the hope that the positive moods of fans towards their favourite sport or entertainment property will be transferred to their corporate or product brand (Dalakas & Levin, 2005), hence increasing brand equity (Cornwell, Roy & Steinard, 2001). A recent experimental study demonstrated how sport sponsorship can change the perceived age and the brand personality of a sponsored brand (Hohenberger & Grohs, 2002). Although a sponsorship contract is typically an agreement between a sponsor and sponsee, the practical reality is that the images of numerous official sponsors and unofficial ambush brands, as well as the brand images of the tournament, venue, and broadcasters, can influence the effectiveness of a sponsorship. In this way, sponsorship can be considered "a network of players" (Chanavat et al., 2016).

Benefits of Sponsorship

A well-managed sponsorship can provide substantial internal and external benefits to the sponsor. These benefits can include typical external brand benefits, such as awareness and preference, external community, and societal reputation benefits, as well as internal benefits, such as employee engagement and branding benefits, and overall business and financial benefits. Sponsorship can communicate an appealing and relevant brand story to multiple audiences and deliver positive returns on the marketing investment.

External Brand Benefits

Brand awareness is considered the foundation of the relationship between a brand and its customers. Awareness has been defined as customer recall and recognition of the brand, and then identification of the products provided by the brand (Cornwell, 2020; Macdonald & Sharp, 2003). Brand awareness is critical to the buying process because it places the brand in the awareness set of the relevant category, without which the brand will not be evaluated, considered, preferred, or purchased. Brand awareness is one of the most mentioned goals of sponsorship (Cornwell, 2020). For example, Shopee, an ecommerce platform in South East Asia included Blackpink, a South Korean music girl group they sponsored, in a 2018 electronics advertising campaign to target Generation Z customers.

In South Africa, a study of sponsors of the country's national men's rugby team demonstrated the positive role sponsorship can play in delivering brand awareness and positively influencing the target customers' reaction to the brand (Sephapo & Erdis, 2016). In India, numerous sponsors have used extensive coverage and affinity for cricket to raise awareness of their brands. The Chinese smartphone manufacturer OPPO signed a five-year sponsorship deal with the BCCI in early 2017 to sponsor the Indian national men's cricket team and hoped to use the sponsorship to increase their brand awareness and usage (Venugopal, 2017). A market commentator argued:

> When the likes of Oppo and Vivo (for Indian Premier League) picked up sponsorships, they were relatively unknown brands. And they were hungry. And we can all see how they became national. Another angle that most of us miss is that besides consumers, there is an equally important community - the sales team and the trade. Such associations and visibility give a lot of boost to the sales team and trade. Confidence starts building among the traders on relatively unknown brands and orders start pouring in. (Bansal, 2019, para. 6)

The Chinese consumer electronics brand Hisense has used sponsorship to increase its brand awareness domestically and internationally. The brand is seen as a global partner of the Union of European Football Associations

(UEFA) and the International Federation of Association Football (FIFA) for their regional and global tournaments. According to an Ipsos FIFA World Cup pre-and post-match survey, Hisense TV's domestic brand recognition had increased by 12%, while Hisense TV's overall international recognition had increased by 6% (Hisense, 2019, p. 11).

- **External community reputation benefits**

Corporate social responsibility, which has also been described as social responsibility, corporate citizenship, or community relations, has been defined as: "Both the philosophy and practice of for-profit organisations voluntarily acting to positively assist society in ways beyond that required to obtain profit objectives" (Phillips, 2006, p. 69). In addition to sponsorship's commercial objectives, brands can use sponsorships to contribute to societal goals. For example, Banco Itaú Unibanco S.A., a Brazilian financial services company, sponsors the Brazilian Cultural Center as part of its advocacy for diversity, inclusion, and cultural legacy.

An analysis of 1473 CSR cases within the Financial Times Stock Exchange 100 Index companies found that almost half of the cases were recorded as sponsorship (Bason & Anagnostopoulos, 2016, p. 15). In East Asia, sponsorship is believed to conform to the "Humanity (Ren)" theory in Confucianism (Ho, 2011, p. 216). Through sponsorship, sponsors can address their social responsibilities before opening the local market (Ho, 2011). In Poland, sport sponsorship has been seen as a manifestation of CSR implementation, leading to benefits for internal and external investors (Sudolska & Lapinska, 2020). In addition, research suggests that customers perceive brands that sponsor sports events, leagues, and teams as more socially responsible, with the level of alignment between the brand's tone and the sponsored subject increasing the perceptions of social responsibility (Hino & Takeda, 2020).

For example, Brandhouse Beverages in South Africa used the Celebrating Strides campaign to identify and profile individuals whose life stories imitated and reflected the brand values of the Johnnie Walker brand: entrepreneurship, creativity, and striving for success. Through its Celebrating Strides Awards, Johnnie Walker empowered acclaimed actor, writer, producer, and entrepreneur, Welcome Msomi, to spark a revival of the Stable Theatre in Durban, South Africa. It was expected that the partnership would act as a catalyst to inspire a new generation of artists. Rhys Lindstrom, Johnnie Walker's Marketing Manager, stated:

> This initiative fitted perfectly with the vision for the Celebrating Strides Awards. We wanted to recognise and honour individuals like Msomi who had made great strides in achieving their dreams. But in doing, so we also wanted to, through their success, inspire others and empower those around them who might not have had the same opportunities. The way Msomi has ploughed his win back into the Stable Theatre in the community from which he hails will hopefully act as a catalyst and inspire a whole new generation of artists dreaming of a chance to embark on their own journeys. (Business and Arts South Africa, n.d, p. 14)

China Pacific Insurance Company (CPIC), an official partner of the Chinese national women's volleyball team, recently increased their brand value by 31% to an estimated $14 billion, without a dramatic increase in marketing spending (Brand Finance, 2020). After the team's historic victory at the 2019 International Federation of Volleyball (FIVB) World Cup in Japan, Chinese President Xi Jinping welcomed the team as guests of honour at the Great Hall of the People in Beijing and attended the 70th Anniversary Reception of China (FIVB, 2019). The CPIC brand was perceived very favourably as a result of the team's performance and reception, which contributed to their political capital and social relevance.

Internal Benefits

The success of many companies depends on the extent to which their employees are committed to achieving the goals of the organisation, and the level of emotional connection employees have with each other and the corporate brand. Intellectual property rights are an important aspect of sponsorship, which allows a sponsor to use the property's marks and content to communicate internally and externally (Cornwell, 2020). A sponsorship rights package can, therefore, include internal employee-focused assets that can be used for internal marketing purposes. Research has found that employee perception, attitude, and behaviour can be positively influenced by sport sponsorship and that employees who are interested in the company's sponsorship will likely have a strong sense of firm identification and will be committed both to their work in general and to satisfying customer needs (Hickman et al., 2005). Activating a sponsorship internally can improve the employees' "esprit de corps", contributing to increased productivity and retention (Cornwell, 2020, p. 47-55).

The Standard Bank Group's pan-African sponsorship of the African Cup of Nations included a specific set of activities focused on employees and had a stated objective to create meaningful connections with customers, staff, and other stakeholders through unique experiences. Standard Bank's internal activations included Trophy Tour events, AFCON Ambassador breakfasts, a fantasy league, Football Friday team-building events, and in-branch ambient media. Jenny Pheiffer, Standard Bank's head of Brand and Sponsorship, stated:

> We are proud to be able to have a long-standing commitment to CAF which showcases Africa's accomplishments in the sport through competitions that attract continental and global audiences. This is a major opportunity to connect with our customers, football fans and our employees, in all of the eighteen countries in which we operate, through our shared passion for Africa and African football. (Moorhouse, 2013, para. 29)

Financial Benefits to the Sponsor

As a strategic marketing communications tool, sponsorship should be expected to deliver financial benefits to the sponsor. In one study of more than 50 US-based corporations, Jensen and Hsu (2011) found that, as a group, companies that consistently invested in sport sponsorships outperformed market averages and that those with higher sponsorship spend on rights and activation achieved higher returns. In South Africa, research indicated that consistent sport sponsors were able to grow earnings per share faster than other listed firms, while consumer services and sport sponsors were able to grow revenues faster than the other firms in that sector, although no evidence was found that sponsoring companies' share price growth rates were different from the market (Blake et al., 2018). A recent meta-analysis of 20 years of research on event studies in sponsorship found that overall, share prices of sponsors increased in the pre-announcement period, suggesting that information about the impending sponsorship announcement was received positively by the financial markets (Kwon & Cornwell, 2020).

For example, in addition to Hisense's brand awareness growth discussed earlier, the Chinese consumer electronics brand used sponsorship to increase sales volumes in the United States by over 50%, in Mexico by more than 30%, in Germany by almost 40%, in the United Kingdom by over 30%, and in Spain by almost 30% (Hisense, 2019).

Nissan demonstrated the market share benefit of sponsorship through its deal with the IOC for the 2016 Olympics and Paralympics Games held in Rio de Janeiro, Brazil. The company launched a new model inspired by the urban Brazilian context, the Nissan Kicks, to coincide with the Summer Games and registered 2000 down payments for the vehicle during the event. The brand used a personal sponsorship of Usain Bolt to create content that received almost nine million views, which contributed to 2.4 billion impressions of Nissan Olympic-specific hashtags on Twitter. Nissan planned hospitality events in a rebranded Nissan Kicks hotel on Copacabana Beach, provided 4200 vehicles for the official Olympic fleet, and hosted a 40-metre bungee jump used by more than 1000 people. The business in Brazil saw a one percentage point increase in market share during the event, with François Dossa, President of Nissan Brazil, confirming:

> We are thrilled with the impact our sponsorship has had throughout Latin America and on fans around the globe. This has been a big win for Nissan and we are excited to continue to build on this momentum in the region. (Harrington, 2016, para. 8)

Risks Associated with Sponsorship

As with all marketing communication investments, there are risks associated with using sponsorships. These risks are typically related to ambush marketing activities by competitors and cluttered sponsorship environments.

* **Ambush marketing**

Typically, ambush marketing occurs in larger sporting events that attract substantial media attention, although it is becoming increasingly common in smaller events (Cornwell, 2014). Discussion around ambush marketing began in 1984, when the organisers of the Los Angeles Olympics restructured the sale of sponsorship rights to reduce the number of official sponsors and increase the financial value of sponsoring an International Olympic Committee event (Burton & Chadwick, 2018). These changes encouraged other non-sponsoring brands to attempt to take advantage of the event, sometimes illegally and unethically. The concept has been defined as "the incursive, obtrusive, or associative activities of a brand intended to yield a range of benefits similar or comparable to those typically achieved by brands that have a formal, contractual sponsorship agreement with an event" (Burton & Chadwick, 2009, p. 289).

For example, Beats Electronics headphones have been banned since 2014 from all official FIFA World Cup events because Sony was an official partner. However, athletes were still seen wearing them during their leisure time. The five-minute "The Game Before the Game" piece of content that Beats by Dre released just days before the start of the FIFA World Cup in Brazil in 2014 featured football stars Neymar Junior, Cesc Fabregas, and Luis Suarez, as well as LeBron James, Serena Williams, Nicki Minaj, and Lil Wayne. Beats by Dre had previously ambushed the 2012 London Olympics when numerous swimmers were seen on live TV walking to the starting blocks wearing the brand's unmistakable headphones. These and other ambush marketing activities attract the attention of audiences and have been shown to create doubt among spectators and viewers about which brands are official sponsors of events (Brownlee, Greenwell & Moorman, 2018). To mitigate the risk of ambush marketing, official sponsors need to do more than just rely on their association with the official marks of the event. Sponsors need to ensure a strong and authentic fit between their brand and the sponsored athlete, team, or event, and ensure that their highly creative executions reach their target audiences (Simpson, 2018). A sponsor's credibility can be based on a long historical association with the property, the natural fit or congruence between the product and the property, and a compelling message that is of interest and relevance to the target audience (Farrelly et al., 2005).

In response to ambush marketing activities by non-sponsors, rights holders have strengthened the intellectual property protections provided to official sponsors. FIFA, for example, created the Rights Protection Programme, with the purpose to protect official sponsors and disrupt ambush marketing actions, and require hosting countries to have laws in place to protect these rights (Blackshaw, 2010). Despite these protections, Bavaria Beer famously ambushed Budweiser, the official sponsor at the 2010 FIFA World Cup in South Africa. The Dutch beer company was accused of hiring 36 young blonde women to sit together at the Netherlands vs. Denmark first-round game, while wearing short orange dresses that were sold as a gift pack by Bavaria Beer. Although the outfits drew some attention of the spectators and media, the ambush attempt generated the most attention when the authorities removed the women from the game and threatened legal action against the organisers of the attempt. Some studies have suggested that customer attitudes can turn negative when they realise that a brand is using ambush marketing (Mazodier & Quester, 2010). The public interest in creative ambush marketing and the related competitive and legal questions contribute to the "controversy and excitement" of the tactic (Cornwell, 2014, p. 162).

- **Clutter**

The substantial role of sponsorship in the financial sustainability of sports and entertainment events means that there are often numerous sponsors with official associations for an event. The large number of featured brands can result in clutter, or a "high level of competing communications" (Donlan, 2014, p. 6), which can negatively impact the effectiveness of sponsorship (Cornwell et al., 2005). A cluttered sponsorship communication environment can be perceived as simply just noise (Donlan, 2014) and "may reduce the consumer's ability to recall the brand's involvement in the event" (Jensen & Cornwell, 2017).

Similar to responding to ambush marketing, a sponsor can employ more creative and congruent sponsorship communication and activations to stand out from the crowd. For example, OMO Sports, a Unilever laundry detergent brand, used hydro-chromic ink for their logo on the jerseys of the Corinthians football team in Brazil in 2018. As the jerseys absorbed the players' sweat during the game, the logo became visible, which attracted more attention and provided an opportunity for spectators, viewers, players, and the media to talk about the sponsorship. The initial results included 120 million social media impressions and a TV audience of 18 million people. Giovanna Gomes, Marketing Director of OMO, described their efforts to avoid sponsorship clutter:

> The brand is constantly innovating and bringing remarkable moments to its consumers. And just as Omo is one of the most remembered and used brands of the Brazilians, football is one of the favorite sports. Nothing better than showing that every drop of sweat marks, than being associated with a sport that connects and excites people. (McCarthy, 2018, para. 3)

Sponsorship Issues in Emerging Markets

The dynamic nature of many emerging markets presents unique sponsorship issues for companies hoping to use sponsorship as a marketing communications platform. In addition to the typical sponsorship benefits and risks, sponsors in these fast-changing countries and regions need to cautiously consider the strategic use of soft power and sports betting.

- **Soft power**

Countries, and the organisations representing these nation brands, can use sponsorships as an instrument of soft power to achieve a number of geopolitical and economic objectives. Soft power sponsorship stands distinct from other forms of sponsorship as governments utilise it as a means of accentuating the attractiveness of a nation's culture, political ideals, and policies. Political theorist Joseph Nye drew a distinction between coercive power, wherein entities "influence the behaviour of others to get the outcomes one wants", from that of soft power, described as an actor's potential to "attract and co-opt them to want what you want" (Nye 2004). Nye argued that states would increasingly rely on softer or abstract

5 Sponsorship: Practices and Benefits in Emerging Markets

sources of power, such as culture, ideology, and institutions, which are based on the power of attraction. Sponsorship and hosting events, especially sport events, have been shown to help improve a "nation's image, profiling and showcasing themselves globally and 'attracting' others through inbound tourism, increased trade and a growing sense of national pride" (Grix, 2013, p. 17). Emerging market countries have increasingly been using international sponsorships to extend their influence.

For example, Russia's state-owned natural gas producer, Gazprom, has been a substantial football sponsor, including the FIFA World Cup and UEFA Champions League. The company is also the jersey sponsor of Russian club Zenit Saint Petersburg, Red Star Belgrade in Serbia, English Premier League team Chelsea FC, and the German Bundesliga club FC Schalke 04. Gazprom decided to sponsor Schalke in 2006 because the company believed that the club had "lots of connections with the German energy sector and has lots of supporters" (Vox, 2020). The German football club is located in the country's Ruhr Valley region, which is a domestic industrial heartland. At the time, Gazprom was facing negative media coverage and public perceptions about its impending Nord Stream pipeline, which planned to directly link Russia and Germany. In this way, Gazprom used its football sponsorship as a means of soft power to improve its image and appeal, extend its gas network in Europe, and "by extension, extend the influence of Russia" (Schneider, 2020, para. 2). Gazprom demonstrated how to use prominent sport sponsorships as a "way around bad publicity by winning approval on the field" (Vox, 2020).

Krzyzaniak (2018) argued that there are three main determinants of the success of a sponsorship in garnering soft power: the number of elite teams a country sponsors, the strength of the team's brand prior to the sponsorship, and the brand that the country uses for the sponsorship. Emirates Airlines is another example of a country-owned brand that has successfully used sponsorship to achieve business and soft power objectives for the United Arab Emirates and Dubai. The airline has been a sponsor of numerous strong regional and global sports brands with positive brand associations such as Chelsea FC, Arsenal, Real Madrid, AC Milan, Hamburger SV, FC Benfica, Paris Saint Germain, New York Cosmos, Formula 1 racing, and US Tennis, thereby reaching a substantial number of enthusiastic fans. The airline brand also sponsors the Australian and San Francisco symphonies, as well as Dubai's Festival of Literature and Jazz Festival. By using the Emirates Airlines brand, Dubai's government and ruling families, as well as the sport, arts, and entertainment businesses involved, have also avoided any potential negative attention that may be directed at the city state.

- **Sport betting sponsorships**

Sport betting companies have increasingly used sponsorship as a key marketing communications tool (Day, 2011; Hing et al., 2013; Meenaghan, 2013). Competitors in this category use sponsorship and sponsorship-linked advertising to leverage their association with sport and engage current and prospective customers (Chang & Liu, 2012). Individuals involved in sport betting perceived that sponsorship had a powerful effect on them (Johnston & Bourgeois, 2015). For example, embedded promotions and the use of athletes in betting promotions have been seen by young people to link sport and betting, and to nurture positive attitudes towards sport betting (Pitt et al., 2016). In spite of these benefits and practices, sponsorship by sport betting companies continues to be controversial.

For example, Dream11's sponsorship of the IPL in 2020 faced questions due to the potentially unhealthy close relationship between fantasy sport companies, illegal sport betting in India and the United Arab Emirates, and cricket players and teams in India (Raza & Shekhar, 2020). In 2000, India's Central Bureau of Investigation found extensive evidence of a "major organised racket" to manipulate and "fix" matches (CBI, 2000, p. 8), while a judicial commission in the country had proposed legalising betting with strict licences in 2016.

Evidence of match-fixing and corruption related to sport betting has also been found in Uganda (Richard, 2013). In neighbouring Kenya, habitual betting among the youth has been driven by limited regulations, unemployment, peer pressure, early exposure to betting games, advertisements, and a desire to escape from reality (Wachege & Mugalo, 2019). Advertising spending by betting and gambling companies in Kenya grew from 0.3% of total advertising spending in the country in 2014 to 22% of spending by 2018, the year in which betting and gambling advertising overtook all other categories (Reelforge, 2019). Within this context, SportPesa was launched in Kenya as a sport betting and news technology company in 2014. The brand was able to exploit the growth in mobile penetration and affordable data services before sponsoring domestic and national football and rugby teams in the East African country. SportPesa's signed on as title sponsor of the Kenyan Premier League in 2015, followed by deals with the Kenyan Football Federation, as well as two of the biggest clubs in Kenyan football, Gor Mahia and AFC Leopards. SportPesa became the first Kenyan company to sponsor an English Premier League team, when it signed a deal with Hull City in 2016, followed by agreements with Southampton FC and Everton Football Club, as well as club sponsorships in Tanzania and South Africa (Capital FM Kenya Sports, 2019). SportPesa's sponsorships in Kenya were called into question in June 2017. The sponsorship relation soured, however, after Kenyan President Uhuru Kenyatta signed a new finance bill into law that included a new 35% tax rate on all gambling revenue in addition to the existing 30% corporate tax. As a result, SportPesa suspended its sponsorships and terminated most of them in 2020 (Olobulu, 2019). With SportPesa withdrawing their sponsorships, a number of other sport betting companies acquired some of the sponsorship rights, including BetKing's five-year deal with the Kenyan Football Federation (O'Boyle, 2020).

Brazil is expected to allow legal sport betting from early 2022 and could then become the largest sport betting market in the world (O'Connor, 2021). Waldir Eustaquio Marques Jr., from the Brazilian Ministry of Economy, cautioned that sport betting "must be studied quite a bit, such as the integrity of the sport, the prevention of money laundering, [and] the prevention of pathologies among vulnerable players" (O'Connor, 2021, para. 4). Recent research pointed to a set of risk factors for gambling problems, specifically associated with sports betting. One study found that companies involved in sports betting need to pay most attention to:

> younger people with some disposable income, who are more engaged sports bettors (and gamblers in general), who gamble for a variety of motivations but particularly for money, have higher gambling urges and more erroneous cognitions, who experience alcohol issues, and have lower self-control. (Russell et al., 2019, pp. 1224-1225)

Conclusion

From BBVA Argentina's use of sport, music, art, and entertainment sponsorships to acquire and grow customers, to Gazprom's use of football sponsorship to improve its influence in Europe, this chapter has provided an understanding of sponsorship as a powerful marketing communications tool. The benefits of sponsorship include the achievement of externally focused brand goals, such as awareness, preference, and loyalty, as well as positively influencing a sponsor's reputation with stakeholders in its community and operating environment. Sponsorship benefits discussed also include internal marketing goals and the achievement of financial goals. The chapter detailed the mechanisms that explain how sponsorship works, such as exposure, fit, and image transfer. This sponsorship chapter included numerous examples of how brands have used sponsorship in emerging market country contexts and discussed the special sponsorship issues of soft power and sports betting.

References

Bansal, S. (2019). Do brands pay too much for Indian cricket team? *Mint*. Retrieved from https://www.livemint.com/opinion/columns/opinion-do-brands-pay-too-much-for-indian-cricket-team-1565199263698.html

Blackshaw, I. (2010). 2010 FIFA world cup South Africa: Legal protection of the marks and the event. *International Sports Law Review Pandektis, 3*(4), 32–41.

Brand Finance. (2020). Chinese brands grow eight times faster than global average. Retrieved from https://brandfinance.com

Burton, N., & Chadwick, S. (2009). Ambush marketing in sport: An analysis of sponsorship protection means and counter-ambush measures. *Journal of Sponsorship, 2*(4), 303–315.

Burton, N., & Chadwick, S. (2018). Ambush marketing is dead, long live ambush marketing: A redefinition and typology of an increasingly prevalent phenomenon. *Journal of Advertising Research, 58*(3), 282–296.

Chanavat, N., Desbordes, M., & Dickson, G. (2016). Sponsorship networks: Toward an innovative model. *Sport, Business and Management: An International Journal, 6*(4), 424–439.

5 Sponsorship: Practices and Benefits in Emerging Markets

Charbonneau, J., & Garland, R. (2010). Product effects on endorser image: The potential for reverse image transfer. *Asia Pacific Journal of Marketing and Logistics, 22*(1), 101–110. https://doi.org/10.1108/13555851011013182

Central Bureau of Investigation. (2000). *CBI's report on cricket match fixing and related malpractices*. Retrieved from http://docshare02.docshare.tips/files/5470/54707971.pdf.

Charlton, A. B., & Cornwell, T. B. (2019). Authenticity in horizontal marketing partnerships: A better measure of brand compatibility. *Journal of Business Research, 100*, 279–298.

Cornwell, T. B. (2014). *Sponsorship in marketing: Effective communication through sports, arts and events*. Routledge.

Cornwell, T. B., Weeks, C. S., & Roy, D. P. (2005). Sponsorship-linked marketing: Opening the black box. *Journal of Advertising, 34*(2), 21–42.

Crompton, J. L. (2014). Potential negative outcomes from sponsorship for a sport property. *Managing Leisure, 19*(6), 420–441.

Donlan, L. (2014). An empirical assessment of factors affecting the brand-building effectiveness of sponsorship. *Sport, Business and Management: An International Journal, 4*(1), 6–25.

Farrelly, F., Quester, P., & Greyser, S. A. (2005). Defending the co-branding benefits of sponsorship B2B partnerships: The case of ambush marketing. *Journal of Advertising Research, 45*(3), 339–348.

Guttmann, A. (2019). Global sponsorship spending by region from 2009 to 2018 (in billion U.S. dollars). Retrieved from https://www.statista-com/statistics/196898/global-sponsorship-spending-by-region-since-2009/

Harrington, J. (2016, August 22). Nissan: Rio 2016 sponsorship grew our marketing share in Brazil. *PR Week*. Retrieved from https://www.prweek.com/article/1406357/nissan-rio-2016-sponsorship-grew-market-share-brazil.

Hickman, T. M., Lawrence, K. E., & Ward, J. C. (2005). A social identities perspective on the effects of corporate sport sponsorship on employees. *Sport Marketing Quarterly, 14*, 148–157.

Hino, Y., & Takeda, F. (2020). Market reactions to sport sponsorship announcements: Comparison between sponsors and their rivals. *Sport Management Review, 23*(3), 401–413.

Hohenberger, C., & Grohs, R. (2002). Old and exciting? Sport sponsorship effects on brand age and brand personality. *Sport Management Review, 23*(3), 469–481.

IEG. (2020). *IEG outlook 2020: Forecasting the future of the sponsorship industry*. Retrieved from https://www.sponsorship.com/Latest-Thinking/Sponsorship-Infographics/IEG-Outlook-2020%2D%2DForecasting-the-Future-of-the.aspx

Jensen, J. A., & Cornwell, T. B. (2017). Why do marketing relationships end? Findings from an integrated model of sport sponsorship decision-making. *Journal of Sport Management, 31*(4), 401–418.

Krzyzaniak, J. S. (2018). The soft power strategy of soccer sponsorships. *Soccer & Society, 19*(4), 498–515.

Kwon, Y., & Cornwell, T. B. (2020). Sport sponsorship announcement and stock returns: A meta-analytic review. *International Journal of Sports Marketing and Sponsorship, 1*, 1. https://doi.org/10.1108/IJSMS-05-2020-0085

McCarthy, J. (2018, May 15). Laundry powder Omo's Corinthians logo only appears on a sweaty jersey. *The Drum*. Retrieved from https://www.thedrum.com/news/2018/05/15/laundry-powder-omos-corinthians-logo-only-appears-sweaty-jersey.

Moorhouse, S. (2013). Afcon 2013 sponsors delight. *Ojeikere Aikhoje's Blog*. Retrieved from https://ojeksaikhoje.blogspot.com/2013/02/afcon-2013-sponsors-delight.html.

Nielsen. (2019). *Esports playbook for brands 2019*. Retrieved from https://www.nielsen.com/us/en/insights/report/2019/esports-playbook-for-brands.

O'Connor, D. (2021, January 18). Sports betting in Brazil to launch next year ahead of 2022 World Cup. *Casino.org*. Retrieved from https://www.casino.org/news/sports-betting-in-brazil-to-launch-next-year-ahead-of-2022-world-cup.

Pitt, H., Thomas, S. L., & Bestman, A. (2016). Initiation, influence, and impact: Adolescents and parents discuss the marketing of gambling products during Australian sporting matches. *BMC Public Health, 16*(967), 1–12. https://doi.org/10.1186/s12889-016-3610-z

Raza, M. R., & Shekhar, R. (2020). Dream11 and IPL 2020: Illegal gambling and Indian sports. *Jurist*. Retrieved from https://www.jurist.org/commentary/2020/09/raza-shekhar-ipl-bookmaker.

Reelforge. (2019). *Kenya media landscape report*. Retrieved from https://www.reelforge.com/PublicFiles/Media-Landscape-in-Kenya-2019-Report-(Reelforge-and-TIFA)-10.07.2019.pdf.

Russell, A. M. T., Hing, N., & Browne, M. (2019). Risk factors for gambling problems specifically associated with sports betting. *Journal of Gambling Studies, 35*, 1211–1228.

Schneider, M. (2020, January 31). Why this Russian gas company sponsors soccer teams. *Vox*. Retrieved from https://www.vox.com/videos/2020/1/31/21117233/gazprom-russia-soccer-sponsor.

Vox. (2020, January 31). *Why this Russian gas company sponsors soccer teams* [YouTube video]. Retrieved from https://www.youtube.com/watch?v=utUOJ64X7u0.

6

Sports Marketing Communications in South America

Raúl A. Rosales and Roger G. Tito

Introduction

Professional sport started becoming an important content for the growing television industry since the mid-1980s. Whannel (2009) opines that sports played a key role in the development of television, especially between 1950 and 1980. Several aspects of the competition at both club and country level had an impact on the television industry, and therefore, it was able to grow into a multimillion industry, whose primary income comes from the television broadcast of matches. In this context, each match is analysed as an event and provided the level of entertainment required to make it an interesting content for the public.

As tournaments were drawing audience's attention, sports events became an interesting event for many TV stations; they began to set aside more resources to obtain exclusive broadcasting rights in major

R. A. Rosales (✉) • R. G. Tito
Universidad Peruana de Ciencias Aplicadas, Lima, Peru
e-mail: raul.rosales@upc.pe; u201515095@upc.edu.pe

tournaments (Taylor, 2016). As sports continued to grow as a global spectacle, professional soccer has become one of the contents of main coverage worldwide at both club and country levels. This has translated to more income streams from soccer through national and international competitions. It has also led to consolidation of soccer as a global professional sport.

In Latin America, soccer has become a national treasure. In this chapter, we analyse the relevance of the audience of the Peru national soccer team's matches in the World Cup Qualifiers to Russia 2018, as well as its participation in the same event. This is even more relevant because Peru national soccer team took part in a Fédération Internationale de Football Association (FIFA) World Cup after 36 years.

An important aspect to consider is the way in which qualification processes are undertaken for the FIFA World Cup. The qualification process is different for each sport, even more when we talk about a team sport in comparison to other types of sports, such as individual sports (Feu et al., 2018). It will explain in brief the process to achieve the qualification for the most important soccer event among countries.

We will also analyse the audience and some aspects which influence demand by different segments. Based on the research, this chapter will analyse the several motivations that make spectators follow these events by television.

Sports as Media Content

Sports is a social phenomenon whose growth has been associated with growing media coverage. As Bryant and Holt (2009) noted, the connection between sports and media in the United States is much older than the beginning of sports in the Modern Age in the early twentieth century. This fact can be verified before the Industrial Revolution of the mid-seventeenth century.

In that sense, Boyle and Haynes (2012) noted that sport as a media scene is a product of modernity. They indicated that the sport's first stage of development was through institutions such as the church, armed forces, public schools, anh8d universities because they encourage modern practices. In 1936 in the United States, a journalist affirmed that soccer is probably one of the biggest sports on earth; it engages millions of people, captivating their minds and emptying their pockets.

Brown and Bryant (2012) noted that in the case of the United States, sports is an important part of television content, occupying 13 of 30 programmes with a large audience on cable television. According to them, an important milestone was the creation of the specialised sports channel ESPN in 1979. It is evident that the contents are not only of sports events, but also of key aspects around the sports such as news programmes and panel discussions. For his part, Gastaldo (2014) makes reference to the fact that in Brazil, soccer and media arrived at the same time by the end of the nineteenth century. In the same way as previous authors, they also indicated that both elements are part of modernity and that they helped to shape that sense of identity with the Brazilian-ness. This identity has a distinctive element: the "malandro" or "bad boy", a popular hero similar to the American cowboy or the Japanese samurai. This "malandro" represents resistance to discipline and labour exploitation, a rebel attitude which is valued in spaces as soccer.

By helping countries consolidate and create their national sport identity, while growing media engagement alongside, the professional sport went from a basic productive activity to becoming a worldwide multimillion-dollar industry (Borges, 2019). Competition among different television networks to obtain television rights of those events increased prices and, therefore, translated to higher income for the competing clubs.

In Australia, soccer, like other team sports, started to grow due to large media coverage, especially of professional tournaments. As in other countries, the development of alternative ways such as cable television created an opportunity for growth and consolidation of sports contents in developed markets, as the case in Australia (Rowe & Gilmour, 2009). Just like in Brazil, the international competitions of national teams helped to consolidate rituals of national identity to go with their team at the time.

This aspect of soccer as an element that creates a national identity was considered an argument about whether soccer broadcasts should be done by open signal channels or payment channels. Spain's national soccer team matches had a particular national regulation in which the government required the matches of national interest to be broadcast by open signal television, that is without any cost to the audience. Open signal channels prioritised payment channels to define which matches would be broadcast for free (Martin & Rennhoff, 2015).

Sports Events as Communication Platform

Sports Events: Definition of Events and Sports Events

According to the Royal Spanish Academy, an event is an important and organised occasion of social, academic, artistic, or sports nature (Real Academia Española, 2021). Other academic publications about events are more practical, and they define it as the process of planning, organisation, and management. They refer to economic resources, human resources, communication, marketing, promotion, sponsorship, logistic control, and project management (Galmés Cerezo, 2010). On the other hand, Shone (2001) defines events in general as those phenomena that arise from non-routine activities and that have leisure, cultural, personal, and sports goals whose objective is to illustrate, celebrate, entertain, or challenge the experience of a group of people. From these assumptions, it can be pointed out that sporting events aim at arousing interest from a part or all target audience of a group of people. The business scope aims to share, communicate, or strengthen products, services, or a brand through direct contact with potential or current clients; meanwhile, in the sports scope, it seeks to give experiences, promote sport, bring tourism, and even generate profitability through social impact. According to Añó (2003), sports events are activities that have a high level of social impact, which in turn is translated through a strong presence in media and that generates economic income by itself.

There are several classifications for defining the nature of a sports event, for example, based on its audience. Another classification involves the type and intensity of the exercise performed (Mitchell et al., 1985). From international events such as the World Cup or the Olympic Games, which are called major sporting events, to events led for a region such as Pan American Games or Conmebol (South American Football Confederation) America Cup, or at national level such as swimming competitions organised by the federation, and even to local community level such as the soccer tournament of Miraflores (district of Lima, Peru), one sees different evident classifications.

Considering these definitions, it can be described that an event is a set of actions that develop from different manners (nature) according to the needs and goals of the organisation or institution of a particular industry. It is a group of people who have interests in common about a specific topic and who look for engaging unique and once-in-a-lifetime events with a high level of interaction and during a limited time which cause a strong presence in media and economic resources (Cerezuela, 2005).

Use of Sports Events as Part of Marketing

Bryant and Holt (2009) noted that both the sport and media are institutions which aim for profitability, and for that reason, they have been able to develop in a capitalist system. It is from this premise that sport products, in particular sporting events, can be analysed from a marketing perspective.

Thrassou et al. (2012) presented a traditional definition of marketing as "an organisational management process that emphasises customers' needs, wants, and exchange processes" (p.279). In addition, they noted that four (4) key elements should be taken into account: "organisational goals, profitability, need satisfaction, and integrative marketing activities". Liu (2017), after reviewing several definitions of marketing that have been suggested from its beginning, defines marketing as "the activities and value creation processes that facilitate exchanging offerings within the domain of business and benefit the society at large" (p.3).

The concept of the marketing mix has been developed along with the development of the concept of marketing. A marketing mix is a management tool that allows us to identify strategies from certain key aspects. Traditionally four (4) elements have been considered; they are called 4Ps: price, product, promotion, and place. This traditional approach has evolved since its beginning in the 1950s until today, and it has adapted to the different needs that have existed. As Wu and Li (2018) noted, if one would like an approach focused on the consumer for niche segments, the

4Cs could be used: communication, consumer and their needs, cost, and convenience. Meanwhile, Yi (2017) says there are two models of marketing mix with 4Ps and 7Ps, respectively; the goal is to provide a combination of methods that will be used by parts of the organisation in order to achieve its objectives in pursuit of placing effectively their products or services for a specific group of clients.

Based on the proposal of the 4Ps for marketing mix, promotion is the element that we are going to pay more attention. According to Thrassou et al. (2012), promotion is "the means through which the marketer communicates data about the product, place, and price" (p.284). We can also say that promotion is the method to place a product in consumer's mind through different marketing activities. This objective can be achieved through advertising activities, personal selling, or sales promotion, such as fairs and events.

As there are different definitions for marketing and marketing mix, there are also different definitions for Sports Marketing. Cristóbal Fransi (2003) defines it as those activities designed to face the needs of sports product consumers through exchange processes (p.2). For example, Thrassou et al. (2012) indicated that one of the definitions is related to the activities led to meet particular needs of sports consumers through exchange processes. Similarly, Coutinho Da Silva et al. (2017) noted that sport is seen as that space in which the connection between a consumer or fan and their club is given in a particular way. For that reason, it is necessarily a specific analysis of this connection.

One of the more relevant aspects to take into account in sports marketing is that it has been developed to promote sports events and teams who participate in those competitions, just like the promotion of products and services related to sports events (Coutinho Da Silva et al., 2017).

In that way, we have to ask ourselves what kind of product is a sports event. Thrassou et al. (2012) noted that, regarding soccer, the product is "essentially a service of entertainment; along with its auxiliary characteristics, such as excitement, fun, etc." However, it is important to note that, from this service, other products and services related to it are generated. On the other hand, from the point of view of income generation, broadcasting rights have become the main source of income for team sports, such as soccer. Caruso et al. (2019) pointed out that income for broadcasting matches represents 53% of the English Premier League and 61% of the Italian Serie A for the season 2014/2015.

It is for this reason that Borges (2019) indicated that clubs which take part in professional competitions in the European soccer league are multinational. Through this entertainment service, they have a presence in many different countries outside of their home country, and they have become authentic media organisations, as a large part of their activities are covered by media.

In addition to national-level tournaments, sporting events of international nature awoke the interest of different stakeholders that see a way to promote their cities or countries in these events (Vassiliadis et al., 2021). This pragmatic approach to sporting events is promoted mainly for the governments that see a positioning strategy for their country in this kind of events, which draws global attention, especially for businesses within their country.

Lenskyj (2009) noted that there was not always considerable interest in these events, such as the Olympic Games. During the 1960s and 1970s, it was noted that there was a decline in the interest in hosting these sporting events. However, the tipping point was Los Angeles 1984 Olympic Games hosted in the United States. It was the first game to announce an economic surplus. Since Los Angeles 1984, the interest in becoming a host city has increased. It is important to note that in the last few years, this interest has been moderated due to the high costs associated with the organising of these events.

The tourism sector uses destination marketing in order to promote a specific destination through the organisation of a major sports event (Cabanilla et al., 2020). These sports events are organised to attract tourism. For this reason, it is necessary to analyse tourists' motivations to visit a particular destination, either directly or indirectly related to a sports event (Andersson et al., 2021).

Sports Tournaments: World Cups and their Qualifiers

Major sports events are tournaments that can attract spectators through tourism, a large audience, and media, as in the Summer and Winter

Olympic Games, Super Bowl, FIFA World Cup, Formula 1, and so on (Santiago et al., 2016). FIFA World Cup, also known as World Cup, is the main international soccer tournament where the best soccer teams around the world compete. It is held every four years by a host country chosen by different FIFA bodies.

The first World Cup (Uruguay 1930) was the only one that did not have a qualification stage because all countries affiliated with FIFA were invited to compete and given a deadline of February 28 to submit their response. Due to the refusal by the European countries justifying their absence by the costly ship trip to cross the Atlantic, only 13 teams participated in that event. The South American participating countries were Argentina, Chile, Brazil, Bolivia, Peru, and Paraguay (Sanchez, 2015).

For the Switzerland World Cup of 1954, the qualifiers match started in South America. In the previous editions of this tournament, teams qualified by invitations or withdrawals (Conmebol, 2015). The qualification format was all against all and play-off matches. In this edition, three national soccer teams participated (Brazil, Chile, and Paraguay), and the first place (Brazil) qualified. It also had Uruguay as defending champion. In the following edition, eight teams participated in the 1958 Sweden World Cup; due to the withdrawal of Venezuela, the qualification format was divided into two groups of three teams and one group of two teams. The first place in each group automatically qualified for the World Cup. The qualifying teams were Argentina, Brazil, and Paraguay.

Conmebol (2015) also points out that for the 1962 Chile World Cup, the Conmebol had three available places. The qualification format was three fixtures in two legs for a total of six teams. In the 1974 Germany World Cup, the qualification format had the play-off match for the first time as a way of qualification. Chile faced the Soviet Union and qualified for the World Cup after the latter withdrew due to political issues. For this edition, the qualifying teams were Argentina, Chile, Uruguay, and Brazil as the defending champion.

Until 1994 USA World Cup, qualifiers for South American countries had a group format in which the winners qualified directly for the World Cup, while the other team had a play-off match with non-American teams. In France 1998, the Conmebol had four available places, and unlike previous qualification processes, the format was all against all in two-leg matches, and the first four places qualified for the World Cup, and the fifth place had a play-off match.

According to Conmebol (2015), from France 1998 to the present, the qualification format is the same. The nine members (Argentina, Bolivia, Chile, Colombia, Ecuador, Peru, Paraguay, Uruguay, Venezuela) compete in qualifiers in two-leg matches. The four first places qualify automatically, while the fifth place has a play-off match against a country that does not belong to the Conmebol, that is, countries from the Oceania Football Confederation, Asian Football Confederation, or Concacaf (Confederation of North, Central America, and Caribbean Association Football).

An important event in soccer is television broadcast; even in the present times, there is no other sport that has become a worldwide television product. According to Asociación Nacional del Fútbol Profesional (2014), Switzerland 1954 was the first World Cup broadcast due to the joint work of eight European countries that created the continental television network Eurovision. This edition was broadcast in all Europe; more than 50 million people watched the final between Hungary and West Germany. In the 1966 England World Cup, the inauguration and the final were broadcast via satellite all over the world. This was the beginning of repetitions and slow-motion in official soccer matches, and a change of the rules due to the incident during the final between England and Argentina, where the Argentinian captain Antonio Rattín was verbally sent off (red or yellow cards did not exist before this World Cup) by the referee after 30 minutes of stopping the game.

The 1970 Mexico World Cup was the first worldwide colour event broadcast via a communication satellite. However, given the expensive minute rate for broadcasting, FIFA and television networks got together to review Antonio Rattín's sending off, and that game was not stopped for more than 30 minutes, so they decided to use red and yellow cards (FIFA, 1997).

According to Aranguiz (2020), Mexico 1970 is the beginning of satellite colour television. It was the first time in history that 32 matches were broadcast live and in colour through eight cameras set on the stadium, reaching more than 700 million people all over the world.

The significance of soccer matches of a country's national team reached a milestone in television history when, at 3a.m in the morning of June 21, 2002, the largest TV audience for a sports event was registered. In Brazil, 98% of the homes were watching the semi-finals against England during the 2002 Korea/Japan World Cup (Gastaldo, 2014).

Television Audience of the Qualification Matches: The Case of Peru

Audience: Motivations and Measuring Ways

Since the 1950s, the economic analysis of the aspects that determine the demand for sports has been related to the concept of uncertainty of the results. It is in this sense that the more competitive a competition is, the more interest it will attract from consumers (Caruso et al., 2019). In addition to the technological advances in broadcasting, the events that were broadcast on television increased, particularly professional-level events.

Pérez et al. (2017) analysed the audience of the matches of Spain's professional soccer league, as well as the probabilities of the results associated with bets. They found that the uncertainty of the outcome did not lead to a larger audience, but only in important matches such as Real Madrid versus Barcelona.

Caruso et al. (2019) performed a review of the research carried out on the relationship between television audiences and specific factors that determine the outcome of the competition. A study of the English Premier League between 1993 and 2003 found a relevant positive relationship between the uncertainty of the result and the television audience. In the case of the National Football League (NFL) of the United States, a study carried out in 2005 showed that the audience increased when there was a black quarterback in the game.

The traditional way to measure the audience is from the official organisations that are in charge of measuring the audience (Bergmann & Schreyer, 2019). Another way to measure the audience of sports events is through telephone surveys, which will allow not only quantitative aspects but also qualitative aspects. McDaniel (2002) applied this methodology to analyse the profile of the North American audience of the 1996 Olympic Games. He found that those who followed the competitions had a higher level of patriotism and religiosity than those who did not, as well as a greater willingness to enjoy advertising than those who were less interested in sports events.

An approach to take into account is the one proposed by Ramchandani et al. (2014) on the willingness of spectators to start practising sport. An analysis carried out on the attendees who were attending an event of a particular sport for the first time showed that a positive experience as a spectator did not necessarily translate into an active sports practice. This research was carried out in England in 2010.

On the other hand, Bergmann and Schreyer (2019) analysed the television audience in Germany of the German national team between August 2004 and July 2017. This exploratory study revealed that the interest in the matches of their national team is different depending on the age group considered. Clearly, seniors (65+) are those with different motivations than the other groups.

Audience of the Matches of Peru in the World Cup Qualifiers for Russia 2018

After 36 years of not attending the World Cup, on October 10, 2017, Peru played the most important match against Colombia that would allow it to go to a play-off match. According to Kantar IBOPE Media (2017a), this game was broadcast by the ATV (open signal) and Movistar Deportes (cable signal) channels in Peruvian territory, getting ratings of 53.2% in homes. It was watched by 3,499,490 people.

After a tie against Colombia, the Peruvian national soccer team was able to access the play-off match against the New Zealand national soccer team. This match took place in Oceania and got ratings of 63.1%, and it was watched by 3,775,500 people nationwide, according to the report made by Kantar IBOPE Media (2017c). However, the match played in Lima was watched by 4,086,270 people and got ratings of 61.4% in Peruvian homes. This event also generated 182,210 tweets that resulted in 20.7 million reactions in the match, which qualified Peru to the most important soccer event (Kantar IBOPE Media, 2017b).

The increase in the number of viewers meant Peruvians were able to actualise their desire and were given an opportunity to see Peru play in the World Cup, as the expectant situation from the last matches increased in all the cities of Peru and of Peruvians living abroad. A study on behaviour towards television programming analyses a matrix that has variables as soccer represents "more reach" and "more loyalty" as the programming genre with the greatest reach compared to contests, films, magazines, newscast, miniseries, talk shows, soap operas, and comedy shows; however, there is a lower loyalty to these last three genres (Kantar IBOPE Media, 2020).

The beneficiaries of attending the World Cup or having high ratings are not only the fans but also the sponsoring companies and television channels that, through advertising spots, generate an outreach to millions of people. According to Carrillo (2015), leading companies of products and services for mass consumption, such as Movistar or Cristal beer, seek to associate their brands with the Peruvian national soccer team to create an emotional bond with their consumers and to widen their brand penetration.

Conclusion

Sport has established itself as a relevant content for television in South America. This fact is particularly evident in the competitions associated with professional soccer at the club level, as well as the competitions of the national soccer teams. This audience behaviour related to soccer matches can also be seen in European countries such as Germany and Spain. In the case of Peru, the matches of the national soccer team in the World Cup Qualifiers are the television content with the largest audience. Based on the research carried out, it can be verified that this situation also occurs in other countries of the region, such as Brazil and Argentina.

This relationship between the media and professional soccer in South America was able to develop in a context in which both elements were considered as particular elements of modernity. Based on the information reviewed, we can affirm that both grew together from the end of the nineteenth century to the present day. Currently, there are new forms of communication that should be the subject of analysis in future research on the matter.

One aspect to highlight is that soccer understood its role as a media content. This fact motivated a professionalisation of the sport in its different aspects: from the competition calendar and its rules to the image management of the elements that make up the event: stadiums, players, and so on.

From the literature reviewed on the characteristics of the audience or the motivations for watching soccer matches, there was a shortage of information for the South American case. Based on the information found in European countries, this is a topic to which attention should be paid since it is possible that the motivations of the audience will change over time given that professional sports are entertainment-type content.

Television has allowed higher income to several stakeholders of professional soccer. This income is not only for television rights but also for the sponsorships that can be generated from the broadcast. Organisers at international and national levels such as FIFA, Conmebol at the South American level, or the National Soccer Federations along with their members are the ones who have benefited from this consolidated industry.

References

Andersson, S., Bengtsson, L., & Svensson, Å. (2021). Mega-sport football events' influence on destination images: A study of the of 2016 UEFA European football championship in France, the 2018 FIFA world cup in Russia, and the 2022 FIFA world cup in Qatar. *Journal of Destination Marketing & Management, 19*, 100536.

Añó, V. (2003). Organización y gestión de actividades deportivas Los grandes eventos. INDE. https://n9.cl/eu5gr

Aranguiz, E. (2020). Mexico 1970 el comienzo del fútbol como lo conocemos. El equipo Deporte online. https://elequipo-deportea.com/2020/05/21/mexico-1970-el-comienzo-del-futbol-como-lo-conocemos/

Asociación Nacional del Fútbol Profesional. (2014, May 7). La evolución de los mundiales por tv: el estadio más grande del mundo. https://www.anfp.cl/noticia/20977/la-evolucion-de-los-mundiales-por-tv-el-estadio-mas-grande-del-mundo

Bergmann, A., & Schreyer, D. (2019). Factors that shape the demand for international football games across different age groups. *International Journal of Sport Finance, 14*(1), 13–23. https://doi.org/10.32731/IJSF.141.022019.03

Borges, F. (2019). Soccer clubs as media organizations: A case study of Benfica TV and PSG TV. *International Journal of Sport Communication, 12*(2), 275–294. https://doi.org/10.1123/ijsc.2019-0001

Boyle, R., & Haynes, R. (2012). Sport, the media and popular culture. *Power Play, 1*(2009), 1–18. https://doi.org/10.3366/edinburgh/9780748635924.003.0001

Brown, D., & Bryant, J. (2012). Chapter 5 - sports content on U.S. television. *Routledge Online Studies on the Olympic and Paralympic Games, 1*(46), 80–110. https://doi.org/10.4324/9780203873670_chapter_5

Bryant, J., & Holt, A. M. (2009). A historical overview of sports and media in the United States. *Handbook of Sports and Media, 2006*, 22–45. https://doi.org/10.4324/9780203873670-8

Cabanilla, E., Bravo, L., & X., Pazmiño, J., & Burbano, M. (2020). Análisis del perfil demográfico y consumo turístico en eventos deportivos en la ciudad de Quito. Caso de estudio: Roger Federer (analysis of the demographic profile and tourist consumption in sporting events in the city of Quito. Case of study: Roger Federer). *Retos, 2041*(40), 27–40. https://doi.org/10.47197/retos.v1i40.82749

Carrillo, L. (2015, June 29). *El curioso caso de la selección peruana de fútbol y sus enormes ratings televisivos | Blogs | GESTIÓN.* https://gestion.pe/blog/el-deporte-de-hacer-negocios/2015/06/el-curioso-caso-de-la-seleccion-peruana-de-futbol-y-sus-enormes-ratings-televisivos.html/

Caruso, R., Addesa, F., & Di Domizio, M. (2019). The determinants of the TV demand for soccer: Empirical evidence on Italian Serie a for the period 2008-2015. *Journal of Sports Economics, 20*(1), 25–49. https://doi.org/10.1177/1527002517717298

Cerezuela, B. (2005). *La información y documentación deportiva y los grandes eventos deportivos.* http://olympicstudies.uab.es/pdf/wp086_spa.pdf

CONMEBOL. (2015, October 5). *Historia de las eliminatorias.* https://www.conmebol.com/es/05102015-1328/historia-de-las-eliminatorias

Coutinho Da Silva, E., Luzzi, A., & Casas, L. (2017). Sports marketing plan: An alternative framework for sports Club. *International Journal of Marketing Studies, 9*(4). https://doi.org/10.5539/ijms.v9n4p15

Cristóbal Fransi, E. (2003). Marketing deportivo: la comercialización del producto de deporte. *Alta Dirección, 39*(230), 11–16. https://www.researchgate.net/publication/40966685_Marketing_deportivo_la_comercializacion_del_producto_de_deporte?enrichId=rgreq-d9d75e02acc162f6427bf60121cb94c8-XXX&enrichSource=Y292ZXJQYWdlOzQwOTY2Njg1O0FTOjE0OTE5NTk5MDI0NTM3N0AxNDEyNTgyNTA0NTI5&el=1_x_

Feu, S., García-Rubio, J., Antúnez, A., & Ibáñez, S. (2018). Coaching and coach education in Spain: A critical analysis of legislative evolution. *International Sport Coaching Journal, 5*(3), 281–292.

FIFA. (1997). *Fútbol y Televisión - una historia de gran éxito.* https://es.fifa.com/news/futbol-television-una-historia-gran-exito-76069

Galmés Cerezo, M. A. (2010). *La organización de eventos como herramienta de comunicación de marketing.* http://riuma.uma.es

Gastaldo, É. (2014). Soccer and media in Brazil. *Soccer and Society, 15*(1), 123–131. https://doi.org/10.1080/14660970.2013.854576

Kantar IBOPE Media. (2017a). *¡Estamos un paso más cerca de #Rusia2018! Estamos felices de compartir con ustedes el rating del partido de ayer en Perú.* https://www.facebook.com/KantarIBOPEMediaPeru/photos/279491615875678

Kantar IBOPE Media. (2017b, October 16). *Después de 180 minutos jugados con garra y corazón, ¡Ya estamos en el Mundial Rusia 2018!* https://www.facebook.com/KantarIBOPEMediaPeru/photos/291705821320924

Kantar IBOPE Media. (2017c, November 13). *¡Estamos un paso más cerca de #Rusia2018! Compartimos con ustedes el rating del partido del viernes y el impacto de este evento en Twitter.* https://www.facebook.com/KantarIBOPEMediaPeru/photos/290723198085853

Kantar IBOPE Media. (2020, October 18). *El comportamiento frente a la programaciónentvesdiversificado.* https://www.facebook.com/KantarIBOPEMediaPeru/photos/965311487293684

Lenskyj, H. J. (2009). Alternative media versus the Olympic industry. *Handbook of Sports and Media, 2006,* 219–230. https://doi.org/10.4324/9780203873670-19

Liu, R. (2017). A reappraisal of marketing definition and theory. *Journal of Eastern European and Central Asian Research, 4*(2), 1–8. https://doi.org/10.15549/jeecar.v4i2.170

Martin, H. J., & Rennhoff, A. D. (2015). Spanish TV regulations and audiences for soccer matches, factors influencing utility from watching TV, and how media coverage influences financial returns for Australian companies. *Journal of Media Economics, 28*(1), 1–3. https://doi.org/10.1080/08997764.2015.1004894

McDaniel, S. R. (2002). An exploration of audience demographics, personal values, and lifestyle: Influences on viewing network coverage of the 1996 summer Olympic games. *Journal of Sport Management, 16*(2), 117–131. https://doi.org/10.1123/jsm.16.2.117

Mitchell, J. H., Blomqvist, C. G., Haskell, W. L., James, F. W., Miller, H. S., Miller, W. W., & Strong, W. B. (1985). Classification of sports. *Journal of the American College of Cardiology, 6*(6), 1198–1199.

Pérez, L., Puente, V., & Rodríguez, P. (2017). Factors determining TV soccer viewing: Does uncertainty of outcome really matter? *International Journal of Sport Finance, 12*(2), 124–139.

Ramchandani, G., Kokolakakis, T., & Coleman, R. (2014). Factors influencing the inspirational effect of major sports events on audience sport participation behaviour. *World Leisure Journal, 56*(3), 220–235. https://doi.org/10.1080/16078055.2014.938296

Real Academia Española. (2021). *Diccionario de la Lengua Española*. Real Academia Española. https://dle.rae.es/evento

Rowe, D., & Gilmour, C. (2009). Getting a ticket to the world party: Televising soccer in Australia. *Soccer and Society, 10*(1), 9–26. https://doi.org/10.1080/14660970802472635

Santiago, C., Ladino, C., Camilo, G., Corredor, P., & Asistente, P. (2016). *LOS MEGA-EVENTOS DEPORTIVOS, UNA ESTRATEGIA DE LAS POTENCIAS EMERGENTES: Los casos de los Juegos Olímpicos de Invierno Sochi (2014), el Mundial de Fútbol de la FIFA Brasil (2014) y los Juegos Olímpicos de Río (2016) como herramientas de imagen internacional*.

Taylor, N. T. (2016). Now you're playing with audience power: The work of watching games. *Critical Studies in Media Communication, 33*(4), 293–307.

Thrassou, A., Vrontis, D., Kartakoullis, N. L., & Kriemadis, T. (2012). Contemporary marketing communications framework for football clubs. *Journal of Promotion Management, 18*(3), 278–305. https://doi.org/10.1080/10496491.2012.696454

Vassiliadis, C. A., Mombeuil, C., & Fotiadis, A. K. (2021). Identifying service product features associated with visitor satisfaction and revisit intention: A focus on sports events. *Journal of Destination Marketing & Management, 19,* 100558. https://doi.org/10.1016/j.jdmm.2021.100558

Whannel, G. (2009). Television and the transformation of sport. *The Annals of the American Academy of Political and Social Science, 625*(1), 205–218.

Wu, Y. L., & Li, E. Y. (2018). Marketing mix, customer value, and customer loyalty in social commerce: A stimulus-organism-response perspective. *Internet Research, 28*(1), 74–104. https://doi.org/10.1108/IntR-08-2016-0250

Yi, Z. G. (2017). Marketing services and resources in information organizations. *Proquest Ebook Central.* https://doi.org/10.1016/b978-0-08-100798-3.00005-2

7

Social Media-Driven Consumer–Brand Interactions in Mexico: Healthy Food Brands Versus Indulgent Food Brands

Gricel Castillo, Lorena Carrete, and Pilar Arroyo

Introduction

Social media literature has substantially increased over the last few years because it provides businesses with the opportunity to increase sales and brand awareness, establish better communication with consumers, use analytics to learn about the consumers and adjust branding strategy (Felix et al., 2017; Kamboj, 2019). In social settings, many people have adopted social media because it enables them to set up personal profiles, generate content and interact with friends or other online users (Ahmed et al., 2019; Carr & Hayes, 2015; Liu et al., 2019). The segment of young adults aged between 18 and 29 years has the highest social media adoption rates (Perrin, 2015). Social media also provides an ideal environment for companies to connect with their consumers and enhance brand engagement (Beukeboom et al., 2015; Jayasingh & Venkatesh, 2016).

G. Castillo (✉) • L. Carrete • P. Arroyo
EGADE Business School, Tecnologico de Monterrey, Monterrey, Mexico
e-mail: gricel.castillo@tec.mx; lcarrete@tec.mx; pilar.arroyo@tec.mx

© The Author(s), under exclusive license to Springer Nature Switzerland AG 2022
O. Adeola et al. (eds.), *Marketing Communications and Brand Development in Emerging Economies Volume I*, Palgrave Studies of Marketing in Emerging Economies,
https://doi.org/10.1007/978-3-030-88678-3_7

Companies can attract the interest of potential customers and develop personalised relationships (Chen et al., 2011; Fournier et al., 2012; Pate & Adams, 2013).

Generally, social media is any site that enables people to make connections and be part of a network (Warner-Søderholm et al., 2018). Main subdomains include social networking sites (SNS) (e.g. Facebook), video-sharing sites (e.g. YouTube), photo-sharing sites (e.g. Flickr) and microblogging sites (e.g. Twitter), but several other domains exist (Whiting & Williams, 2013). Facebook is the predominant social networking site with an increasing branded content (Berezan et al., 2020; Estrella-Ramón et al., 2019; Kang et al., 2014; Luarn et al., 2015), and it provides the option to create *brand fan pages* (De Vries et al., 2012). Brand managers can distribute and exchange information about the brand and its products on brand fan pages. If this information is sufficiently attractive, consumers can turn into 'fans', publish 'likes' and even express their sentiments towards the brand (Heinonen, 2011; Hossain et al., 2019). The consumers' satisfaction with brand fan pages boosts brand engagement and, consequently, consumer–brand interaction (Chen & Tsai, 2020; Gan & Li, 2018; Phua et al., 2017; Sabate et al., 2014).

Nevertheless, the underlying reasons for individuals to interact with brand fan pages call for further research that enhances the understanding of consumers' motivation to use this specific social media site (Rasheed Gaber et al., 2019; Rohm et al., 2013). Based on the Uses and Gratification Theory (UGT) (Katz et al., 1973), this chapter explores whether companies of an emerging country are providing the content (i.e. emotional, informational, relational and remunerative content) that consumers seek when deciding to interact with Facebook brand fan pages. Specifically, consumers' interaction with the firm, as a result of the information posted by brand managers in brand fan pages, is compared for two brand categories, namely, healthy food brands (e.g. cereals) and indulgent food brands (e.g. potato chips and soft drinks).

A qualitative mixed-method approach was used to contrast the level of consumer interaction with the platform for the two brand categories under study. Data were collected in Mexico via netnography and in-depth interviews. The in-depth interviews encompass a personal interaction with participants, whereas netnography is a marketing methodology

(Del Vecchio et al., 2020; Sharma et al., 2018) that allows collecting data without interfering with the actions of the observed subjects. The healthy brand fan pages analysed are Special K, All-Bran and Nestlé Fitness, and the indulgent brand fan pages are Doritos and Coca-Cola. By using a convenience sampling method, the five most commented posts from each brand fan page were selected for analysis.

The remainder of this chapter is organised as follows. In the next section, we develop the theoretical framework and describe the research methodology. Then, we present the study results and discuss how our findings challenge the assumption that brand fan page managers are capable of using social media to engage consumers and motivate interaction. We then relate our findings with the extant literature on social media to explain consumer–brand interactions as a function of the gratifications received by consumers of the two contrasting brands. Finally, we state the theoretical and managerial implications that can support food manufacturing companies of emerging countries in the design of fan brand pages that engage consumers and stimulate them to interact with the brand.

Theoretical Framework

Consumer Motivations to Use Social Networks

Interactions of consumers with social media platforms could be motivated by multiple drivers. The UGT proposed by Katz et al. (1973) is a media theory that responds to the question of why people engage with different media. UGT proposes that people use media to gratify specific wants and needs, such as cognitive and affective needs, personal and social integration and recreation (Katz et al., 1973). Unlike other media theories that view individuals as passive users, UGT recognises media users as active in their media selection. Under this perspective, people are attracted and motivated by media and are aware of the reasons for selecting among media options. Although the UGT was initially applied in the field of traditional communications, the gratification categories proposed by Katz et al. (1973) have been reviewed, confirmed and complemented in the context of social media to extend the external validity of the theory to social networks (Gan & Li, 2018; Phua et al., 2017).

The extant literature related to UGT and social media has advanced into two research avenues (Athwal et al., 2019). The first focuses on the evaluation of individuals' needs in social settings (Gan & Li, 2018; Griffin et al., 2015; Karnik et al., 2013; Phua et al., 2017) and the second explores the evaluation of the consumers' needs in a commercial context (Athwal et al., 2019; Gao & Feng, 2016; Whiting & Williams, 2013). This chapter contributes to the body of knowledge of the second avenue based on the assumption that consumers look for interesting content about their preferred brands on social media.

Several studies have addressed the question of what needs and gratifications influence consumers to use media, create and share information about products and brands? Whiting and Williams (2013) confirmed and identified the following additional gratifications that motivate people: information seeking, social interaction, passing time, entertainment, relaxation, expression of opinions, information sharing, communicatory utility, convenience and surveillance/knowledge gathering of others. Other motivations to consume media include brand engagement, timeliness of information and service responses, product information, incentives and promotions (Froget et al., 2013; Rohm et al., 2013).

Dolan et al. (2016) developed an integrative model of social media content and engagement behaviour. Their model proposes that social media content facilitates social media engagement behaviour that has positive consequences such as value co-creation, consumption and positive contributions. Social media content was categorised into four groups: *information, entertainment, remunerative* and *relational content*. The information content is related to how much resourceful and helpful information can consumers extract from the content. Meanwhile, entertainment content refers to the fun and enjoyment provided to users, thus fulfilling their hedonistic and pleasure needs. Remunerative content is related to the rewards expected by contributing to online communities (economic incentives, prizes or personal wants). Finally, relational content satisfies the consumer needs for integration, sense of belonging and expression of feelings and experiences. The delivery of these contents is viewed as gratifications that consumers receive when using social media to interact with brands. Positive outcomes resulting from these interactions include engagement behaviours and consumer–brand relationship (Sabate et al., 2014).

Consumers' Use of Facebook Brand fan Pages

Empirical studies have confirmed the elements of the social media content framework proposed by Dolan et al. (2016) in the case of brand fan pages (Hossain et al., 2019). For example, Ho et al. (2013) found that informational content and social interactions have positive effects on brand fan page usage. Choi et al. (2016) also found the positive influence of informational content on customers' usage of brand fan page. Other gratifications such as convenience (which refers to the simplicity and friendliness of the page) and self-expression (related to the possibility of posting pictures, updating the consumer profile information and design of wall content) also affected the participation and satisfaction of a hotel's Facebook page. Estrella-Ramón et al. (2019) evaluated the effect of several content dimensions of Facebook fan pages on brand equity. For the content domain, posts with affective content (emotional appeal) were found to generate higher levels of brand equity compared to posts with informational/transactional content (rational appeal).

Research on the usage of brand fan pages in the context of emerging countries has also been conducted. For instance, Thongmak (2015) analysed 1577 posts from 183 brand fan pages in Thailand and found that content on product prices, promotions and emotional messages resulted in a larger number of comments, likes and shares. Moreover, Rasheed Gaber et al. (2019) explored why Egyptian consumers interact with Facebook brand fan pages. They identified eight motivators: information search, complaints, socialisation, incentives, entertainment, emotional aspects, brand promotions and social image. In addition, Nyekwere et al. (2013) showed that Facebook promotes an open, transparent environment for free discussion between consumers and advertisers in the Nigerian context. The findings of the study indicate that consumers support products advertised on social media based primarily on referrals from trusted sources, such as their friends. Furthermore, Chen and Tsai (2020) studied the effect of the value perceived by the consumer for participating in brand fan pages in Taiwan. The analysis of survey data demonstrated that utilitarian, hedonic and monetary values have a positive effect on consumers' participation. The previous studies have confirmed that consumers in general obtain different types of gratifications from their participation in brand fan pages. These gratifications can be categorised as utilitarian (e.g. product information), hedonic (e.g. entertainment), socio-psychological (e.g. community belonging) and monetary (e.g. promotions and coupons).

However, each social media site has unique features that satisfy consumer's needs in different ways; hence, research is not conclusive, and more studies are desirable. According to Paul (2019) and Sheth (2011), emerging markets have specific characteristics, such as market heterogeneity, chronic shortage of resources and market volatility that influence the consumption patterns and behaviours of individuals. Therefore, more studies in emerging economies must advance managerial understanding of how to take full advantage of social media. The framework proposed by Dolan et al. (2016), based on the UGT, is the theoretical reference to answer the following research questions: (1) Do consumers receive the desired gratifications from participating in brand fan pages in the context of emerging countries? (2) Are the gratifications received by consumers from their participation in brand fan pages the same for healthy food brands and indulgent food brands? A brief discussion about the concepts of healthy and indulgent food brands is presented in the following section before describing the methodology followed to answer the research questions stated.

Healthy and Indulgent Food Brands

Although a health brand has no standard definition, the general consensus is that a health food brand is more than a brand that claims its products have nutritional and health benefits (Centeno et al., 2017; Liñan et al., 2019). Several food classification systems and diet guidelines have been developed worldwide to assist the population in better understanding what food healthiness symbolises (Robinson et al., 2019). For example, the Food Classification System developed by the National Heart, Lung and Blood Institute and the Dutch Guidelines for Food Choice (Ravensbergen et al., 2015) categorises products into three groups: '(1) Go or preference products that are low in calories, fat and sugar and can be eaten daily; (2) Slow or occasional products that are higher in fat, sugar or calories but can still be part of a healthy diet if consumed few times per week in smaller amounts and (3) Whoa or exceptional products that are the highest in fat, salt, sugar and energy and should be eaten only in special circumstances' (Liñan et al., 2019).

An increasing trend to communicating brand benefits through declarations in the form of claims, such as 'low sugar', 'without trans fats' or 'may help reduce cholesterol', has been registered in the last years. These claims deliver information either by declaring the presence or absence of nutritional/undesirable ingredients (low sugar) or suggesting a health outcome or result (may help reduce cholesterol). These product-based definitions are complemented by the consumer's conceptualisation of 'healthy food'. For example, the results of the national survey of 2100 US consumers conducted by Lusk (2019) showed how individuals define natural and healthy food. The first dimension used by US customers to judge the healthiness of food is their animal origin: animal products are judged unhealthier than products of vegetal origin. The second dimension is the degree of preservation and processing of products: foods that are naturally produced and free of additives are considered healthier than those that contain preservatives or have been chemically processed.

Although visualising product healthfulness as a continuum with two extremes, that is, healthy and unhealthy, is challenging, the general agreement is that products have different degrees of healthiness (Centeno et al., 2017; Liñan et al., 2019). A multi-cultural study was conducted in US, China and Brazil that aimed to increase the understanding of consumers' mindset about healthy and indulgent foods. The study concluded that snacks and treats were considered indulgent foods that are markedly appealing and comforting and are consumed to satisfy cravings or hunger (GutCheck, 2015). Additionally, consumers declared that indulgent brands make them feel guilty if they are consumed regularly. Although indulgent food is not judged nutritious, it is perceived as delicious, palatable and with emotional attributes (Demetrakakes, 2018).

Methodology

A qualitative mixed approach was used to explore the level of consumer interaction with brand fan pages of the following brand categories: Special K, All-Bran and Nestlé Fitness as healthy food brands, and Doritos and Coca-Cola as indulgent food brands. Data were collected via a netnography study and in-depth interviews with Mexican consumers. Interviews provided rich and in-depth information about the motivations of consumers to use social media, particularly, Facebook brand fan pages. Then, netnographies were performed to cross-validate and complement the information collected through interviews (Kozinets, 2010). Netnography allows a better understanding of the phenomenon under study without interfering or altering the behaviour of the studied subjects (Chung & Kim, 2015; Del Vecchio et al., 2020; Kozinets, 2010; Sharma et al., 2018).

Twenty-seven interviews were conducted with individuals who are between 24 and 40 years of age. A purposive sampling approach was adopted to ensure participants were consumers of the selected brands and active users of the social media platform (i.e. they interacted at least once per day). The interviews lasted about 40 minutes on average. Appendix 1 provides detailed information about the participants. The names of participants were replaced with nicknames to guarantee anonymity.

An interview guide was designed to support the interviews. In the first part of the interview, the consumer's experience with the selected brand was explored. During the second part of the interview, the consumer's underlying motivations to interact with the healthy brand fan pages were assessed. Interviews were recorded and transcribed to perform a thematic analysis (Boyatzis, 1998) that consisted of two activities: (1) the identification of initial themes based on the four content components proposed by Dolan et al. (2016) according to the UGT (i.e. level of information, entertainment, remunerative and relational content) and (2) coding and validation of themes. The main themes identified are described in the

Results section. Verbatim quotations are included to illustrate and endorse these themes. We translated quotations from Spanish to English as literally as possible but preserved the meaning of the original statement.

A convenience sample was also selected to perform the netnography by picking the most commented threads of each brand fan page. Most of the threads consisted of an initial post of the brand manager and only a few subsequent comments made by consumers. Therefore, we decided to analyse only the five posts that received a relatively large number of comments (more than 100). The selection provided a total of 5991 comments corresponding to brand fan pages of healthy brands distributed as follows: 3628 comments for Special K, 1168 for Nestlé Fitness and 1195 for All-Bran. For indulgent food brand fan pages, 10,746 comments were selected, with 6157 comments corresponding to Coca-Cola and 4589 comments to Doritos. Appendix 2 provides a brief description of each brand fan page. Following the recommendations of Spiggle (1994), we conducted a content analysis to interpret the netnography data. First, we read all comments and then organise them into categories with the support of an Excel spreadsheet.

Results

In general, findings show lower participation of consumers in healthy brand fan pages than indulgent brand pages. The results of the two analyses (thematic and content analyses) are described in the following sections, which are organised according to the four components of the conceptual model proposed by Dolan et al. (2016).

Informational content. During the interviews, consumers of healthy food brands expressed that the nutritional information of products on the fan brand page is already available on the package. Therefore, they did not find the information available in the brand social networks to be useful. Participants indicated they would like the pages to include information on how to balance their diets and prepare recipes with the brand products to help them achieve their health goals. Meanwhile, consumers of indulgent brands declared they are interested in knowing about new product launches and new ingredient developments, and even learn more about the nutritional characteristics of indulgent products. The following quotations support these findings:

No, I did not know about the brand fan page; it does not attract my attention. I just buy the cereal because it is rich and nutritious. [Ivan, 31, Nestlé Fitness]
I would like that on the fan page they to [sic] put more recipes. [Victoria, 38, Special K]
I follow the Doritos fan page. It has interesting information about flavours, but it does not contain any information about the product's ingredients, and I would like it to have that information. [Michael, 36, Doritos]

Netnography confirmed the low interest of healthy brand consumers to participate in the company pages. In contrast, the indulgent food brand fan pages recorded many comments about the brand's posts. The following comments exemplify these results:

The new flavour, Coca-C with coffee, is very cool when you need to study for an exam. [John, Coca-Cola]
The new flavour, Coca-Cola with coffee, is the best I have ever tasted; it has become my addiction. [Chen, Coca-Cola]
Uncle Doritos take me!... to the concert ViveLatino2020, I found them! the new flavour of Doritos: DoritosAlive. [Jane, Doritos]

Entertaining content. Health food brand fan pages are not fulfilling adequately the users' need for entertainment. Most consumers view these pages as informative rather than enjoyable. Additionally, consumers of healthy food brands were concerned about their privacy if they participate in fan pages (Eisingerich et al., 2015). Indulgent food brand fan pages seem to satisfy the entertainment needs of consumers better because they post activities that provide distraction, pleasure and enjoyment. The UGT indicates that content entertainment is the primary motivator for the use of online sites (Raacke & Bonds-Raacke, 2008). An important finding in the case of indulgent food brands is that consumers were aware of various marketing campaigns that promote entertainment through various events such as games. The following quotes from interviews support these findings:

> *I remember [entering] the fan page recently on Facebook because there was a game and I wanted to win. [Sara, 32, Doritos]*
> *I don't follow the brand page... I follow any funny post if it appears at some point, but as far as I'm aware, I haven't seen anything about that page. [Rodrigo, 31, Special K]*

The netnography analysis confirmed that indulgent brands do provide entertaining content by giving consumers more opportunities for distraction, recreation and amusement, as expressed in the following comments:

> *I have participated in many events of this type, and I have won very good prizes. This time I did not have the time to participate, but I collected many stamps for the next time, but Uncle Doritos always does what he says. [William, Doritos]*
> *Thanks for the experience and the tickets to the Coca-Cola Flow Fest; I hope next year they bring back the Ivy Queen. [Bruce, Coca-Cola]*

Relational content. Healthy food brand fan pages again did not fully meet the relational needs of their consumers. Participants think pages do not promote a sense of community. If these brand pages have promotions, consumers share the publications because of the economic reward but not to establish links with other consumers. According to Leung (2009) and Muntinga et al. (2011), one of the key motivators of using social networking sites is to obtain a sense of belongingness (sharing with others). Indulgent food brand fan pages make a great effort to offer relational gratifications to their consumers, such as being with family, being part of a community and promoting the integration of minorities. The following quotes support these findings:

> *I like they [sic] brand fan page, have, for example, a campaign against racism. I feel that I am helping others. [Daniel, 28, Coca-Cola]*
> *They are donating virtual kisses on their brand fan page to include LGBT people. [Sara, 32, Doritos]*

I do not follow any brand page. I can only share my brand's experience with my family and contacts. [Ulises, 37 years, Nestlé Fitness]

The netnography confirmed that consumers of indulgent food brands believe that these brands try to create community ties. The following comments exemplify this appreciation:

I really love its inclusion, it's great. People should already remove their prejudices; love is love [Charles, Doritos]
Coca-Cola always seeks to make us smile and be optimistic in these times that people must be more united [Henry, Coca-Cola]

Remunerative content. Consumers of health food brand pages specified only a few posts related to contests but without economic rewards. In the case of indulgent brands, consumers stated that companies post promotions and games to entice them in winning prizes that include products and even cash. Extant research on the use of social media has shown that consumers use social media sites to earn some rewards or economic incentives (Muntinga et al., 2011), but this strategy was recognised as a potential motivator to engage consumers with their pages only by indulgent brands (Kang et al., 2015). The following quotes confirm this conclusion:

By participating in contests, I have the chance to win prizes if I share the publications of the page. [Celia, 29, Doritos]
I would like them to put contest or promotion [sic] on the brand's fan page so I can search for it and be able to participate. [Fabiola, 30, All Bran]
I think I would look for the page if they put promotions or coupons that I can use, even with other related companies, such as milk. [Ivan, 31, Nestlé Fitness]

The netnographic analysis indicates consumers of indulgent food brands are taking advantage of this motivator to interact with the brand fan pages:

I have been in the two weeks in the first 5 places, thanks! [Kevin, Doritos]
Uncle Doritos, where do I win the prizes? [Sam, Doritos]

Discussion

This study explored whether the information posted by brand managers on healthy and indulgent food brand fan pages supports consumers' interaction. Using the UGT as the theoretical framework, we explained the participation of consumers in brand pages in terms of the gratifications attained. In the case of healthy brand pages, the analysis of qualitative data indicates that consumers are not obtaining sufficient gratifications from participating in these sites. Although the literature on social media has shown the significant effect of informative content and advertising creativity on behavioural responses and purchase intention (Lee & Hong, 2016), this study's findings indicate that healthy brand managers are not attentive to this strategy. The informative posts on these brand pages are judged to be reiterative of the package information or easily acquired from personal referrals or other media (Choi et al., 2016; Whiting & Williams, 2013).

For the entertainment content, several studies have concluded that although this content is not the primary motivator, it has a positive influence on social media usage, brand engagement, customer attitudes and purchase intentions (Athwal et al., 2019; Raacke & Bonds-Raacke, 2008; Shareef et al., 2018). In particular, Rohm et al. (2013) found that entertainment is a primary motivational factor to use Facebook or Twitter among youngsters (20–21 years) but not for individuals over 21 years of age who are motivated to use these sites because of their information content. Despite this evidence, the entertainment, social interaction and remuneration contents on the advertisement of health brand pages were judged limited by participants. Although the main objective of users of healthy brand pages is to care for their health, they are also interested in sharing their thoughts and fears with others and in being part of a community. Therefore, companies should fulfil the recreation expectations of consumers and provide pleasant experiences on their brand pages.

Indulgent food brand pages are better at satisfying the needs of their consumers, specifically in terms of the relational and remunerative content. Brand managers of these companies put a greater emphasis on providing gratifying relational content, such as the sense of being part of a social group and participating with family or friends. Indulgent food brand fan pages also provide more interesting remunerative content through promotions, including gifts of the brand. The results of this study are consistent with the findings of previous studies. Shi et al. (2016) highlighted that economic rewards and benefits are significant to consumers. Offering prizes, promotions or free products motivates consumers to use the brand fan pages. The games included in the indulgent brand page advertisement tempt consumers to interact with the brand. The analysis of the qualitative information provides evidence that consumers receive different types of rewards depending on the brand category, namely, healthy and indulgent.

Some concurrences were also identified; in particular, consumers of both brand categories stated they do not like to see irrelevant messages posted by other consumers (Hur et al., 2017), but they appreciate the extra information provided about new product launches and attractive posts of other users (Choi et al., 2016; Ho et al., 2013). Meanwhile, the negative comments posted by some consumers, not adequately handled by brand managers, decrease the perceived gratification and promote co-destruction (Dolan et al., 2016; Kang et al., 2014). The interaction of the brand with consumers via comment replies, solutions to service problems and participation support generates feelings of connection and enhances the quality of the relational experience (Hudson & Thal, 2013).

Conclusion

The current global trend towards healthy foods extends to emerging economies. In the case of Latin America the increasing rates of obesity, diabetes and heart disease drive the demand for natural, healthy and organic products. Although the healthy food market is small compared with the indulgent food market, some outstanding companies are contributing to its expansion. For example, Aires de Campo is a Mexican company managed by a network of organic producers that develop healthy products, including frozen foods and groceries that are distributed in the national and international market. Currently, food companies need to take care of both healthy and indulgent markets by applying tailored social media advertising strategies. To design these differentiated advertising strategies, companies must know their audience, understand their needs and wants and provide the expected gratifications on their brand fan pages to stimulate engagement and interaction.

This chapter contributes to the extant literature on consumer–brand interactions driven by social media by identifying what gratifications consumers receive when they use brand fan pages in the context of emerging economies. As far as we know, this is the first study that uses UGT to determine whether food companies of two contrasting categories, indulgent and healthy brands, provide the content (i.e. emotional, informational, relational and remunerative) consumers expect to get when they decide to interact with their favourite brands via brand pages.

The results of the study indicate that consumers of indulgent brands obtain greater gratifications from participating in brand fan pages than consumers of healthy brands. Therefore, manufacturers of healthy foods should determine how to deliver more exciting and novel informational content to brand page users. Moreover, although the main objective of healthy consumers is to maintain a healthy lifestyle, they expect healthy brand pages to also satisfy their need for entertainment, social interaction and rewards. Based on these findings, this chapter provides some recommendations to brand managers to enhance the gratification obtained by consumers of emerging economies when interacting with brands on social media.

Managerial Implications for Emerging Economies

Healthy food brands have fewer followers than indulgent food brands. Therefore, healthy food manufacturers should invest more in designing useful and engaging content for their followers. Currently, healthy brand pages mainly provide nutritional information content (Chrysochou, 2010). However, the present study's findings reveal that this information needs to be more attractive and different from the information provided by other means, for example the product package. Consumers want timely information about new product flavours and presentations and ideas about how to use the products in healthy dishes. Brand managers can launch a campaign named 'Design Your Happy Healthy Menu', which requires consumers to upload photos or videos of their recipes using the company's products. Asking influencers to be the first to submit their menus can be an appropriate strategy to maximise reach and visibility. This campaign would further add to the entertainment and relational content. Companies should also try fulfilling the inspirational mood of people via the power of sports, as practising a sport is part of a healthy lifestyle. Thus, promoting the discussion around large sports events can increase social interaction and informational content.

To enhance the entertainment and relational content, we suggest companies engage audiences with fun and pop culture from their countries. Mexico and other Latin American countries, for example, Brazil and Colombia, are well known to be friendly countries, with plenty of traditional festivals that brands could include in their social media advertising. Healthy living influencers could become a proper communication channel between consumers and the brand and promote a sense of belonging to a group, which is critical for individuals (Leung, 2009; Muntinga et al., 2011).

Regarding the remunerative content, which is another relevant content (Shi et al., 2016), especially for the consumers from emerging economies, our recommendation to healthy food brand managers is to sponsor TikTok challenges and reward consumers with promotions, discounts and prizes. Managers must continuously change the remunerative content of brand fan pages by including streaming events or games that consumers can play with their friends to take advantage of the collectivist culture that characterises countries such as Mexico.

Indulgent food brands seem to work harder to provide consumers with the expected remunerative and relational content. For example, both Coca-Cola and Doritos promote relational content by encouraging the inclusion of all individuals, regardless of colour, gender or sexual orientation; this puts them at an advantage to have more followers than healthy food brands. Indulgent brand managers should continue to apply this and other similar strategies to assure the loyalty of the brand followers. They can select events of interest (e.g. animal care and public health problems) to grab the attention of consumers, give them the opportunity to learn about topics, and inform how the brand supports and economically back them. These events also provide the time and space to get people together and increase the affinity with the brand.

Regarding public health problems as COVID-19, the indulgent brand may reinforce the notion of closeness by emphasising the importance of social distancing as a means to contribute to community welfare. Research acknowledges that brands that excel at social media may attract other consumers outside their target market. Thus, indulgent brands can increase the number of users on their brand fan pages with campaigns such as 'Crash the Superbowl' (Doritos) and 'Share a Coke' (Coca-Cola).

Indulgent brand managers can even generate more entertaining content by creating and sharing humorous stories involving daily life events. For example, Memac Ogilvy's campaign of Coca-Cola in Turkey became a viral phenomenon because it used humour to address consumers' addiction to smartphones. Finally, the participation of influencers could also be a proper strategy for indulgent food brands to respond to the negative comments about their product's unhealthiness. Designing a sound strategy requires knowing how to respond to media platforms, especially when a problem arises. Therefore, instead of a defensive strategy, influencers can respond humorously or recall the product's sensory experience. Managers should not be afraid to show the brand as it is, with its strengths and limitations, because people prefer to relate to authentic brands.

We hope managers find the chapter's recommendations useful and provide the needed gratification consumers are looking for on social media. The use of social media advertising especially in Mexican cities with limited Internet infrastructure may be complementary to traditional mass communication given the Internet penetration rate in the country (71%) is lower than the percentage of Internet users in developed countries (87%) and America (77%).

Appendix 1 Informant Profile

No.	Name	Age	Gender	Education	Status	Brand selected	Occupation
1	Ana	31	Female	Master	Married	Special K	HR specialist
2	Caro	38	Female	College	Married	All-bran	Business owner
3	Diana	28	Female	College	Married	Special K	Teacher assistant
4	Elizabeth	29	Female	Master	Single	Special K	Business owner
5	Fabiola	30	Female	Master	Single	All-bran	HR specialist
6	Gabriel	24	Male	College	Single	Nestlé Fitness	College student
7	Hilda	28	Female	PhD	Single	Special K	PhD student
8	Ivan	31	Male	PhD	Married	Nestlé Fitness	PhD student
9	Juan	40	Male	College	Married	Special K	Teacher
10	Liliana	30	Female	Master	Single	Special K	IT analyst
11	Mario	28	Male	College	Married	All-bran	IT analyst
12	Nora	38	Female	College	Married	Special K	HR specialist
13	Oliva	28	Female	College	Single	All-bran	Photographer
14	Pablo	38	Male	College	Divorced	Special K	Unemployed
15	Rodrigo	31	Male	Master	Single	Special K	IT analyst
16	Alberto	28	Male	College	Single	Special K	Employee
17	Sergio	31	Male	College	Single	All-bran	Graphic designer
18	Ulises	37	Male	High school	Married	Nestlé Fitness	Business owner
19	Victoria	38	Female	High school	Single	Special K	Lab assistant
20	Tania	36	Female	PhD	Single	All-bran	Business owner
21	Bruno	31	Male	College	Married	All-bran	Business owner
22	Cesar	36	Male	College	Single	All-bran	Quality analyst
23	Daniel	28	Male	College	Divorced	Coca-Cola	Employee
24	Flavio	22	Male	High school	Single	Coca-Cola	Student
25	Sara	32	Female	High school	Single	Doritos	Secretary
26	Michael	36	Male	College	Married	Doritos	Business owner
27	Celia	29	Female	High school	Married	Doritos	Unemployed

Appendix 2 Description of Selected Brand fan Pages

Health Food Brand fan Pages

	Special K	*Nestlé Fitness*	*All-Bran*
General data	3,311,495 people liked this. 3,306,155 people followed this.	5,291,958 people liked this. 5,290,188 people followed this.	32,312 people liked this. 32,169 people followed this.
Marketing campaign	It suggested that everyone was powered by inner strength and increase the capabilities of women.	It suggested the positive care of oneself, trying to promote mental well-being and exercise.	It suggested making dinners based on this product because it contained fibre and helped people sleep well.
Slogan	'I am strong'	'My summer fitness'	'Eat fibre'
Demographics	Adults over 18 years of age	Adults over 18 years of age	Adults over 18 years of age
Personal disclosure	Participants are identified by their Facebook nickname. Their photo or avatar is shown with each comment.		

Indulgent Food Brand fan Pages

	Coca-Cola	*Doritos*
General data	106.047.086 people like the page. 106.056.379 followers	16.473.577 people like the page. 16.466.280 followers
Marketing campaign	It suggested all persons are equal and promote respect and love between people.	It suggested that all individuals have an inner strength that makes us better people.
Slogan	'Feel the taste'	'Discover your true strength'
Demographics	Adults between 18 and 40 years of age	Adults between 18 and 40 years of age
Personal disclosure	Participants are identified by their Facebook nickname. Their photo or avatar is shown with each comment.	

References

Ahmed, Y. A., Ahmad, M. N., Ahmad, N., & Zakaria, N. H. (2019). Social media for knowledge-sharing: A systematic literature review. *Telematics and Informatics, 37*, 72–112.

Athwal, N., Istanbulluoglu, D., & McCormack, S. E. (2019). The allure of luxury brands' social media activities: A uses and gratifications perspective. *Information Technology & People, 32*(3), 603–626.

Berezan, O., Krishen, A. S., Agarwal, S., & Kachroo, P. (2020). Exploring loneliness and social networking: Recipes for hedonic well-being on Facebook. *Journal of Business Research, 115*, 258–265.

Beukeboom, C. J., Kerkhof, P., & de Vries, M. (2015). Does a virtual like cause actual liking? How following a brand's Facebook updates enhances brand evaluations and purchase intention. *Journal of Interactive Marketing, 32*, 26–36.

Boyatzis, R. E. (1998). *Transforming qualitative information: Thematic analysis and code development.* Sage Publications Inc.

Carr, C. T., & Hayes, R. A. (2015). Social media: Defining, developing, and divining. *Atlantic Journal of Communication, 23*(1), 46–65.

Centeno, E. Carrete, L., Arroyo, P., & Peñaloza, L. (2017, April). *Delivering a health food brand promise through a proposed value co-creation model.* Paper presented at the Global Brand Conference of the Academy of Marketing (AM), Kalmar, Sweden.

Chen, M. H., & Tsai, K. M. (2020). An empirical study of brand fan page engagement behaviors. *Sustainability, 12*(1), 434.

Chen, Y., Fay, S., & Wang, Q. (2011). The role of marketing in social media: How online consumer reviews evolve. *Journal of Interactive Marketing, 25*(2), 85–94.

Choi, E. K., Fowler, D., Goh, B., & Yuan, J. (2016). Social media marketing: Applying the uses and gratifications theory in the hotel industry. *Journal of Hospitality Marketing & Management, 25*(7), 771–796.

Chrysochou, P. (2010). Food health branding: The role of marketing mix elements and public discourse in conveying a healthy brand image. *Journal of Marketing Communications, 16*(1–2), 69–85.

Chung, J. Y., & Kim, Y. G. (2015). A netnographic study of eWOM motivations to articulate dining experiences. *Journal of Internet Commerce, 14*(4), 455–475.

De Vries, L., Gensler, S., & Leeflang, P. S. (2012). Popularity of brand posts on brand fan pages: An investigation of the effects of social media marketing. *Journal of Interactive Marketing, 26*(2), 83–91.

Del Vecchio, P., Mele, G., Passiante, G., Vrontis, D., & Fanuli, C. (2020). Detecting customers knowledge from social media big data: Toward an integrated methodological framework based on netnography and business analytics. *Journal of Knowledge Management, 24*(4), 799–821.

Demetrakakes, P. (2018). *Products Strive for a Balance of Health and Indulgence.* Retrieved from https://www.foodprocessing.com/articles/2018/balance-of-health-and-indulgence/

Dolan, R., Conduit, J., Fahy, J., & Goodman, S. (2016). Social media engagement behaviour: A uses and gratifications perspective. *Journal of Strategic Marketing, 24*(3–4), 261–277.

Eisingerich, A. B., Chun, H. H., Liu, Y., Jia, H. M., & Bell, S. J. (2015). Why recommend a brand face-to-face but not on Facebook? How word-of-mouth on online social sites differs from traditional word-of-mouth. *Journal of Consumer Psychology, 25*(1), 120–128.

Estrella-Ramón, A., García-de-Frutos, N., Ortega-Egea, J. M., & Segovia-López, C. (2019). How does marketers' and users' content on corporate Facebook fan pages influence brand equity? *Electronic Commerce Research and Applications, 36*, 100867.

Felix, R., Rauschnabel, P. A., & Hinsch, C. (2017). Elements of strategic social media marketing: A holistic framework. *Journal of Business Research, 70*, 118–126.

Fournier, S., Breazeale, M., & Fetscherin, M. (2012). *Consumer-brand relationships: Theory and practice.* Routledge.

Froget, J. R. L., Baghestan, A. G., & Asfaranjan, Y. S. (2013). A uses and gratification perspective on social media usage and online marketing. *Middle-East Journal of Scientific Research, 15*(1), 134–145.

Gan, C., & Li, H. (2018). Understanding the effects of gratifications on the continuance intention to use WeChat in China: A perspective on uses and gratifications. *Computers in Human Behavior, 78*, 306–315.

Gao, Q., & Feng, C. (2016). Branding with social media: User gratifications, usage patterns, and brand message content strategies. *Computers in Human Behavior, 63*, 868–890.

Griffin, E., Ledbetter, A., & Sparks, G. (2015). *A first look at communication theory.* McGraw-Hill.

GutCheck. (2015). *Healthy vs. indulgent foods: Consumers in the U.S., China, and Brazil help us identify differences and similarities among countries.* Retrieved from https://www.gutcheckit.com/blog/healthy-vs-indulgent-foods-consumers-in-the-u-s-china-and-brazil-help-us-identify-differences-and-similarities-among-countries/

Heinonen, K. (2011). Consumer activity in social media: Managerial approaches to consumers' social media behavior. *Journal of Consumer Behaviour, 10*(6), 356–364.

Ho, K. K., See-To, E. W., & Chiu, G. T. (2013). How does a social network site fan page influence purchase intention of online shoppers: A qualitative analysis. *International Journal of Social and Organizational Dynamics in IT, 3*(4), 19–42.

Hossain, M., Kim, M., & Jahan, N. (2019). Can "liking" behavior Lead to usage intention on Facebook? *Uses and Gratification Theory Perspective. Sustainability, 11*(4), 1166.

Hudson, S., & Thal, K. (2013). The impact of social media on the consumer decision process: Implications for tourism marketing. *Journal of Travel & Tourism Marketing, 30*(1–2), 156–160.

Hur, K., Kim, T. T., Karatepe, O. M., & Lee, G. (2017). An exploration of the factors influencing social media continuance usage and information sharing intentions among Korean travellers. *Tourism Management, 63*, 170–178.

Jayasingh, S., & Venkatesh, R. (2016). Determinants of customer brand engagement in social media sites: A conceptual framework. *International Business Management, 10*(15), 2802–2807.

Kamboj, S. (2019). Applying uses and gratifications theory to understand customer participation in social media brand communities. *Asia Pacific Journal of Marketing and Logistics, 32*(1), 205–231.

Kang, J., Tang, L., & Fiore, A. M. (2014). Enhancing consumer–brand relationships on restaurant Facebook fan pages: Maximizing consumer benefits and increasing active participation. *International Journal of Hospitality Management, 36*, 145–155.

Kang, J., Jun, J., & Arendt, S. W. (2015). Understanding customers' healthy food choices at casual dining restaurants: Using the value–attitude–behavior model. *International Journal of Hospitality Management, 48*, 12–21.

Karnik, M., Oakley, I., Venkatanathan, J., Spiliotopoulos, T., & Nisi, V. (2013, February). Uses & gratifications of a Facebook media sharing group. *In Proceedings of the 2013 Conference on Computer Supported Cooperative Work* (pp. 821–826).

Katz, E., Blumler, J. G., & Gurevitch, M. (1973). Uses and gratifications research. *The Public Opinion Quarterly, 37*(4), 509–523.

Kozinets, R. V. (2010). *Netnography: Doing ethnographic research online*. Sage Publications Inc.

Lee, J., & Hong, I. B. (2016). Predicting positive user responses to social media advertising: The roles of emotional appeal, informativeness, and creativity. *International Journal of Information Management, 36*(3), 360–373.

Leung, L. (2009). User-generated content on the internet: An examination of gratifications, civic engagement and psychological empowerment. *New Media & Society, 11*(8), 1327–1347.

Liñan, J., Arroyo, P., & Carrete, L. (2019). Conceptualizing healthy food: How Consumer's values influence the perceived healthiness of a food product. *Journal of Food and Nutrition Research, 7*(9), 679–687.

Liu, X., Min, Q., & Han, S. (2019). Understanding users' continuous content contribution behaviours on microblogs: An integrated perspective of uses and gratification theory and social influence theory. *Behaviour & Information Technology, 39*(5), 525–543.

Luarn, P., Lin, Y. F., & Chiu, Y. P. (2015). Influence of Facebook brand-page posts on online engagement. *Online Information Review, 39*, 505–519.

Lusk, J. L. (2019). *Consumer Perceptions of Healthy and Natural Food Labels*. Retrieved from https://static1.squarespace.com/static/502c267524aca01df475f9ec/t/5c4df49440ec9a53af435ab4/1548612761167/report_revised.pdf

Muntinga, D. G., Moorman, M., & Smit, E. G. (2011). Introducing COBRAs: Exploring motivations for brand-related social media use. *International Journal of Advertising, 30*(1), 13–46.

Nyekwere, E. O., Kur, J. T., & Nyekwere, O. (2013). Awareness and use of social media in advertising: The case of Facebook among residents of Port Harcourt, Nigeria. *African Research Review, 7*(4), 174–194.

Pate, S. S., & Adams, M. (2013). The influence of social networking sites on buying behaviors of millennials. *Atlantic Marketing Journal, 2*(1), 7.

Paul, J. (2019). Marketing in emerging markets: A review, theoretical synthesis and extension. *International Journal of Emerging Markets, 15*(3), 446–468.

Perrin, A. (2015). *Social Media Usage: 2005–2015*. Pew Research Center. Retrieved from http://www.pewinternet.org/2015/10/08/2015/Social-Networking-Usage-2005-2015/

Phua, J., Jin, S. V., & Kim, J. J. (2017). Uses and gratifications of social networking sites for bridging and bonding social capital: A comparison of Facebook, twitter, Instagram, and snapchat. *Computers in Human Behavior, 72*, 115–122.

Raacke, J., & Bonds-Raacke, J. (2008). MySpace and Facebook: Applying the uses and gratifications theory to exploring friend-networking sites. *Cyberpsychology & Behavior, 11*(2), 169–174.

Rasheed Gaber, H., Elsamadicy, A. M., & Wright, L. T. (2019). Why do consumers use Facebook brand pages? A case study of a leading fast-food brand fan page in Egypt. *Journal of Global Scholars of Marketing Science, 29*(3), 293–310.

Ravensbergen, E. A., Waterlander, W. E., Kroeze, W., & Steenhuis, I. H. (2015). Healthy or unhealthy on sale? A cross-sectional study on the proportion of healthy and unhealthy foods promoted through flyer advertising by supermarkets in the Netherlands. *BMC Public Health, 15*(1), 470.

Robinson, L., Segal, J., & Segal, R. (2019). *Help Guide. Healthy Eating*. Retrieved from https://www.helpguide.org/articles/healthy-eating/healthy-eating.htm

Rohm, A., Kaltcheva, V. D., & Milne, G. R. (2013). A mixed-method approach to examining brand-consumer interactions driven by social media. *Journal of Research in Interactive Marketing, 7*(4), 295–311.

Sabate, F., Berbegal-Mirabent, J., Cañabate, A., & Lebherz, P. R. (2014). Factors influencing popularity of branded content in Facebook fan pages. *European Management Journal, 32*(6), 1001–1011.

Shareef, M. A., Mukerji, B., Alryalat, M. A. A., Wright, A., & Dwivedi, Y. K. (2018). Advertisements on Facebook: Identifying the persuasive elements in the development of positive attitudes in consumers. *Journal of Retailing and Consumer Services, 43*, 258–268.

Sharma, R., Ahuja, V., & Alavi, S. (2018). The future scope of netnography and social network analysis in the field of marketing. *Journal of Internet Commerce, 17*(1), 26–45.

Sheth, J. N. (2011). Impact of emerging markets on marketing: Rethinking existing perspectives and practices. *Journal of Marketing, 75*(4), 166–182.

Shi, S., Chen, Y., & Chow, W. S. (2016). Key values driving continued interaction on brand pages in social media: An examination across genders. *Computers in Human Behavior, 62*, 578–589.

Spiggle, S. (1994). Analysis and interpretation of qualitative data in consumer research. *Journal of Consumer Research, 21*, 491–503.

Thongmak, M. (2015, June). Engaging Facebook users in brand pages: Different posts of marketing-mix information. In Proceedings of the *International Conference on Business Information Systems* (pp. 299–308). Springer, Cham.

Warner-Søderholm, G., Bertsch, A., Sawe, E., Lee, D., Wolfe, T., Meyer, J., ... Fatilua, U. N. (2018). Who trusts social media? *Computers in Human Behavior, 81*, 303–315.

Whiting, A., & Williams, D. (2013). Why people use social media: A uses and gratifications approach. *Qualitative Market Research: An International Journal, 16*, 362–369.

8

Health and Lifestyle Branding

Emmanuel Silva Quaye
and Leeford Edem Kojo Ameyibor

Introduction

Corporate bodies in emerging markets have resorted to healthy lifestyle branding through the creation of promotional message appeals using healthy lifestyle mediums for non-health-related products and direct health-related taglines created for branding and promoting health-related products (Global Wellness Summit Report, 2020). Unhealthy lifestyle

---

E. S. Quaye (✉)
Wits Business School, University of the Witwatersrand, Johannesburg, South Africa
e-mail: emmanuel.quaye@wits.ac.za

L. E. K. Ameyibor
Wits Business School, University of the Witwatersrand, Johannesburg, South Africa

University of Professional Studies, Accra, Madina, Ghana
e-mail: leeford.ameyibor@upsamail.edu.gh

and its antecedent consequences continue to dominate global economies' health budgets (Saraswat, 2013). The global picture of lifestyle-related diseases indicates a continuous surge in obesity, diabetes, high blood pressure, and cardiac issues (World Health Organization, 2020). These can be traced to lack of physical activity, ever-increasing fast foods eatery chains, and the complex nature of work–life balance brought by the demands of today's corporate operational architecture (Ashakiran & Deepthi, 2012). The World Health Organization (WHO), for example, estimates that in the next ten decades, there will be a 40% surge in the already existing 1.6 billion overweight adults across the world (World Health Organization, 2020).

In emerging economies, an unhealthy lifestyle is largely promoted by sprawling urban developments and adaptation to modern cosmopolitan lifestyles including gated communities with a full complement of social goods like shopping centres, fast food dinners, and easy access to transportation (Herzog, 2015). Admittedly, these new developments make living comfortable; however, people living in such communities still do not find the urge to engage in physical activities, even though facilities for physical activity have been adequately provided. Urban living and a healthy lifestyle do not only relate to the affluent and their bad food and physical activity decisions, but also have much to do with the high rate of rural–urban migration in emerging economies. For example, the increasing urbanisation as a result of large rural-urban migration has profound consequences for obesity as a non-communicable disease (Cockx et al., 2018). This is due to governments' inability to equally distribute resources to these new peri-urban settlements, therefore forcing people to make unhealthy food choices due to healthy food price differentials (Sanders et al., 2008). In South Africa, for example, people who migrated from rural areas to urban centres in Cape Town linked changes in eating patterns and levels of physical activity to socioeconomic and environmental constraints (Stern et al., 2010).

In response to these seemingly public health crises brought by unhealthy lifestyles, governments worldwide, including those in emerging economies, have initiated interventions that seek to alter attitudes and norms regarding healthy lifestyle behaviour (Arena et al., 2015). Corporate organisations have complemented these efforts from the beginning as part of their corporate social responsibilities. However, corporate bodies in contemporary times are beginning to find a strategic fit to bridge the gap between creating awareness, changing unhealthy habits, and branding and communicating these while also promoting corporate brands. This synergy was highlighted throughout the COVID-19 pandemic as companies used their marketing to showcase their brand while also promoting COVID-19 protocols awareness and adherence (He & Harris, 2020; Sheth, 2020).

Thus, this chapter contributes to a deeper understanding of consumers' healthy lifestyle motivations and how these motivations may serve as essential ingredients for branding and marketing communications. Segmentation theory is considered equally vital in social and health marketing to determine an ideal clustering of unhealthy and healthy lifestyle consumers for marketing attention. The next section begins with a brief conceptualisation of lifestyle and healthy lifestyle. The rest of the chapter focuses on how corporate organisations promote healthy lifestyle behaviour and its impact on their brand(s). It also explores the key factors that predispose consumers to adopt desirable healthy lifestyle behaviours, serving as the basis for segmentation, targeting, and positioning healthy lifestyle branding and communication efforts.

Healthy Lifestyle: The Creation of a Healthy Lifestyle Consumer

Lifestyle generally describes how people live and spend their time and money. It portrays patterns of actions that differentiate people. For example, some people go to the gym every morning before work. Others resolve to eat only organic products, whereas others integrate health-promoting technologies into their daily routines and self-identity (Dean et al., 2012; Gupta et al., 2020). Lifestyle helps us understand what people do, why they do what they do, and the meaning of their actions to themselves and others (Vyncke, 2002). People's actions to maintain health-promoting behaviours, their rationale, and what those actions imply constitute healthy lifestyle choices (Chen, 2011; Mai & Hoffmann, 2015).

Many habits, activities, interests, and behaviours constitute an unhealthy lifestyle. Bloch (1984) provided a classical definition of a healthy lifestyle as a signpost of what is acceptable "as an orientation toward the prevention of health problems and the maximization of personal wellbeing". von Bothmer and Fridlund (2005) describe a healthy lifestyle as comprising not smoking, alcohol consumption avoidance, healthy food habits, physical activity, and stress management. Chen (2009) conceptualises a healthy lifestyle as containing three underlying features: natural food consumption, health care, and life equilibrium. Specifically, natural food consumption relates to consuming fresh fruits and vegetables and an interest in reducing one's consumption of red meat, processed food, or food with additives (Gil et al., 2000). Health care focuses on consumers' interest in keeping themselves healthy by engaging in sports, pursuing natural diets, controlling salt intake, and regularly checking their health (Gil et al., 2000). Lastly, life equilibrium concerns consumers' real interest in maintaining a positive work–life balance, living in a methodical and ordered fashion, and seeking to minimise stress (Gil et al., 2000).

Risk Factors Associated with Unhealthy Lifestyle

Poor and unhealthy lifestyle diseases manifest risk factors similar to four modified lifestyle behaviours: unhealthy eating, smoking, excessive alcohol consumption, and physical inactivity. These can result in the development of chronic diseases such as stroke, diabetes, obstructive pulmonary diseases, obesity, metabolic syndromes, and, recently, some forms of cancer (WHO, 2003). To minimise these risks, many consumers have increasingly begun avoiding harmful products and have turned their attention towards green or eco-friendly products to improve their health and health behaviours (Sharma et al., 2020).

However, before personal wellbeing is maximised, there is the need for alignment between how people perceive themselves (self-identity) and their behavioural intent (action) as the basis for predicting behaviour (Oyserman et al., 2012). For example, people who see themselves as fitness enthusiasts make great efforts to sustain physical activities.

Self-identities move beyond their group and social affiliations to present a more dynamic underlying influence that drives people's emotions, thoughts, and behaviours in varying contexts (Dominick & Cole, 2020). The underlying crux of the self-identity theory is to explain behavioural action and intent as a function of the congruence between the behaviour, action, and trait identified self-emotions and thoughts that eventually drive the needed motivation for lifestyle changes.

Therefore, in describing the healthy lifestyle consumer, it must be noted that the basis of becoming part of this segment is the conscious effort to engage in all choices that sustain such nomenclature. Admittedly, in most developing economies, the statistics on healthy consumer lifestyle adaptations tend to be relatively insignificant compared to those not choosing healthy lifestyle habits, and this is evident in the public health expenditure on lifestyle-based diseases (Jakovljevic et al., 2019). Despite this observation, the healthy lifestyle consumer has been cultivated by the efforts of both national and corporate-led interventions through awareness creation and alternative living choice provisions, as evidenced by the rise of the healthy food market and fitness and exercise businesses (Salter & Dickson, 2020; Essen & Englander, 2013).

Segmentation in Social and Health Marketing

Market segmentation is commonly used in commercial sector marketing but is gaining much traction in social marketing (French., 2017). Market segmentation describes "the process of dividing up the market into homogenous segments and then developing unique marketing programs for individual target segments" (Rundle-Thiele et al., 2015, p. 524). Dividing target audiences into homogenous groups within a heterogeneous population is essential for effective targeting and positioning (Arli et al., 2017; Fujihira et al., 2015). The application of segmentation theory to social marketing phenomena is crucial to ensure the effective and efficient use of scarce resources (Rundle-Thiele et al., 2015). Segmentation is based on the first marketing principles that suggest that people in any population are different and change over time. However, since resources are limited, and competition is continuously intensifying, people with similar needs and wants should be identified and targeted with appropriate marketing offerings and interventions to achieve competitive advantage (Palmatier & Sridhar, 2017).

One crucial area where segmentation has proved useful is the domain of healthy lifestyles. The lifestyle concept has become an essential basis for segmenting and targeting consumer groups, and it is broadly defined as an element of psychographic segmentation (Arli et al., 2017; Vyncke, 2002). Lifestyle research generally combines the activities, interests, and opinions and other segmentation bases to develop groups' unique typologies through cluster analysis (Rundle-Thiele et al., 2015). Thus, in generating a rich profile of homogeneous customer groups, brands that promote healthy lifestyles may group people according to more observable criteria such as demographic or geographic basis, or general psychological or behavioural basis relative to maintaining health-promoting lifestyles (Vyncke, 2002).

Therefore, segmentation can be achieved mainly through one or a combination of demographic, geographic, psychographic, and behavioural factors (Kotler & Keller, 2012). Specifically, *demographic segmentation* uses age, income, gender, education, race, generation, occupation, marital status, family size, family life cycle, social class, nationality, and religion to identify the appropriate target audience (Kotler & Keller, 2012). *Geographic segmentation* uses locations where people reside, such as urban, rural, peri-urban, town, municipality, metropolis, city, region, or country, to achieve a suitable target audience (Kotler & Keller, 2012). Similarly, *psychographic segmentation* employs psychosocial factors to divide a heterogeneous population into an ideal target segment based on people's attitudes, knowledge, self-identity, values, emotions, interests, abilities, awareness, personality, social norms, intentions, and other facilitating factors (Kotler & Keller, 2012). Lastly, *behavioural segmentation* utilises habits, occasions, user status, usage rate, benefit sought, and loyalty status to achieve ideal target segments (Kotler & Keller, 2012). The ideal segment formation should be determined based on whether the target audience is measurable, accessible, sustainable, substantial, and differential enough to warrant marketing attention (Arli et al., 2017).

In the next sections, we explain some brands' promotion and communication strategies for positioning healthy lifestyle brands as promoters and representatives of good health.

Brands' Promotion and Communication Strategies for Positioning of Healthy Lifestyle Behaviour in Emerging Economies

Business organisations have adopted a strategic stance of using a healthy lifestyle as a critical theme to brand, communicate, and promote their products and services to enhance brand equity in the long run. The reason for this phenomenon is not farfetched. A cursory look at the healthy lifestyle-driven marketplace shows tremendous growth in healthy lifestyle-related businesses largely driven by the health and wellness movement across the world (Global Wellness Summit Report, 2020). According to the Global Wellness Summit (GWS), the health and wellness market is at $4.3 trillion and is still growing. Some of the critical sectors identified by the GWS include, but are not limited to, wellness tourism, wellness lifestyle, real estate, sleeping well, and sexual wellness. Specifically looking at the food sector, Wunsch (2020) observed that the global health and wellness food market is projected to increase from $701.12 billion in 2016 to $811.82 billion in 2021.

This immense economic value created by the health and wellness movement across the globe has created the right impetus for business organisations to naturally take advantage of these opportunities through the branding, promotion, and communication of products and services. These opportunities relate to health and wellness or the creation of promotional overlays with healthy lifestyle themes in cases where they do not deal directly with health and wellness products and services. There are several ways in which business organisations brand, promote, and communicate health and wellness-related products and services within emerging economies (Bligh, 2018).

In tourism alone, there is a plethora of diversifications in terms of the offerings available for exploring health and wellness leisure. For example, some healthcare facilities within emerging economies have been able to develop niche medical expertise and service provision that attracts persons interested in specific medical care to engage in medical tourism. For example, in the Middle East, the United Arab Emirates in 2014 revealed plans to build 22 hospital facilities to strategically attract tourism and boost its economy by up to approximately USD 704 million from neighbouring countries and Europe (Kannan, 2014).

Major hospitals brand these services as a complete service package of wellness and relaxation to potential clients (Enderwick & Nagar, 2011). Indeed, medical tourism has become popular due to long waiting lists and high costs in developed economies; hence facilities within emerging economies communicate and promote this service as fast, responsive, and dependable to attract clients from wealthy nations (Bookman & Bookman, 2007; Connell, 2006).

Businesses offering culinary services have also carved a niche for destination tourism, offering a one-stop gastro-tourism experience. Not to be confused with the usual food tourism, gastro-tourism is branded as an authentic, memorable food and beverage experience that includes behind-the-scenes observations laced with cultural and specific regional or country insights and hands-on food and beverage participation experience within a festive or casual context (Hall & Mitchell, 2005). Gastro-tourism is branded, promoted, and communicated for its ability to deliver a distinctive food and beverage experience to tourists seeking unique, healthy, and traditional food and beverages, especially for middle-aged travellers in developed economies who form a significant demographic segment for gastro-tourism oriented businesses (Williams et al., 2014). The Carribean Tourism Organisation (2008), for example, reports that large parts of the Caribbean, North Africa, and India and some parts of Asia are progressively reporting a high turnout of culinary tourists through international food festivals such as the Cayman Cookout, the St Croix Food and Wine Experience, the Vegetarian Festival in Thailand, and the National Street Food Festival in India.

An emerging trend in healthy lifestyle branding is to represent functional benefits of products as having efficacy in either promoting or enhancing the health and wellness of consumers (Chrysochou, 2010). In practice, most of these consumable commercial brands tend to use experts in health and nutrition to give their promotional messages credibility with regard to functionalfoods' nutritional claims (Corbo et al., 2014). Other consumable brands also represent their healthy lifestyle products through product differentiations that allow them to have product extensions representing the promotion of a healthy lifestyle to consumers explicitly (Carrete et al., 2018). A global brand like Coca-Cola, for example, has found the need to satisfy a growing segment of its consumers who take their healthy lifestyle seriously by creating a sugar-free Coca-Cola product not only to satisfy them but to continuously keep and attract potential consumers who fall in this segment (Moss, 2013). For example, Coca-Cola South Pacific launched Coca-Cola No Sugar as a major reaction to a public health crisis of obesity and diabetes. The aim was to cater to a segment of the population and health experts calling for business organisations to be responsible for consumable product design by ensuring the promotion of a healthy lifestyle and wellness (Green, 2017). In the promotional campaign brief, Marina Rocha, Group Marketing Manager at Coca-Cola South Pacific, reiterated the need for promoting healthy lifestyle choices by brands by stating:

> We know many of those people who love the taste of Coca-Cola are looking for ways to [decrease] their sugar intake. The new Coca-Cola No Sugar offers a great new choice for those who love the taste of Coke but are conscious of their sugar intake. (Rocha, 2017)

In the organic food market, trust is an important component of driving attitudes and purchase intentions (Teng & Wang, 2015). The organic food industry thrives on consumer trust, in the process leading to organic food production so that businesses promoting organic foods use verifiable production processes for branding, promotion, and communication of organic food brands to consumers through labelling (Anisimova & Sultan, 2014). Organic foods generally have been branded as "healthfulness" and have continuously driven the healthy food market due to consumers' growing health consciousness (Hemmerling et al., 2015). The central theme running through promotional messages for organic foods is the absence of chemicals, pesticides without hormones, and genetically modified organisms (Abrams et al., 2010; Dean, Raats, & Shepherd, 2008). Beyond labelling, organic foods are also branded and promoted based on the moral obligation for environmental concerns and consumption sustainability, as evident in the growing worldwide "green" movements (Lazzarini et al., 2016).

In response to the growing healthy lifestyle consumer movement, Fast Moving Consumer Goods (FMCGs) across emerging markets have resorted to branding and promoting a healthy lifestyle as a strategy for sustainable business continuity (Kemp & Bui, 2011; Tandon & Sethi, 2018). These organisations use different healthy lifestyle branding and promotion strategies. For example, the use of prompting engagements, links to health information, featured fruits, vegetables, and grains, and hashtags were prominent, while others used more facts and statistics and real-world tie-ins and a less optimistic tone (Klassen et al., 2018). For most FMCGs in emerging markets, a healthy lifestyle is branded as an integral part of what either the corporate brand (for umbrella brands) or the product brands represent and stand for, hence positioning themselves as trustworthy brands in the minds of consumers (Kraak et al., 2009). The next section explains critical factors that have been identified as enablers of healthy lifestyle behaviours, which may serve as appropriate bases for segmenting and targeting individuals for practical brand positioning efforts.

Enablers of Healthy Lifestyle Adaptation

In discussing the enablers of healthy lifestyle adaptation, critical attention must be given to the corporations due to their complex role as economic and social agents. Corporations use business practices such as product design, advertising, pricing, and distribution to maximise profit and reach business goals. Consumption in the twentieth century was a marker of modern lifestyles and affluent living, such as sugar consumption, which was driven mainly by the outputs of these vast corporations (Freudenberg, 2012). However, in the twenty-first century, corporations began shifting consumption to low- and middle-income countries to expand their markets due to stiff competition. The result of this move is the changing lifestyle of these so-called low-income countries, such that consumption and lifestyle patterns are beginning to look like those seen in affluent nations (Popkin et al., 2012).

Corporations are therefore massive influencers of lifestyle through their operational activities of producing and marketing goods and services that either promote or inhibit healthy life choices (Freudenberg, 2012). Furthermore, they wield enormous capacity to use big data, artificial intelligence, and data analytics to predict and describe consumer behaviour in ways that allow for demographic, psychographic, and geographic zoning, segmentation, and economic development purposes (Freudenberg, 2012).

Admittedly, although other forces such as culture, religion, governments, and family influence health-related behaviour, corporations continue to dominate the space of health-related behaviour influence primarily due to their enormous economic power (MacLachlan, 2006; Mathers et al., 2010). Socioeconomic factors also present far-reaching consequences for healthy lifestyle adaptation. Persons with poorer socioeconomic status are most likely to have poorer health choices and shorter life expectancy than persons with improved socioeconomic standing (Mackenbach et al., 2008). The influence of poor socioeconomic status on healthy lifestyle is manifested through the inability to afford balanced diets, fruits and vegetables, access to gym facilities, and access to quality health care and the cost of exploring organic foods and alternative medicine.

Here, we turn our attention to some prior studies that report findings on the role of specific and psychographic factors in explaining attitudes and intentions towards a healthy lifestyle and their implications for branding.

Demographic Factors

Age. The findings regarding the relationship between age and a healthy lifestyle are mixed. Whereas Geen and Firth (2006) find that committed organic food consumers were generally older in the UK, Magnusson et al. (2001) show that younger people expressed a more positive attitude towards organic foods and expressed higher purchase intentions for organic foods. Yet, older Australians reported higher motivation to exercise and experienced fewer exercise barriers (Newson & Kemps, 2007). Notably, as one advances in age, they will be more concerned about their health and may commit to health-promoting and prevention behaviours. In South Africa, organic food brands are shifting towards younger consumers using healthy lifestyle themes for branding organic food products such as wines, fruits and vegetables, confectionaries, and pastries (Kisaka-Lwayo & Obi, 2014).

Gender. Aertsens et al. (2009) provide several studies that support the view that women are generally more favourably predisposed towards maintaining good health and positive attitudes and purchase intentions for organic foods. In a study regarding the motivation to exercise, men rated the desire for a challenge as a more critical driver for exercise than women. In contrast, women rated health concerns as a more critical driver for exercise than men (Aertsens et al., 2009). In terms of barriers to exercise, women rated health concerns and facilities/knowledge more highly than men (Newson & Kemps, 2007). Healthy lifestyle-oriented brands such as organic foods in some Latin American countries have focused more on women because they are more proactive and motivated, while men pay attention to their social circumstances in the consumption of organic foods (Olivas & Bernabéu, 2012).

Income. Grinstein and Riefler (2015) reported that income was positively related to willingness to pay for environmentally friendly fast-moving consumer goods. One would expect that higher socioeconomic status would enable people to engage in discretionary consumption of products and brands that enhance healthy lifestyles. The decision regarding a gym membership, purchase of wearable watches, and healthy eating habits may be costly, requiring consumers to commit resources to such lifestyles. In emerging economies such as South Africa, India, and Brazil, healthy lifestyle brands have used price discrimination strategy to offer consumers of different income brackets the chance to stay healthy (UNDP Human Development Report, 2019). Decathlon India, for example, has found innovative ways to reduce cost via its supply chain and R&D and is therefore able to offer competitive prices on its sports equipment to the Indian population (Kumar et al., 2018).

Education. Many studies do not confirm a significant positive relationship between education and organic food consumption or healthy lifestyles (Aertsens et al., 2009). However, one would expect that the more a person is educated, the better their ability in reviewing information related to a healthy lifestyle (Aitken et al., 2020; Tanner & Kast, 2003), appreciating the perceived benefits of leading a healthy lifestyle (Gupta et al., 2020), and following through with health-promoting behaviours (Mai & Hoffmann, 2012). Indeed, healthy lifestyle brands are mostly positioned as an extension of enlightened awareness of general wellbeing for productivity. The educated understand health literature and are better placed to make more informed choices. In India and South Africa, governments are striving to provide adult education to the illiterate adult population as a means of empowering them to make better health choices (Vamos et al., 2020).

Psychological Factors

Self-Identity

Self-identity (or self-concept) describes a person's concept or perceptions of themselves (Singh, 2016; Sparks & Shepherd, 1992). Oyserman (2009) explains that people maintain consistent behaviours with their self-identity because choices are identity-based. Identity-based motivations provide the readiness to engage in identity-consistent actions (Lewis & Oyserman, 2016). Self-identity is a crucial driver of consumer behaviour (Reed et al., 2012). Previous studies report that people choose healthy lifestyles as a mechanism to enact healthy lifestyles. For example, Essen and Englander (2013) found that young Swedish consumers chose organic diet consumption as an identity marker and healthy lifestyle experience.

Sharma et al. (2020) also find that green self-identity and green self-concept are related to green purchase intentions and actual purchase behaviour among some Indian consumers. These individuals use organic food consumption to express their personality and communicate how they desire to be identified by others. Notably, a person's identity, based on their choice of diet, physical activity, and healthy lifestyle, may serve as a motivational basis to establish a sense of uniqueness, group membership, and connection to nature (Essen & Englander, 2013; Sharma et al., 2020). Wearable watches such as Fitbit Versa Lite and Samsung Galaxy Watch Active have become important identity markers in Africa and other emerging markets among young and adult consumers; they have become essential objects for communicating one's fitness personality and healthy lifestyle. Thus, people with healthy self-identity will be more receptive to brands imbued with healthy lifestyle cues (Kirmani, 2009; Singh, 2016).

Self-Efficacy and Perceived Behavioural Control

Drawing on Social Cognitive Theory (SCT), researchers establish that perceived self-efficacy significantly influences consumers' health-related behaviours (Luszczynska et al., 2005). SCT maintains that self-efficacy is a primary and proximal driver of behaviour (Bandura, 1999). Self-efficacy refers to the extent to which "a person is convinced that (s)he is able to achieve and sustain a desired goal" (Mai & Hoffmann, 2012, p. 317). Luszczynska et al. (2005) describe self-efficacy as a trait-like variable that highlights "people's beliefs in their capabilities to perform a specific action required to attain a desired outcome" (p. 439) and relates to a broad range of health behaviours. High levels of self-efficacy beliefs contribute to increased exertion of effort to achieve set goals (Bandura, 1999). Mai and Hoffmann (2012) report that health-conscious consumers who maintain nutrition self-efficacy apply more cognitive effort to consider health-related information more favourably. Jackson et al. (2007) find that health self-efficacy significantly predicted health-promoting lifestyles among college students in the USA; thus, people who are convinced that they can reduce their weight and commit to an exercise regime are more likely to achieve their goals than those who are convinced that they will be unsuccessful no matter what they do.

Unlike perceived self-efficacy, which is considered internally driven, perceived behavioural control is externally driven. Perceived behavioural control (PBC) describes "the perceived ease or difficulty of performing the behaviour" (Ajzen, 1991). One's beliefs determine their PBC, which may enhance or hinder the performance of a certain behaviour (Aertsens et al., 2009). Previous studies show that PBC favourably predisposes consumers to positively evaluate green products (Aitken et al., 2020; Paul et al., 2016). Thus, people who perceive previous or future obstacles in engaging in healthy lifestyles may be more reluctant to engage in healthy behaviours. Consequently, marketing practices and brand communications should encourage heightened self-efficacy and behavioural control to enact the right behaviours.

Health Consciousness

Health consciousnesses refers to "the degree to which a person plays an active role in maintaining his or her health" (Mai & Hoffmann, 2015, p. 65). Health-conscious people demonstrate a strong desire and commitment to enhance or sustain the state of their physical wellbeing through preventive behaviours and healthcare (Michaelidou & Hassan, 2008). For example, health-conscious consumers may use wearable smart watches to monitor the condition of their health purposively and pursue actions that will improve or maintain their health and wellbeing (Mai & Hoffmann, 2015). Notably, they may decide to seek health-related information, join a gym, or engage periodically in running, swimming, cycling, and following nutritious dieting; all actions derive from their health-conscious beliefs. Michaelidou and Hassan (2008) empirically confirmed that health-conscious consumers had a positive attitude towards healthy lifestyles and expressed positive intentions to purchase of organic foods. In a study among German consumers, Mai and Hoffmann (2015) found that health-conscious consumers are more interested in gathering appropriate information about healthy and natural foods and are engaged in frequent shopping for healthy rather than unhealthy products. Health consciousness encourages searching for nutritional information and purchasing organic products (Rana & Paul, 2017). Using data from Taiwan, Chen (2009) reports that health consciousness leads to healthy lifestyles and influences positive attitudes towards organic foods.

Thus, increasing consumers' health consciousness may contribute to their healthy lifestyle behaviours.

Susceptibility to Interpersonal Influence and Subjective Norms

Consumer susceptibility to normative influence concerns "the need to identify or enhance one's image with significant others through the acquisition and use of products and brands, and the willingness to conform to the expectations of others regarding purchase decisions, and/or the tendency to learn about products and services by observing others and/or seeking information from others" (Bearden et al., 1989, p. 474). Interpersonal influences are strong predictors of consumer behaviour in many consumption contexts (Martin et al., 2008; Shukla, 2011). Bearden et al. (1989) highlight two characteristics of susceptibility to interpersonal influences: (a) normative interpersonal influence, that is, the tendency to conform to the expectations of others to enhance their self-image and (b) informational interpersonal influence, that is, the tendency to accept information from others as evidence about reality (Bearden et al., 1989, p. 474). Thus, consumers who are highly susceptible to interpersonal influence often use reference group cues as self-appraisal standards, self-image enhancement, or as a source of personal norms and attitudes (Batra et al., 2001).

Barauskaite et al. (2018) explain that some consumers opt for healthy foods to impress others. They confirm that high susceptibility to interpersonal influence has a strong impact on functional food choices (i.e. foods laden with vitamins, minerals, and active cultures to enhance bodily functions and improvements in health and wellbeing). This, in turn, influences purchase rates for functional foods. Khare (2014) found that normative and informational susceptibility to interpersonal influence differentially influences green attitudes and ecologically conscious purchase behaviour of Indians. Gupta et al. (2020) show that social comparison tends to influence the perceived health outcomes and user satisfaction of smart wearable watches. Thus, since emerging markets are generally collectivist and interdependent cultures (cf. Markus & Kitayama, 1991), healthy lifestyles can be encouraged through the mechanisms of interpersonal influences from reference groups. They can shape health-related behaviours by enacting norms of appropriate health behaviours and providing health-relevant information.

Environmental Concerns and Sustainability Issues

Environmental concerns relate to "consumer awareness about the negative effect of development on the environment" (Gil et al., 2000, p. 212). The growing trend favouring the consumption of organic foods and healthy lifestyles may be linked to increased environmental concerns (Dean et al., 2012). More consumers in the West and recently in emerging markets are becoming more interested in green marketing (Borin et al., 2011; Strizhakova & Coulter, 2013). Because more consumers are demanding environmentally friendly food products, many firms are responding by producing and marketing foods sourced and marketed in an environmentally sustainable manner (Khare, 2014; Strizhakova & Coulter, 2013). Environmental consciousness refers to "the degree to which an organisation produced a product which is advantageous to the natural environment while minimising negative impacts on the environment" (Kang & James, 2007, p. 310). There is growing concern about the use of pesticides and chemicals in farming and additives in food processing, causing environmental concerns to influence ecological food considerations (Rana & Paul, 2017). Thus, ecologically conscious consumers find a firm's green branding and sustainability practices very important in influencing their green consumption behaviour and healthy lifestyles (Khare, 2014). Many firms find green marketing in emerging markets a welcome trend and embrace it to influence corporate social responsibility and strategy considerations (Ofori & Hinson, 2007).

Global Consumption Orientation

Many consumers worldwide are resorting to common health-promoting behaviours as an expression of their global consumption orientation.

Globally oriented consumers maintain a strong preference for global brands and lifestyle alternatives (Westjohn et al., 2016). Globalisation of healthy lifestyles has produced globally oriented consumer segments that are concerned about their health. They tend to seek common healthy lifestyle behaviours on a global rather than a national basis (Westjohn et al., 2016). Social media platforms amplify health-promoting behaviours, where many people frequently share their health milestones (e.g. calories burned, running or cycling miles achieved) with like-minded global consumers (Makri et al., 2019). Such behaviours include yoga clubs, gym memberships, and organic food patronage to enact their healthy lifestyles. There is a growing trend worldwide for smart fitness watches to monitor the state of one's health, track activities (e.g. walking, running, and cycling), provide hedonic benefits, and act as fashion accessories (Gupta et al., 2020). In their study of six emerging markets from South East Asia and Latin America, Salnikova and Grunert (2020) found that globally oriented consumers place greater importance on sustainability attributes and environmental concerns in their food choices. Moreover, cosmopolitan consumers are more concerned about sustainability and environmental issues than less cosmopolitan consumers (Grinstein & Riefler, 2015). Thus, consumers who desire global citizenship through global brands may find smart wearable watches appealing and are attracted to green marketing since they promote health-promoting behaviours on a global scale (Strizhakova et al., 2008).

Consumer Knowledge

Limited knowledge about the benefits of sustainable consumption and healthy lifestyles triggers negative consequences for the environment and human health effects (Xie et al., 2015). Consumers with actionable knowledge about environmental issues and health-related behaviours are more likely to overcome barriers that impede their decisions to make pro-environment behaviour choices and take health-promoting actions. Tanner and Kast (2003) reported that being sufficiently knowledgeable to decide between environmentally friendly and environmentally harmful products encouraged appropriate green consumption actions.

Consumers armed with useful information about the benefits of living healthy lifestyles through organic consumption and physical activity are more likely to consider their decisions essential and increase their organic food consumption. A deeper understanding of organic foods as good for the environment and healthier than traditional foods promotes positive attitudes and purchase intentions for organic foods (Aitken et al., 2020; Tanner & Kast, 2003).

Attitudes Towards a Healthy Lifestyle

Since attitudes strongly influence healthy lifestyle behaviours, they can be called upon to explain consumers' food choices and physical activity initiation, and to provide purposeful monitoring of alcohol and tobacco consumption, as well as the maintenance of life equilibrium (Gil et al., 2000; Tuorila, 1997). An attitude can be defined as "a psychological tendency that is expressed by evaluating a particular entity with some degree of favour or disfavour" (Eagly & Chaiken, 1993). Attitudes may include the evaluation of objects or behaviours for their hedonic function (pleasant or unpleasant, good or bad, negative or positive) or utilitarian function (useful or useless, important or unimportant, beneficial or harmful) (Batra & Ahtola, 1991). Previous studies report that consumers' attitudes towards a healthy lifestyle (e.g. organic food consumption) lead them to buy healthy foods (Chen, 2009; Dean et al., 2012). For example, Chen (2011) reports that Taiwanese consumers' willingness to purchase functional foods was heavily influenced by their attitudes defined by the perceived rewards, necessity, confidence, and safety of functional foods. These attitudes exerted more significant influence when consumers were more health-conscious and sought to lead a healthy lifestyle. Thus, when consumers maintain a positive attitude towards physical exercise or vegetarian food, they are more likely to behave consistently with their attitudes by engaging in regular exercise, recycling, and buying and eating organic foods (Paul et al., 2016).

Recommendations for Healthy Lifestyle Branding and Promotions

Thus far, the review provides many bases on which brands may position themselves in the healthy lifestyle domain to achieve competitive advantage. Health-related issues are gaining attention due to many factors examined in this chapter. This section provides insights into how brands may benefit from developing appropriate brand positioning strategies to improve brand equity.

Target Older and Younger Consumers with Unique Brand Propositions

There are studies that show that older consumers are generally more likely to purchase products and brands that support consumers' healthy lifestyles (Magnusson et al., 2001; Newson & Kemps, 2007). Similarly, younger consumers are also found to seek healthy lifestyles due to globalisation influences and an orientation towards the globalised marketplace. Thus, brand communications should be designed with unique propositions that focus on specific needs and attitudes towards healthy lifestyles. Older consumers may pursue health-promoting behaviours to improve their current health conditions or avoid future health problems. In contrast, younger consumers may look at a healthy lifestyle as a means of achieving a particular self-identity (Dean et al., 2012).

More Focus on Female Consumers

Female consumers are generally more likely to lead healthy lifestyles than their male counterparts (Aertsens et al., 2009). Brand positioning communications that encourage healthy lifestyles should target female consumers first, before their male counterparts. Females are more likely to be concerned about their health and deliberately take actions to improve it. This knowledge should guide health-promoting brands to target appropriately.

Socioeconomic Status Is Relevant for Identifying Health-Conscious Consumers

People in the high-income bracket are more likely to buy organic foods and purchase smart wearable watches to gauge their health. Thus, income should be included in selecting appropriate target segments, as higher income levels have been associated with organic food consumption and propensity to engage in physical exercise. Firms that promote gym equipment sales may target high-income consumers.

More Education to Promote Healthy Lifestyles

People with high education do not necessarily engage in healthy lifestyles. Aertsens et al. (2009) report a lack of sufficient basis to establish a strong link between higher education and health-promoting behaviours. To achieve brand prominence among highly educated consumers in the health products space, firms should provide a more compelling rationale for why educated consumers should engage in health-promoting behaviours. This approach should be aligned with more general psychological factors, such as their values, personality, interpersonal influences, and social norms and ethics, to ensure behavioural change.

Linking Health Self-Identity to Brand Identity

The review shows that people tend to maintain consistency between their self-identity and domain-specific behaviours (e.g. Oyserman, 2009; Singh, 2016). To improve healthy lifestyle branding, firms need to imbue their brands with identifiers that reinforce consumers' health or green self-identity. Torelli et al. (2012) explain that brand concepts reinforcing consumers' self-identity and values are more effective than those that do not reinforce their ideas about their self-conception and values. Emerging market brands in the healthy lifestyle sector should use health self-identity cues to convey their brand messages.

Commit to Promoting Health Consciousness

We document that health consciousness profoundly impacts healthy lifestyles (cf. Mai & Hoffmann, 2015; Michaelidou & Hassan, 2008; Rana & Paul, 2017). Thus, message appeals should make invitations, specifically targeting health-conscious consumers about specific health behavioural changes. For example, organisations seeking to change people's behaviour regarding adherence to COVID-19 protocols should promote health consciousness to achieve better outcomes. In contrast, individuals who are not health conscious need to be encouraged to take steps to enhance their health and wellbeing. Brands may highlight life situations where health consciousness improved health-promoting and health-debilitating behaviours.

Communicate "Yes, you Can" Messages

Furthermore, self-efficacy and perceived behavioural controls are important routes that emerging market brands may follow to engender appropriate health behaviour change and healthy lifestyles. People who think they can overcome any obstacles in their lives resolve to lead healthier lifestyles and are more likely to be successful than those who believe they cannot (Jackson et al., 2007; Luszczynska et al., 2005; Mai & Hoffmann, 2012). Hence, brands may initiate campaigns that encourage "Yes, you can" self-beliefs for positive health behaviours.

Use Reference Groups to Encourage Healthy Lifestyles

The reviewed documents concluded that interpersonal influences or subjective norms influence many behaviours, including organic food consumption and health-promoting lifestyles (Barauskaite et al., 2018; Gupta et al., 2020; Khare, 2014). Thus, brand communication messages from significant others and influential reference groups such as celebrity endorsers, key opinion leaders, and important organisations may be used as information sources to influence behaviour change. Influential reference group members who engage in healthy lifestyles such as physical exercise, organic food eating, stress management, social distancing, mask-wearing, and alcohol and tobacco avoidance may be effective communicators in campaigns to achieve health behaviour change.

Put Environmental Concerns and Sustainability at the Forefront of Brand Strategy

As concerns for the environment and sustainability intensify, brands may capitalise on these concerns to position their brands. A healthy lifestyle is a trend in many countries. Brands seeking to be strong, unique, and favourable in consumers' minds should take a stand about environmental concerns and commit to sustainability as a source of competitive advantage (Khare, 2014; Ofori & Hinson, 2007; Rana & Paul, 2017). Brands such as The Body Shop and Nedbank South Africa emphasise strong sustainability and environmental focus in their strategy, thereby contributing as points of difference in brand strategy (Keller, 2008).

Encourage Global Connectivity through Healthy Lifestyles

Many people buy brands as instruments to achieve membership in a global community of like-minded people (Westjohn et al., 2016). Emerging market brands that seek to promote healthy lifestyles should capitalise on global consumption orientation and cosmopolitan values to encourage health-promoting behaviours. Global smartwatch brands in emerging markets such as Apple, Huawei, Samsung, Fossil, and Fitbit that encourage healthy lifestyles should target people with positive globalisation attitudes and a strong global identity. These consumers would find brand appeals with emphasis on global healthy lifestyle trends to be more rewarding. Likewise, local brands in emerging markets may also target local consumers with positive globalisation attitudes with similar appeals of global healthy lifestyle trends. The use of aspiration to global citizenship may work equally effectively for local and global brands in emerging markets (Strizhakova et al., 2008).

Help Consumers to Understand Health Issues Better

The more knowledgeable people are about the perceived benefits of participating in a healthy lifestyle, the more likely they are to engage in health-promoting behaviours (Aitken et al., 2020; Tanner & Kast, 2003; Xie et al., 2015). Thus, brand interventions should contribute to educating people about the importance of engaging in specific health behaviours. For example, since many misconceptions surround COVID-19, social enterprises and companies should educate the public about the negative consequences of contracting the disease and the importance of maintaining COVID-19 protocols. Commercial-based brand equity may appropriate from brand image benefits by being at the forefront of a grave global health concern.

Build Positive Attitudes about a Healthy Lifestyle

Attitudes are fundamental to many social behaviours, especially in the healthy lifestyle domain (Batra & Ahtola, 1991; Eagly & Chaiken, 1993; Paul et al., 2016). Effective brand positioning strategies recommend that firms and organisations should contribute to promoting positive attitudes towards healthy lifestyles. This can be achieved by touting the benefits of adopting health-promoting behaviours (Aertsens et al., 2009; Chen, 2011; Dean et al., 2012). The utilitarian, hedonic, and symbolic attitudinal functions of leading a healthy lifestyle should be integrated into firms' brand concepts to develop positive health attitudes (Batra & Ahtola, 1991; Keller, 1993).

Conclusion

This chapter reviews various studies related to healthy lifestyles and how they may improve our understanding of consumer behaviour and lifestyle branding in emerging markets. The review draws on many studies from different countries and relates them especially to emerging markets. Primarily, we document the role of segmentation in social and health marketing and highlight some fundamental bases upon which segmentation strategies are dependent, and how they benefit targeting decisions and brand positioning outcomes. This chapter principally shows that many demographic and psychographic factors are crucial to understanding the propensity towards health-promoting behaviours. Together with theoretical approaches and conceptual underpinnings of healthy lifestyle behaviours, this chapter provides some insights into the key factors influencing people to eat organically, exercise periodically, and embrace certain products with the aim of improving their health and preventing disease.

Furthermore, this chapter's insights enable both commercial and not-for-profit brands to design effective marketing interventions and brand-building strategies to encourage healthy behaviours while achieving marketing effectiveness. Given the enormous power corporations have in new product development, pricing, promotion, and distribution, this chapter recommends a health approach to a strategy where products are designed and marketed in response to the health and wellness movements which increasingly embrace health-oriented products. A health-oriented branding strategy would significantly reduce societal health problems, such as unhealthy lifestyle or burden of diseases.

References

Abrams, K., Meyers, C., & Irani, T. (2010). Consumers' perceptions of all-natural and organic pork products. *Agriculture and Human Values, 27*(3), 365–374.

Aertsens, J., Verbeke, W., Mondelaers, K., & Huylenbroeck, G. V. (2009). Personal determinants of organic food consumption: A review. *British Food Journal, 111*(10), 1140–1167.

Aitken, R., Watkins, L., Williams, J., & Kean, A. (2020). The positive role of labelling on consumers perceived behavioural control and intention to purchase organic food. *Journal of Cleaner Production, 255*, 120334.

Ajzen, I. (1991). The theory of planned behavior. *Organizational Behavior and Human Decision Processes, 50*(2), 179–211.

Anisimova, T., & Sultan, P. (2014). The role of Brand Communications in consumer purchases of organic foods: A research framework. *Journal of Food Products Marketing, 20*, 511–532.

Arena, R., Lavie, C., Hivert, M., Williams, M., Briggs, P., & Guazzi, M. (2015). Who will deliver comprehensive healthy lifestyle interventions to combat non-communicable disease? Introducing the healthy lifestyle practitioner discipline. *Expert Review of Cardiovascular Therapy, 14*(1), 15–22.

Arli, D., Dietrich, T., Tkaczynski, A., & Rundle-Thiele, S. (2017). Indonesian healthy living intentions: Segmentation study insights. *International Journal of Nonprofit and Voluntary Sector Marketing, 22*, 1–9.

Ashakiran, S., & Deepthi, R. (2012). Fast foods and their impact on health. *Journal of Krishna Institute of Medical Sciences University, 1*(2), 7–13.

Bandura, A. (1999). Social cognitive theory of personality. In L. P. O. John (Ed.), *Handbook of personality* (Vol. 2, pp. 154–196). Guilford Publications.

Barauskaite, D., Gineikiene, J., Fennis, B. M., Auruskeviciene, V., Yamaguchi, M., & Kondo, N. (2018). Eating healthy to impress: How conspicuous consumption, perceived selfcontrol motivation, and descriptive normative influence determine functional food choices. *Appetite, 131*, 59–67.

Batra, R., & Ahtola, O. T. (1991). Measuring the hedonic and utilitarian sources of consumer attitudes. *Marketing Letters, 2*(2), 159–170.

Batra, R., Homer, P. M., & Kahle, L. R. (2001). Values, susceptibility to normative influence, and attribute importance weights: A nomological analysis. *Journal of Consumer Psychology, 11*(2), 115–128.

Bearden, W. O., Netemeyer, R. G., & Teel, J. E. (1989). Measurement of consumer susceptibility to interpersonal influence. *Journal of Consumer Research, 15*, 473–482.

Bligh, S. (2018, May 04). *How big brands are helping consumers shift to healthier eating options*. Retrieved from Reuters Evens sustainable business: https://www.reutersevents.com/sustainability/how-big-brands-are-helping-consumers-shift-healthier-eating-options

Bloch, P. (1984). The wellness movement: Imperatives for health care marketers. *Journal of Health Care Marketing, 4*(Winter), 9–16.

Bookman, M., & Bookman, K. (2007). *Medical tourism in developing countries*. Palgrave Macmillan.

Borin, N., Cerf, D. C., & Krishnan, R. (2011). Consumer effects of environmental impact in product labeling. *Journal of Consumer Marketing, 28*(1), 76–86.

von Bothmer, M., & Fridlund, B. (2005). Gender differences in health habits and in motivation for a healthy lifestyle among Swedish university students. *Nursing and Health Sciences, 7*, 107–118.

Carrete, L., Arroyo, P., & Centeno, E. (2018). Are brand extensions of healthy products an adequate strategy when there is a high association between the brand and unhealthy products? *Review of Business Management, 1*, 1–22.

Carribean Tourism Organisation. (2008). *Developing a niche tourism market database for the Carribean*. Acorn Consulting Partnership Ltd.

Chen, M.-F. (2009). Attitude toward organic foods among Taiwanese as related to health consciousness, environmental attitudes, and the mediating effects of a healthy lifestyle. *British Food Journal, 111*(2), 165–178.

Chen, M.-F. (2011). The joint moderating effect of health consciousness and healthy lifestyle on consumers willingness to use functional foods in Taiwan. *Appetite, 57*, 253–262.

Chrysochou, P. (2010). Food health branding: The role of marketing mix elements and public discourse in conveying a healthy brand image. *Journal of Marketing Communications, 16*(1–2), 69–85.

Cockx, L., Colen, L., & Weerdt, J. (2018). From corn to popcorn? Urbanization and dietary change: Evidence from rural-urban migrants in Tanzania. *World Development, 110*, 140–159.

Connell, J. (2006). Medical tourism: Sea, sun, sand and …surgery. *Tourism Management, 27*(6), 1093–1100.

Corbo, M., Bevilacqua, A., Petruzzi, L., Casanova, F., & Sinigaglia, M. (2014). Functional beverages: The emerging side of functional foods commercial trends, research, and health implications. *Comprehensive Reviews in Food Science and Food Safety, 13*(6), 1192–1206.

Dean, M., Raats, M. M., & Shepherd, R. (2012). The role of self-identity, past behavior, and their interaction in predicting intention to purchase fresh and processed organic food 1. *Journal of Applied Social Psychology, 42*(3), 669–688.

Dominick, J., & Cole, S. (2020). Goals as identities: Boosting perceptions of healthy-eater identity for easier goal pursuit. *Motivation and Emotion, 44*, 410–426.

Eagly, A. H., & Chaiken, S. (1993). *The psychology of attitudes*. Harcourt Brace.

Enderwick, P., & Nagar, S. (2011). The competitive challenge of emerging markets: The case of medical tourism. *International Journal of Emerging Markets, 6*(4), 329–350.

Essen, E. V., & Englander, M. (2013). Organic food as a healthy lifestyle: A phenomenological psychological analysis. *International Journal of Qualitative Studies on Health and Well-Being, 8*(1), 1–10.

French. (2017). The importance of segmentation in social marketing strategy. In T. Dietrich, S. Rundle-Thiele, & K. Kubacki (Eds.), *Segmnetation in social marketing* (Vol. 1). Springer.

Freudenberg, N. (2012). The manufacture of lifestyle: The role of corporations in unhealthy living. *Journal of Public Health Policy, 33*(2), 244–256.

Fujihira, H., Kubacki, K., Ronto, R., Pang, B., & Rundle-Thiele, S. (2015). Social marketing physical activity interventions among adults 60 years and older: A systematic review. *Social Marketing Quarterly, 21*(4), 214–229.

Geen, N., & Firth, C. (2006). *The comitted organic consumer, Joint Organic Congress.* Odense, Denmark.

Gil, J. M., Gracia, A., & Sanchez, M. (2000). Market segmentation and willingness to pay for organic products in Spain. *International Food and Agribusiness Management Review, 3*, 207–226.

Global Wellness Summit Report. (2020). *Global wellness trends report: The future of wellness 2020.* Global Wellness Summit. Retrieved from Global Wellness Summit.

Green, R. (2017). Coca Cola to promote sugar free product with "Say yes to the taste you love" Work via Ogilvy. *Campaign Brief.* https://campaignbrief.com/coca-cola-promotes-new-sugar-f/

Grinstein, A., & Riefler, P. (2015). Citizens of the (green) world? Cosmopolitan orientation and sustainability. *Journal of International Business Studies, 46*, 694–714.

Gupta, A., Dhiman, N., Yousaf, A., & Arora, N. (2020). Social comparison and continuance intention of smart fitness wearables: An extended expectation confirmation theory perspective. *Behaviour & Information Technology, 1-15.* https://doi.org/10.1080/0144929X.2020.1748715

Hall, C., & Mitchell, R. (2005). Gastronomic tourism: Comparing food and wine tourism experiences. In M. Novelli (Ed.), *Niche tourism: Contemporary issues, trends and cases.* Elsevier Butterworth-Heinemann.

He, H., & Harris, L. (2020). The impact of Covid-19 pandemic on corporate social responsibility and marketing philosophy. *Journal of Business Research, 116*, 176–182.

Hemmerling, S., Hamm, U., & Spiller, A. (2015). Consumption behavior regarding organic food from a marketing perspective–a literature review. *Organic Agriculture, 5*(4), 277–313.

Herzog, L. (2015). *Global Surburbs: Urban sprawl from the Rio Grande to Rio de jenerio.* Routledge.

Jackson, E. S., Tucker, C. M., & Herman, K. C. (2007). Health value, perceived social support, and health self-efficacy as factors in a health-promoting lifestyle. *Journal of American College Health, 56*(1), 69–74.

Jakovljevic, M., Timofeyev, Y., Ekkert, N., Fedorova, J., Skvirskaya, G., Bolevich, S., & Reshetnikov, V. (2019). The impact of health expenditures on public health in BRICS nations. *Journal of Sports Health Science, 8*(6), 516–519.

Kannan, P. (2014). Dubai Reveals Master Plan for 500,000 Medical Tourists a Year. The National http://www.thenational.ae/uae/tourism/dubai-reveals-master-plan-for-500-000-medical-tourist-a-year.

Keller, K. L. (1993). Conceptualizing, measuring, and managing customer-based brand equity. *Journal of Marketing, 57*(1), 1–22.

Keller, K. (2008). *Strategic Brand Management: Building, measuring and managing brand equity* (3rd ed.). Prentice-Hall.

Kemp, E., & Bui, M. (2011). Healthy brands: Establishing brand credibility, commitment and connection among consumers. *Journal of Consumer Marketing, 28*(6), 429–437.

Khare, A. (2014). Consumers susceptibility to interpersonal influence as a determining factor of ecologically conscious behaviour. *Marketing Intelligence & Planning, 32*(1), 2–20.

Kirmani, A. (2009). The self and the brand. *Journal of Consumer Psychology, 19*(3), 271–275.

Kisaka-Lwayo, M., & Obi, A. (2014). Analysis of production and consumption of organic products in South Africa. *Organic Agriculture Towards Sustainability, 26-50.* https://doi.org/10.5772/58356

Klassen, K., Borleis, E., Brennan, L., Reid, M., McCaffrey, T., & Megan, S. (2018). What people "like": Analysis of social media strategies used by food industry brands, lifestyle brands, and health promotion organizations on Facebook and Instagram. *Journal of Medical Internet Research, 20*(6), 1–9.

Kotler, P., & Keller, K. (2012). *Marketing Management* (14th ed.). Pearson Education.

Kraak, V., Kumanyika, S., & Story, M. (2009). The commercial marketing of healthy lifestyles to address the global child and adolescent obesity pandemic: Prospects, pitfalls and priorities. *Public Health Nutrition, 12*(11), 2027–2036.

Kumar, A., Mishra, V., Anand, R., Kabra, M., & Rao, R. (2018, September). *Indian Habit Of Being Healthy.* Retrieved from https://redseer.com/reports/indian-habit-of-being-healthy/

Lazzarini, G., Zimmerman, J., Visschers, V., & Siegrist, M. (2016). Does environmental friendliness equal healthiness? Swiss consumers perception of protein products. *Appetite, 105,* 663–673.

Lewis, N., & Oyserman, D. (2016). Using identity-based motivation to improve the nation's health without breaking the bank. *Behavioural Science and Policy, 2*(2), 25–38.

Luszczynska, A., Scholz, U., & Schwarzer, R. (2005). The general self-efficacy scale: Multicultural validation studies. *Journal of Psychology, 139*(5), 439–457.

Mackenbach, J., Stirbu, I., Menvielle, G., Leinsalu, M., & Kunst, A. (2008). Socioeconomic inequalities in health in 22 European countries. *The New England Journal of Medicine, 358*, 2468–2481.

MacLachlan, M. (2006). *Culture and health: A critical perspective towards Global Health*. Wiley.

Magnusson, M., Arvola, A., Koivisto, H., Åberg, L., & Sjödén, P. (2001). Attitudes towards organic foods among Swedish consumers. *British Food Journal, 10*(3), 209–227.

Mai, R., & Hoffmann, S. (2012). Taste lovers versus nutrition fact seekers: How health consciousness and self-efficacy determine the way consumers choose food products. *Journal of Consumer Behaviour, 11*(4), 316–328.

Mai, R., & Hoffmann, S. (2015). How to combat the unhealthy tasty intuition: The influencing role of health consciousness. *Journal of Public Policy & Marketing, 34*(1), 63–83.

Makri, K., Papadas, K.-K., & Schlegelmilch, B. B. (2019). Global-local consumer identities as drivers of global digital brand usage. *International Marketing Review, 36*(5), 0265–1335.

Markus, H. R., & Kitayama, S. (1991). Culture and the self: Implications for cognition, emotion, and motivation. *Psychological Review, 98*(2), 224–253.

Martin, B., Wentzel, D., & Tomczak, T. (2008). Effects of susceptibility to normative influence and type of testimonial on attitudes toward print advertising. *Journal of Advertising, 37*(1), 29–43.

Mathers, J., Strathdee, G., & Relton, C. (2010). Action of epigenetic alterations by dietary and other environmental factors. *Advances in Genetics, 71*, 3–39.

Michaelidou, N., & Hassan, L. M. (2008). The role of health consciousness, food safety concern and ethical identity on attitudes and intentions towards organic food. *International Journal of Consumer Studies, 32*, 163–170.

Moss, M. (2013). *Salt, sugar, and fat or branding, marketing, and promotion?* WH Allen/Ebury Publishing.

Newson, R. S., & Kemps, E. B. (2007). Factors that promote and prevent exercise engagement in older adults. *Journal of Aging and Health, 19*(3), 470–481.

Ofori, D. F., & Hinson, R. E. (2007). Corporate social responsibility (CSR) perspectives of leading firms in Ghana. *Corporate Governance: The International Journal of Business in Society*.

Olivas, R., & Bernabéu, R. (2012). Men's and women's attitudes toward organic food consumption. A Spanish case study. Panish or Spanish? Panish. *Journal of Agricultural Research, 10*(2), 281–291.

Oyserman, D. (2009). Identity-based motivation and consumer behavior. *Journal of Consumer Psychology, 19*(3), 276–279.

Oyserman, D., Elmore, K., & Smith, G. (2012). Self, self-concept, and identity. In M. Leary & J. Tangney (Eds.), *Handbook of self and identity*. Guilford.

Palmatier, R. W., & Sridhar, S. (2017). *Marketing strategy: Based on first principles and data analytics*. Macmillan International Higher Education.

Paul, J., Modi, A., & Patel, J. (2016). Predicing green product consumption using theory of planned behavior and reason action. *Journal of Retailing and Consumer Services, 29*, 123–134.

Popkin, B., Adair, L., & Ng, S. (2012). Global nutrition transition and the pandemic of obesity in developing countries. *Nutrition Reviews, 70*(1), 3–21.

Rana, J., & Paul, J. (2017). Consumer behavior and purchase intention for organic food: A review and research agenda. *Journal of Retailing and Consumer Services, 38*, 157–165.

Reed, A., Forehand, M., Puntoni, S., & Warlop, L. (2012). Identity-based consumer behavior. *International Journal of Research in Marketing, 29*(4), 310–321.

Rocha, M. (2017). South Pacific Coca Cola campaign launch. In *Say yes to the taste you love*, Sydney, Australia.

Rundle-Thiele, S., Kubacki, K., Tkaczynski, A., & Parkinson, J. (2015). Using two-step cluster analysis to identify homogeneous physical activity groups. *Marketing Intelligence & Planning, 33*(4), 522–537.

Salnikova, E., & Grunert, K. G. (2020). The role of consumption orientation in consumer food preferences in emerging markets. *Journal of Business Research, 112*, 147–159.

Salter, L., & Dickson, A. (2020). The fantasy of healthy food: Desire and anxiety in healthy food guide magazine. *Critical Public Health, 1-13*, 1. https://doi.org/10.1080/09581596.2020.1724262

Sanders, D., Stern, R., Struthers, P., Ngulube, T., & Onya, H. (2008). What is needed for health promotion in Africa: Band-aid, live aid or real change? *Critical Public Health, 18*, 509–519.

Saraswat, K. (2013, September 16). *How unhealthy lifestyles affect the economy*. Retrieved from The HealthSite.com: https://www.thehealthsite.com/diseases-conditions/how-unhealthy-lifestyles-affect-the-economy-79245/

Sharma, N., Saha, R., Sreedharan, V. R., & Paul, J. (2020). Relating the role of green self-concept and identity on green purchasing behaviour: An empirical analysis. *Business Strategy and the Environment, 29*, 3203–3219.

Sheth, J. (2020). Impact of Covid-19 on consumer behavior: Will the old habits return or die? *Journal of Business Research, 117*, 280–283.

Shukla, P. (2011). Impact of interpersonal influences, brand origin and brand image on luxury purchase intentions: Measuring interfunctional interactions and a cross-national comparison. *Journal of World Business, 46,* 242–252.

Singh, J. (2016). The influence of CSR and ethical self-identity in consumer evaluation of cobrands. *Journal of Business Ethics, 138*(2), 311–326.

Sparks, P., & Shepherd, R. (1992). Self-identity and the theory of planned behavior: Assessing the role of identification with green consumerism. *Social Psychology Quarterly, 55*(4), 388–399.

Stern, R., Puoane, T., & Tsolekile, L. (2010). An exploration into the determinants of noncommunicable diseases among rural-to-urban migrants in Periurban South Africa. *Preventive Chronic Disease, 7*(6).

Strizhakova, Y., & Coulter, R. A. (2013). The "green" side of materialism in emerging BRIC and developed markets: The moderating role of global cultural identity. *International Journal of Research in Marketing, 30*(1), 69–82.

Strizhakova, Y., Coulter, R. A., & Price, L. L. (2008). Branded products as a passport to global citizenship: Perspectives from developed and developing countries. *Journal of International Marketing, 16*(4), 57–85.

Tandon, M., & Sethi, V. (2018). An analysis of the determinants of consumer purchase behavior towards Green FMCG products. *Journal of Marketing Management, 16*(3), 7–21.

Tanner, C., & Kast, S. (2003). Promoting sustainable consumption: Determinants of Green purchases by Swiss consumers. *Psychology & Marketing, 20*(10), 883–902.

Teng, C., & Wang, Y. (2015). Decisional factors driving organic food consumption generation of consumer purchase intentions. *British Food Journal, 117*(3), 1066–1081.

Torelli, C. J., Özsomer, A., Carvalho, S. W., Keh, H. T., & Maehle, N. (2012). Brand concepts as representations of human values: Do cultural congruity and compatibility between values matter? *Journal of Marketing, 76*(4), 92–108.

Tuorila, H. (1997). Attitudes as determinants of food consumption. *Encyclopedia of Human Biology, 1,* 599–606.

UNDP Human Development Report. (2019). *Beyond income, beyond averages, beyond today: Inequalities in human development in the 21st century.* UNDP.

Vamos, S., Okan, O., Sentell, T., & Rootman, I. (2020). Making a case for "education for health literacy": An international perspective. *International Journal of Environmental Research and Public Health, 17*(1436), 2–18.

Vyncke, P. (2002). Lifestyle segmentation: From attitudes, interests and opinions, to values, aesthetic styles, life visions and media preferences. *European Journal of Communication, 17*(4), 445–463.

Westjohn, S. A., Arnold, M. J., Magnusson, P., & Reynolds, K. (2016). The influence of regulatory focus on global consumption orientation and preference for global versus local consumer culture positioning. *Journal of International Marketing, 24*, 22–39.

Williams, H., Williams, R., Jr., & Omar, M. (2014). Gastro-tourism as destination branding in emerging markets. *International Journal of Leisure and Tourism Marketing, 4*(1), 1–8.

World Health Organization. (2020, April 1). Obesity and overweight. *World Health Organisation.* Retrieved from https://www.who.int/news-room/fact-sheets/detail/obesity-and-overweight

Wunsch, N. (2020, November 25). *Health and wellness food market value worldwide from 2016 to 2021.* Retrieved from Statista.com: https://www.statista.com/statistics/502267/global-health-and-wellness-food-market-value/

Xie, B., Wang, L., Yang, H., Wang, Y., & Zhang, M. (2015). Consumer perceptions and attitudes of organic food products in eastern China. *British Food Journal, 117*(3), 1105–1121.

9

Personal Branding

J. N. Halm

Introduction

The study of the phenomenon of personal branding is relatively recent (Zarkada, 2012). However, the practice is not new. Individuals have been engaged in some attempt at influencing the perceptions others have of them ever since the first humans started to communicate with each other. However, many of these attempts have been made without much strategy. Rampersad (2009) argues that everyone has a personal brand. However, most people are unaware of their personal brand and, therefore, do not manage their personal brand strategically and effectively.

The importance of a strong personal brand cannot be overemphasised. Chritton (2012) lists a number of benefits that an individual enjoys in the process of developing a personal brand. These include an increase in self-awareness and self-esteem, development, and one's visibility. A strong personal brand also empowers the individual to want to stand out rather

---

J. N. Halm (✉)
Grit Business Group, Accra, Ghana

than to fit in. With a great personal brand, an individual has control over his or her career. Since corporate brands love to associate with success, having a great personal brand can lead to prosperity for the individual. Finally, a great personal brand gives the individual a sense of fulfilment. Rampersad (2009) adds that a strong personal brand influences how people perceive the individual. It also creates an identity around the individual which makes them easier to recall.

With all that being said, it is imperative for individuals to put in as much effort as needed to create strong personal brands. The principal aim of this chapter is to present a review of the literature regarding various aspects of the concept of personal branding, as well as to provide readers with a way of adopting best practices regarding the subject matter.

This chapter will consider what constitutes branding and, more specifically, personal branding and the personal brand. It will also seek to assess the importance, process, and benefits of personal branding. The idea of a personal brand value is also discussed in this chapter. This chapter concludes with the best examples of personal brands from emerging economies.

Branding and Brands

The attempt to differentiate one product from another, the foundation of the practice of branding, can be traced as far back as 1300 BC (Keller, 2013). By placing distinguishing marks on pottery and other clay products such as lamps, early artisans practised an early form of branding. Through the centuries, these differentiating marks were left on many more products, including loaves of bread. Goldsmiths, silversmiths, and blacksmiths all began to place their marks on their products to ensure easy identification by their customers.

Among the many other products marked by owners were livestock, specifically cattle, and it is generally agreed that it is from marking out one owner's herd from another that the term "branding" came into existence. The practice of the time was to create a unique symbol or mark of cast iron, heat the mark until it was red-hot, and then sear the sides of the livestock with the iron mark, leaving behind a "brand". The word "brand" is said to have been derived from the Old Norse word *brandr*, which literally means "to burn" (Adamson, 2006; Interbrand Group, 1990; Verma, 2002).

There are several disagreements on the definition of a "brand", with several experts adding their own nuances to the definition (Kapferer, 2004). At its most basic, however, a brand refers to a name, term, design, symbol, or any other feature that identifies and differentiates one's offerings from those of others (Khan, 2009). Kapferer (2008) defines a brand as simply a name that influences buyers.

Conversely, a brand is much more.

In differentiating between a product and a brand, Verma (2002) asserts that whereas a product is a physical entity existing in a real world, a brand is a perceptual entity living in the mind of the consumer. The brand embodies the intangible aspects of the product or service, including all the emotions that are associated with or that are generated by that offering. Verma (2002) argues that taking consumers beyond the boundaries of logic and reasoning into the realm of emotions is what branding is all about.

The outward representation of the brand is meant to evoke pleasurable emotions in the consumer to cause one to make a favourable decision towards the brand. In this light, Dube (2011) defines a brand as an emotional perception experienced by a purchaser or consumer of goods and services. Middleton (2012) defines a brand as a set of meanings, arguing that the total of the meanings that a product has in the minds and hearts of consumers is the brand. McNally and Speak (2003) define a brand as "a perception or emotion, maintained by a buyer or a prospective buyer, describing the experience related to doing business with an organisation or consuming its products or services" (p. 4).

The importance of branding is clearly seen in the value placed on brands. It has been argued that the brand is the most valuable and most important asset of a company (Ma'arif, 2008). There is evidence that some businesses have been bought for amounts that are in multiples of their book value simply because of the value of the brand. According to Batey (2008), in 1998, when Nestlé took over the Rowntree Mackintosh Confectionery in the United Kingdom, the price Nestlé paid was $1.5 billion more than the actual value of Rowntree.

It used to be that inanimate products and services were imbibed with human characteristics to create a brand. This is the basis of the Brand Personality Theory. Branding, however, is not limited to just the inert offerings of an organisation. Deckers and Lacy (2013) define a brand as "an emotional response to the image or name of a particular company, product, or person" (p. 7). Individuals can, therefore, also be branded, using the same approach as companies and their products and services. This is what Personal Branding is all about.

Personal Branding

Grzesiak (2018) traces the origins of personal branding as a phenomenon to the early work of Napoleon Hill in his 1937 globally acclaimed bestseller *Think and Grow Rich*. Hill drew a link between financial results and the ability to convince people based on the image of the individual. Clark (2013) claims that the publication of a cover story by Tom Peters in an August 1997 edition of *Fast Company* magazine, titled "The Brand Called You", advanced the concept of personal branding.

From the onset, the adoption of strategies used in building, marketing, and managing commercial brands to enhance the image of individuals was limited to individuals in the public space, such as politicians, scientists, entrepreneurs, royalty, and celebrities. However, times have changed. This has been mainly due to a new appreciation of personal branding.

Whether by design or by accident, every individual has a brand that has been developed over a period of time. Gujarathi and Kulkarni (2018) assert that our personal brands come with us from birth. However, not everyone is aware of the existence of their personal brand. Deming (2007) takes it further to state that every individual is a brand. Whether every individual is a brand or has a brand, the truth is that personal branding is very important for every individual. Kang (2013) states that extreme competition for jobs and the explosion of social media have propelled personal branding from something that was "nice to have" to something that is now a "got to do".

The emotional response is central to almost all definitions of personal branding (Ilieş, 2017). The process by which individuals are able to generate the right kind of emotional response when their names are mentioned or when they appear in public or online is what is referred to as *Personal Branding*. It is a deliberate effort aimed at ensuring that there is always a very specific response whenever the individual (or one's name, image, or symbol) is encountered. Personal branding is an individual's message to the world around that individual.

Gorbatov et al. (2018), after identifying a number of core attributes, define personal branding as "a strategic process of creating, positioning, and maintaining a positive impression of oneself, based in a unique combination of individual characteristics, which signal a certain promise to the target audience through a differentiated narrative and imagery" (p. 6).

McNally and Speak (2003) consider a brand as a relationship. Using that definition as a basis, they defined a personal brand as "a perception or emotion, maintained by somebody other than you, that describes the total experience of having a relationship with you" (p. 4).

Personal or Self-branding is everything an individual does to differentiate and market one's self, such as messages, self-presentation, and marketing tactics (Kaputa, 2005).

Nagpal and Hindustani (2017) define personal branding in terms of what unique value the individual can bring to an employer and what makes that individual different or unique. For employees, a successful personal brand has the potential to rub off on the employer. Customers and other stakeholders will see the organisation in a more positive light due to the presence of a well-branded individual within the ranks of the organisation. Lee (2012) argues that strongly branded employees end up being of help to their employers because they lend credibility to the organisation's efforts.

Incidentally, not everyone manages their brand strategically, effectively, and consistently (Waller, 2020). Kang (2013) describes a lack of a brand goal, strategy, and action plan in personal branding as akin to baking a cake without a recipe. The growing interest in the subject matter (Waller, 2020), however, has made more and more people conscious of and willing to do something about their personal brand. The tools that can turn an individual into a powerful brand are also readily available to all.

People have increasingly become aware that personal branding is not a creation of chance. They know that personal brands must be well-thought through and strategic in nature. Montoya (2002) describes this as the Age of Personal Branding—an age spawned, nurtured, and fed by the media. If the media is responsible for the birth and sustenance of personal branding, then consumers are responsible for providing the raw materials for sustaining personal brands.

Society has always been fascinated by celebrities and popular figures. Individuals with instant recognisability and high visibility are much admired, making them much sought after for endorsements. As consumers and organisations demand the latest celebrity to satisfy their insatiable hunger, the need for personal branding becomes more pronounced.

Individuals with strong personal brands are sought after because consumers tend to believe they know these individuals and, by extension, tend to trust what they say. Therefore, when such an individual endorses a product or becomes a spokesperson for or gives approval to a service or a cause, approval, purchase, and consumption tend to follow an upward trajectory.

Good personal branding eventually births a good personal brand.

The Personal Brand

According to Waller (2020), it is the individualisation of branding that has led to the rise in personal branding. Montoya (2002) defines a great personal brand as "a personal identity that stimulates precise, meaningful perceptions in its audience about the values and qualities that person stands for". A personal brand is a combination of the individual and all the values that accompany that individual as well as the emotions that their name generates in others.

Gorbatov et al. (2018) further define a personal brand as "a set of characteristics of an individual (attributes, values, beliefs, etc.) rendered into the differentiated narrative and imagery with the intent of establishing a competitive advantage in the minds of the target audience" (p. 6).

A personal brand can be viewed as a product that needs to be managed and marketed like any other product. Montoya (2002) describes a personal brand as a "one-person enterprise". Hence, it must be managed as a business. Nagpal and Hindustani (2017) discuss the four elements of the marketing mix—Product, Price, Placement, and Promotion—in relation to a personal brand. In this context, the individual is the product with unique features and a unique selling proposition. The price is the remuneration one receives for services provided. Placement is about the distribution of one's services. Services can be distributed in person, by phone, or online. Promotion of a personal brand is about communicating one's qualities to relevant stakeholders. Tools for promotion include advertising, sales promotion, PR, publicity, and events. The tools to be chosen to promote the personal brand depend on the individual in question and the results one desires to achieve.

In addition to the unique value an individual's personal brand brings to his or her employer, Nagpal and Hindustani (2017) list six other benefits of a personal brand.

* Establishing the individual's reputation as a thought leader in the industry
* Getting buy-in within the company for promotion
* Branding the individual as an expert
* Making it easier to network with top officials such as senior government officials
* Raising one's credibility among stakeholders such as customers and other institutions
* Making the individual into a celebrity in their own right

Rockefeller (2017) adds that not only does personal brand increase one's value in the marketplace and raise the individual's profile within the company, it also attracts like-minded clients and customers who identify with the brand. Personal brand ultimately results in an increase in financial returns.

According to Mobray (2009), what all great brands have in common is the ability to create an expectation of quality, superior benefits, and a defining experience. The advantage of a great brand in this regard is conveying these great qualities in a swift and consistent manner. Through consistent performance, a great brand is able to bypass or short-circuit the normal decision-making process of the average consumer. By extension, therefore, a great personal brand helps an individual to quickly establish an association between themself and a host of positive attributes.

Brands are able to earn trust through consistent performance over a period of time. In the same vein, great personal brands earn trust for individuals. An instantly recognisable personal brand ensures that the individual has less of a need to reiterate what they stand for. Expectations are based on the preconceived notions associated with one's personal brand.

Well-branded individuals are also now, more than ever, able to market themselves and monetise their personal brands using the magic of New Media. Personal branding is no more the exclusive right of sports and entertainment stars, successful entrepreneurs, or recognised business professionals.

Personal Branding in the Workplace

One trend that has become increasingly common in workplaces across the developing world is the increase in educational qualifications. With each passing year, many more qualified individuals are being added to the workforce. Individuals who desire to stand out must necessarily possess strong personal brands. Personal branding as a subject matter must be given serious consideration by both business schools and organisations alike. Having employees with strong personal brands is immensely beneficial for any organisation.

Personal Brand Equity

To be well-branded, one has to make real financial input. However, it is true that any investment made in successful personal branding yields the necessary returns. This leads to a discussion of the notion of Personal Brand Equity. Waller (2020) draws an inextricable link between brand equity and wealth, economic growth, and overall health of the company or individual to which the said brand is attached.

Personal brand equity is a measure of the current and future revenues of the individual in question. It is measured as follows:

$$\text{Brand Equity} = \text{Expectations} \times \text{Experiences} \times \text{Observations}$$

Expectations refer to what individuals anticipate you will do, experiences are what actually happens when people interact with you, and observations are the things people see and note when dealing with you (McNally & Speak, 2003).

The higher an individual's personal brand equity, the greater the future opportunities that are available to that individual. Non-branded individuals do not get the opportunities that are available to their well-branded colleagues.

McNally and Speak (2003), in defining a personal brand as a relationship, draw an analogy between a brand relationship and a bank account. Anytime something negative happens regarding the brand, a withdrawal is made from the relationship account. Whenever something positive happens in the relationship, a deposit is made into the personal brand account. As the relationship is strengthened, the account grows and even earns interest. Rampersad (2009) asserts that the relationship between the individual and its target audience is what builds brand equity, an accumulation of credibility, trust, and value over a period of time.

Personal Brand Loyalty

Buying decisions are said to be based predominantly on emotions. Rational justification comes after purchase. When individuals become emotionally attached to a personal brand, the result is a commitment to that personal brand and a willingness to act towards the brand in ways that might even defy logic. This is the basis of Personal Brand Loyalty.

Personal brand loyalty occurs when people become inspired by a personal brand to the point of defending the brand in any way necessary. When people find that they share common values with an individual, it becomes easier to be inspired by that brand. Personal brand loyalty can inspire individuals who have never met the branded individual.

Personal brand loyalty can be defined as a willingness of someone to make a personal sacrifice to strengthen a relationship with an individual's brand. People who are loyal to a personal brand will have no problem recommending the said brand to others. In making recommendations about personal brands, individuals make a sacrifice of putting their own reputations on the line. However, it is a sacrifice they are willing to make due to their loyalty to the brand. Without a doubt, brand loyalty accounts for the large following of the strongly branded. However, before the brand garners the kind of following that some command, it is important to consider the elements of a personal brand.

Personal Brand Elements

Putting together an effective brand requires an understanding of a number of elements. Orlic (2016) states that seven key elements are present in every effective personal brand.

- **Authenticity**

Effective brands are true to the character and being of the individual. According to Morgan (2012), being authentic means being who you say you are. Being authentic means doing what one says one will do—delivering on promises made to the brand's audience. With the multiplicity of individuals claiming to be experts in the marketplace, it helps if one is known for consistently delivering on one's promises.

- **Consistency**

Brands are built on the consistency of their actions (Halm, 2020). One-offs do not make a brand. As the brand engages with its audiences across multiple channels and platforms, it is important that it maintains consistency in its actions, packaging, and all of its communications—verbal and non-verbal.

Sellani (2007) points out that consumers rely on consistency. According to her, when the message changes frequently, the audience might be tempted to think that the individual has changed. Peck (2011) states that brand consistency is about communicating messages that do not detract or wander away from the brand's core proposition.

In practical terms, this means using the same or at least a similar logo, stylistic writing, or fonts for one's name, profile photograph, background, or cover images as well as colour schemes across all social media platforms. In many cases, it can mean using the same profile photograph for a long period of time to get audiences used to that look.

* **Story**

Every individual has a story. It is the narrative that traces one's rise from a certain period in the past to the present. For a personal brand to be effective, it must have a story that resonates with its core audience. Some of the most well-branded entertainers have a cult-like following because those people feel an emotional connection to the story of their idol.

The brand story must be brief and simple. Grams (2012) advocates the use of short brand films—at most, five to six minutes in length—to communicate the brand story. The advantage of using moving pictures is to capture an emotional and personal angle of one's story that cannot be adequately captured with words or still images.

* **Value Proposition**

People engage with a brand not just for the aesthetics. A brand must have something of value to offer. In exchange for the time and attention of its audience, a brand must be in a position to offer something valuable to its target audience. This is something that effective personal brands are able to communicate clearly to their audiences. There are certain individuals the mere mention of whose names summons up certain expectations.

* **Expertise**

According to Orlic (2016), it is the expertise of the individual that would keep people committed to the brand after they have been attracted by the value propositions and promotions. Effective brands communicate expertise in an area of vocation or profession. Waller (2020) states that the value of a personal brand built through expertise attaches to a person with expert opinions. Waller (2020) is, however, quick to point out the difference between those who have certain skills and talents that can make them leaders and those who are real "thought leaders". With a thought leader, the strength of the personal brand is less about one's image or lifestyle and more about one's knowledge.

- **Visibility**

Brands thrive on visibility. Montoya (2002) asserts that a great brand must be seen—consistently and repeatedly—by everyone in its domain. It seems apparent that visibility is a necessity when it comes to personal branding. An effective personal brand must be seen repeatedly until it leaves its imprint on the consciousness of its domain. Montoya (2002) even argues that visibility is more important than ability because it is only after the brand is known that the issue of performance comes into play.

- **Connections**

This is the element of the personal brand that has to do with the ability of the brand to employ networks to grow. For professionals who want to develop their careers, networking is valuable and should be considered an essential exercise in personal branding (Burtonshaw-Gunn, 2008). Connections also play a very important role in increasing the visibility of the brand. There are several paths individuals can traverse to connect with others, and by so doing increase their networks. These include joining professional bodies, attending conferences, and volunteering.

Social networking sites such as LinkedIn, Google+, Facebook, and Twitter provide a great opportunity for individuals to build their personal brands. LinkedIn has especially proven to be a good platform to showcase one's personal brand on professional social networking sites. McNally and Speak (2003) advise individuals to be proactive in adding to their social media networks so that they can learn from and be connected to people of influence and impact.

Steps (or Processes) in Personal Branding

Montoya (2002) asserts that personal branding involves the individual taking control and strategically managing the processes that affect how others view him or her. Personal brand development is about taking control of a process that is already taking place. Montoya (2002) argues that without a strategy for personal branding, all an individual has is a personal image. Personal Image is concentrated on just the external packaging of the individual. Personal Brand is much more: it is the external package as well as all the emotions that are generated in others when they see the individual or what he or she represents.

Step 1: Self-Evaluation

According to Montoya (2002), the most critical skill in personal brand development is brutal self-analysis. Mobray (2009) confirms that the first step in personal branding is to start with the "you" that the individual wants to project to the outside world. Eyre (2019) adds that a personal brand is about authenticity, derived from the individual's mind, heart, values, passions, imaginings, and whatever one believes to be true at the core of his or her personal and professional self. Authenticity is about credibility. People must be able to hold on to the word of the individual. This individual must be trusted to deliver as promised.

Hines (2004) prefers to view personal branding as "more in line with bringing forth self-knowledge and self-expression than the creation of a cultivated or false self". An intimate knowledge of one's self is therefore key to effective personal branding. A good SWOT Analysis or a "self-branding audit" on the individual is therefore needed to create a great personal brand.

According to Johnson (2019), four pieces must come together to create a great personal brand. These pieces that must fit like a puzzle are personal proof, social proof, association, and recognition. Personal proof is about undertaking a critical self-evaluation in areas such as one's education, experience, credentials, and achievements.

Mobray (2009) is, however, quick to point out that personal branding goes beyond what the individual does to the external self. Grooming and personal hygiene, important as they might be, are just an aspect of personal branding.

A good self-evaluation produces a list of key characteristics that the individual can refine into attributes. Personal characteristics include age, height, weight, skill, ethnic background, personality type, and education. In crafting a great personal brand, it is important that the characteristic that is of most relevance to the target audience is emphasised. In creating a powerful personal brand, there is nothing wrong with acknowledging personal flaws. According to Montoya (2002), all great brands have three to five attributes that are instantly recognisable to anyone who encounters that brand.

Step 2: Discover Your USP

A great brand must, however, have a leading attribute—one that is powerful with an emotional appeal that instantly enters an individual's mind when they encounter the brand. According to Kaputa (2005), personal branding is about finding one's Big Idea—an individual's unique selling proposition (USP). It is about discovering something special that sets that individual apart from others. It is about finding that X-factor.

What is it that the individual is offering? Is it going to make life better for others? Is it going to make life a little more interesting? Is it going to help others solve a pressing problem? Why should one's offering be considered above all others? The answers to these and many other questions are important for achieving one's USP.

Step 3: Know Your Target Audience

It is true that one cannot be all things to all people, which makes it imperative to identify one's target audience. The purpose of selecting a target audience is to ensure that the right message is crafted for the right audience. Specific audiences also demand specific marketing. Therefore, knowing the target audience enables brands to select the appropriate marketing strategy. Serrano (2017) states that in personal branding, three targets should be the focus. These include those who will pay you, those who influence those who pay you, and your supporters.

Demographic information to be gathered about the target audience includes socio-economic status, age, gender, educational level, and lifestyle. It is also important to know the things that the target audience wants as well as the challenges they face. This is critical because by knowing the aspirations and obstacles faced by the target audience, the individual is able to place the personal brand as a potential solution provider.

Step 4: Know the Competition

Chritton (2012) insists that to build a very solid personal brand, it is important to have an idea of one's competition. Who is also offering something along the same lines as that which the individual is offering, within the same organisation, same industry, or same locality?

Step 5: Craft a Personal Brand Profile

The reason for putting together a personal brand profile is to manage the perceptions others have of the individual. Chritton (2012) views this step as putting together the building blocks of the personal brand. The individual blocks needed include the following: *Needs, Values, Interests, Mission, Vision, Strengths, Freak Factor, Personality Attributes, Education and Work Experience, 360° Feedback, Goals,* and *Target Market Positioning Statement.* Chritton (2012) advocates placing these building blocks in table form to create the Personal Brand Profile.

Creating a personal brand profile also comes with creating an image for the brand. The image is the external features others identify with the individual. The image will be a reflection of the personal brand (Rampersad, 2015). Grzesiak (2018) argues that building a personal brand is about conscious image management, with image personalisation being the most important determinant of personal branding.

Step 6: Create a Balance Scorecard

Rampersad (2015) argues that personal branding will be of no use without goal-setting, continuous improvement of the individual, and a contribution on a day-to-day basis towards the brand. This stage of the personal branding process is the translation of personal ambition into an execution plan. According to Rampersad (2015), both personal ambition and personal brand are right-brain processes which are, by nature, emotional. Creating a Balance Scorecard, on the other hand, is a logical, left-brain action.

Step 7: Be and Remain Visible

This is where the individual repeatedly promotes the personal brand. Cantrice (2013) notes that an individual's personal brand needs to have high top-of-mind awareness, especially among those that the individual is trying to reach. The advice, however, is that promoting the brand must be done without it looking like an act of desperation. Promoting the brand must be tastefully executed.

Remaining visible is also about effective networking. The individual must be seen where it matters and must be seen with people who matter. Brown (2016) proposes a networking strategy which is Random, Accelerated, and "Piggy-backed". Random characterises the early stages of building the network when the individual is not too selective regarding who joins the network. Accelerated is about building and maintaining momentum. Piggy-backed involves using one's network to build one's network. Using this approach is one sure way to get on the radar of as many people as possible within a short span of time.

Building an Online Personal Brand

Frischmann (2014) has a simple but functional model for creating a good personal brand online. The online personal brand is created with a combination of three important elements: *skill set*, *aura*, and *identity*. The skill set refers to all the skills the individual has acquired through education, employment, and other experiences. Aura refers to the combination of the individual's personality, appearance, style, and charisma. Identity refers to the individual's connections and how they project onto one's networks via one's digital footprint.

Personal Branding in the Age of Social Media

A personal brand, successfully created, must be promoted. And what better way to do it than through the magic of social media? Social media has been found to be a very effective way of increasing one's brand presence and loyalty online (Lee, 2012). It is, by far, the fastest way for one to build and maintain one's network (Chritton, 2012).

Reed (2017) argues that for professionals the best place, by far, to showcase one's brand is LinkedIn. Deckers and Lacy (2013) describe the LinkedIn profile as "the window into your professional soul". The platform's popularity rests on the fact that it is solely used by professionals and is the best place for an individual to project a professional personal brand. Chritton (2012) advises all those interested in personal branding for professional purposes to have LinkedIn in their toolbox because the platform is "dynamic, interactive and current". Additionally, the platform provides the same opportunities for new entrants as it does for accomplished business professionals.

Grzesiak (2018) argues in favour of YouTube as the most effective for exerting influence, shaping the taste of viewers as well as shaping a personal image. Reasons given for YouTube's effectiveness include unbridled access to content and the ability to publish videos for free, low level of technical complexity, as well as ease of viewing. YouTube is also very effective for personal branding purposes because its appeal cuts across multiple cultures across the globe, its measurable penetration and scope of content distribution, and its immense popularity by providing many frequent users of the Internet an opportunity to shape their personal brands. Additionally, the production of videos for loading on the platform can be done with next to no budget and without the use of advanced video production and editing skills. Some of the videos that have garnered millions of views are done with nothing more than a mobile phone video camera.

Twitter provides individuals with an opportunity to share their thoughts with millions of readers. According to Deckers and Lacy (2013), Twitter is not only the quickest, easiest way to share information and content, it is also the perfect site for sharing the ideas and passions that make one a unique individual.

As a social media tool that is very personal, Facebook provides a unique opportunity for personal branding. Content shared on Facebook mostly concerns the individual's personal life. The platform is about connecting people and creating a community. The sense of community that is developed on Facebook can provide a backbone on which to launch one's personal brand using social media.

Blogging is another very effective way by which individuals can promote their personal brands. Short for web log, a blog is an online diary that one is willing to let others read and comment on (Deckers & Lacy, 2013). The usefulness of a blog lies in its ability to become the central hub around which the individual's personal brand revolves.

Regardless of the social media platform one chooses, Jain (2019) insists that the most important decision one has to make is choosing one's niche—the niche being the topic or content that one is trying to communicate to the target audience.

Personal Branding Examples from Emerging Markets

It is no coincidence that the best examples of personal brands also turn out to be those of the most successful individuals. This is because the objective of personal branding is to make the individual stand out and be known for something specific. Achieving this would normally result in the success of the individual.

It is, however, important to note that not all people considered in their various fields as very successful are well-branded. For a personal brand to be deemed successful, the element of instant recognisability must not be lost. In this sense, there are many individuals who are doing well in their chosen fields but whose names do not ring a bell to people outside their immediate spheres of influence. A look at the annual *Time* magazine 100 Most Influential People shows lists of very successful politicians, scientists, business people, activists, religious leaders, and so on whose names are lost on many people around the world.

Among the individuals who have been very successful at personal branding, and by so doing have achieved great success, are those from emerging and developing economies. These individuals include some of the most easily recognisable figures in various fields of endeavour such as commerce, sports, entertainment, and politics.

Aliko Dangote

Africa's richest man for ten years in a row, Aliko Dangote, is also one of the most recognised personal brands in the world. One factor that has helped the business magnate to build and maintain a very powerful personal brand is the fact that his business carries his personal name. With business interests spanning cement manufacturing, sugar refining, salt and seasonings, fertilizer, agriculture, automotive, refineries, energy, real estate, mining, shipping, logistics, etc., Dangote Group is a household name in more than ten countries across Africa.

Dangote's personal brand was given a huge global boost with the public announcement of his intended purchase of English Premier League team Arsenal FC. Although the dream is yet to materialise, the news alone was enough to get football lovers in general and supporters of Arsenal FC to begin to take note of the famous Nigerian billionaire.

The Aliko Dangote Foundation, the tycoon's private charitable foundation, has schemes and interventions in several areas including health, education, empowerment, and humanitarian relief. Such philanthropic works go a long way in developing an affinity for the Dangote brand.

Jack Ma

There is no doubt that the co-founder of e-commerce giant Alibaba Group is one of the world's most well-branded individuals. As a business magnate and investor, Jack Ma is the quintessential business brand. There is no ambiguity about what Mr Ma stands for—a free market economy characterised by entrepreneurship and innovation. In his presentations, he ensures that he leaves his target audience with no doubt about what he stands for.

It is also instructive to note that Jack Ma is also known for his philanthropic works. The Jack Ma Foundation has supported communities from various parts of the world, including China, Africa, Australia, and the Middle East.

Consistently regarded as one of the world's most powerful people, Jack Ma has managed to keep his personal brand alive through various conference speeches and online activities.

Priyanka Chopra

The winner of the Miss World 2000 pageant, Priyanka Chopra, is one of India's best known personal brands. She is also one of the highest-paid and most popular entertainers in the world. She has a large social media following, with 27.1 million Twitter followers, 54.7 million Facebook followers, as well as 64.8 million Instagram followers, as of June 2021.

Although Chopra's brand comes across as representing sophistication, she is also very strong on philanthropy. Through The Priyanka Chopra Foundation for Health and Education, she offers support for various causes. Her philanthropic work was given credence when she was appointed a UNICEF Goodwill Ambassador for Child Rights in August 2010.

Davido

Like those of other youthful influencers, the Davido brand is heavily reliant on social media for promotion. Davido's more than 8.7 million followers on Twitter as of January 2021 makes him one of the most followed African personalities on the social media platform.

The Davido brand is that of youth and wealth, characterised by his appearance in expensive attire, adorned with expensive watches and custom jewellery. Quite recently, the artist has added the element of care for humanity to the elements of his personal brand. Philanthropic acts such as directing all proceeds from the sale of his 2019 release D&G to aid in research to develop a vaccine against the Coronavirus responsible for the COVID-19 pandemic is one such initiative.

Neymar

With more than 146 million followers on his Instagram page, Brazilian football player Neymar is one of those personal brands that has greatly benefitted from the use of social media for personal branding. Additionally, he has a huge following on both Facebook (70 million) and Twitter (52 million), giving a combined following close to 270 million as of January 2021.

The evidence of the success of Neymar's brand is seen in the sheer number of product brands associated with him. As of January 2021, brands such as Beats Electronics, DAZN, Electronic Arts, Gillette, Mastercard, Nike, Red Bull, and TCL were all sponsors of Neymar.

Appealing mainly to a youthful audience, Neymar's brand represents fun and living the good life. This is evidenced in the photographs that are constantly shared on his social media platforms, as well as the music and videos on display.

Recommendations for Building Your Personal Brand

From the above examples, the following qualities can be gleaned:

- It pays to build one's personal brand around what one enjoys doing.
- For those in business, as long it is possible, use your personal name to push your corporate brand.
- Make as much use of social media as possible to get the brand into the consciousness of the target audience. It pays to have a presence on multiple social media platforms.
- Add philanthropy to one's activities. It endears the target market or audience to the personal brand.

Conclusion

To be well-branded as a person is to be in the position where the mere mention of your name evokes the right kind of emotional response. The advantages of an effective personal brand are numerous. The proof is visible in the lives of the many well-branded individuals we have in our various workplaces and countries. As can be deduced from the discussions in this chapter, acquiring a strong personal brand is a process that demands work on the part of the individual. However, in the end, a great personal brand will be worth all the effort because it will provide the visibility, authenticity, and credibility required to excel and achieve personal and career goals, making life easier. A great personal brand is indeed an asset worth having.

References

Adamson, A. P. (2006). *BrandSimple: How the best brands keep it simple and succeed*. Palgrave Macmillan.

Batey, M. (2008). *Brand meaning*. Routledge.

Brown, R. (2016). *Build your reputation: Grow your personal brand for career and business success*. John Wiley & Sons.

Burtonshaw-Gunn, S. A. (2008). *The essential management toolbox: Tools, models and notes for managers and consultants.* John Wiley & Sons.
Cantrice, D. (2013). *You! Branding yourself for success.* Regal Innovations.
Chritton, S. (2012). *Personal branding for dummies.* John Wiley & Sons.
Clark, D. (2013). *Reinventing you: Define your brand, imagine your future.* Harvard Business Review.
Deckers, E., & Lacy, K. (2013). *Personal branding. How to use social media to invent or reinvent yourself* (2nd ed.). Pearson Education.
Deming, S. (2007). *The brand who cried wolf: Deliver on your company's promise and create customers for life.* Wiley & Sons.
Dube, I. M. M. (2011). *Stand out by personal branding.* Business, Inc.
Eyre, M. (2019). *Being you: How to build your personal brand and confidence.* Exisle.
Frischmann, R. M. (2014). *Online personal brand: Skill set, aura, and identity.* CreateSpace.
Gorbatov, S., Khapova, S. N., & Lysova, E. I. (2018). Personal branding: Interdisciplinary systematic review and research Agenda. *Frontiers in Psychology, 9*(November), 1–17. https://doi.org/10.3389/fpsyg.2018.02238
Grams, C. (2012). *The Ad-free brand: Secrets to building successful brands in a digital world.* Que Publishing.
Grzesiak, M. (2018). *Personal brand creation in the digital age: Theory, research and practice.* Palgrave Macmillan/Springer.
Gujarathi, R., & Kulkarni, S. M. (2018). Personal branding an answer to employability: A conceptual need base analysis. *Review of Research, 7*(10), 1–10.
Halm, J. N. (2020). Twenty traits of customer service champions. In R. E. Hinson, O. Adeola, T. Lituchy, & A. F. O. Amartey (Eds.), *Customer service management in Africa: A strategic and operational perspective.* CRC Press.
Hines, A. (2004). The personal brand in futures. *Foresight, 6*(1), 60–61.
Ilieş, V. I. (2017). Personal branding. A theoretical framework. In I. Boldea & C. Sigmirean (Eds.), *Debating globalization. Identity, nation and dialogue. Proceedings of the international conference globalization, intercultural dialogue and national identity* (pp. 273–280). Tîrgu-Mureş.
Interbrand Group. (1990). *Brands: An international review.* Mercury Business.
Jain, S. (2019). *#BecomeABrand: Learn the art of branding yourself on social media with case studies & best practices.* Notion Press.
Johnson, C. (2019). *Platform: The art and science of personal branding.* Lorena Jones.

Kang, K. (2013). *Branding pays: The five-step system to reinvent your personal brand*. BrandingPays.

Kapferer, J.-N. (2004). *The new strategic brand management: Creating and sustaining brand equity* (3rd ed.). Kogan Page.

Kapferer, J.-N. (2008). *The new strategic brand management: Creating and sustaining brand equity* (4th ed.). Kogan Page.

Kaputa, C. (2005). *U R a brand! How smart people brand themselves for business success*. Davies-Black.

Keller, K. L. (2013). *Strategic brand management: Building, measuring, and managing brand equity* (4th ed.). Pearson Education.

Khan, B. (2009). Corporate brand management: Past, present and future. *Pranjana: The Journal of Management Awareness, 12*(1), 21–39.

Lee, C. T. (2012). *Good idea. Now what? How to move ideas to execution*. John Wiley & Sons.

Ma'arif, N. N. (2008). *The power of marketing: Practitioner perspectives in Asia*. Salemba Empat.

McNally, D., & Speak, K. D. (2003). *Be your own brand: A breakthrough formula for standing out from the crowd*. Berrett-Koehler.

Middleton, S. (2012). *Brand new you: Reinventing work, life & self through the power of personal branding*. Hay House.

Mobray, K. (2009). *The 10Ks of personal branding: Create a better you*. iUniverse.

Montoya, P. (2002). *The personal branding phenomenon: Realize greater influence, explosive income growth and rapid career advancement by applying the branding techniques of Michael, Martha & Oprah*. Peter Montoya, Inc.

Morgan, J. M. (2012). *Brand against the machine: How to build your brand, cut through the marketing noise, and stand out from the competition*. John Wiley & Sons.

Nagpal, A., & Hindustani, P. (2017). *Personal branding, storytelling and beyond*. StoryMirror.

Orlic, M. (2016, January). The 7 key elements of an effective personal brand. *Entrepreneur.com*, https://www.entrepreneur.com/article/280268

Peck, D. (2011). *Think before you engage: 100 questions to ask before starting a social media marketing campaign*. Wiley.

Rampersad, H. K. (2009). *Authentic personal branding: A new blueprint for building and aligning a powerful leadership brand*. Information Age Publishing.

Rampersad, H. K. (2015). *Authentic personal brand coaching: Entrepreneurial leadership brand coaching for sustainable high performance*. Information Age Publishing.

Reed, C. J. (2017). *Personal branding mastery for entrepreneurs.* Evolve Global.

Rockefeller, J. D. (2017). *Personal brand: How to grow a following, boost your career, and skyrocket your income with a powerful personal brand.* CreateSpace.

Sellani, S. (2007). *What's your BQ? Learn how 35 companies add customers, subtract competitors and multiply profits with brand quotient.* W Business Books.

Serrano, S. J. (2017). *Getting seen, getting heard: How to define your personal brand's target audience.* http://www.sysgen.com.ph/articles/define-your-personal-brand-audience/27319#:~:text=In%20personal%20branding%2C%20there%20are,Your%20supporters

Verma, H. V. (2002). *Brand management: Text and cases.* Excel.

Waller, T. (2020). *Personal brand management: Marketing human value.* Springer Nature Switzerland AG.

Zarkada, A. (2012). Concepts and constructs for personal branding: An exploratory literature review approach. *SSRN Electronic Journal.* https://doi.org/10.2139/ssrn.1994522

Part IV

Contemporary and Futuristic Approaches to Marketing Communications and Brand Development

10

Neuromarketing: The Role of the Executive Function in Consumer Behaviour

Chika Remigious Ezeugwu, Awele Achi, and Chikaodi Francisca Ezeugwu

Introduction

Every year, companies spend millions of dollars on advertising to achieve a competitive advantage (Mian et al., 2018; Venkatraman et al., 2015). This results from efforts to test different marketing strategies suitable for different products and services for varying consumers, depending on their ecosystem characteristics. Moreover, consumer marketing strategies

---

C. Remigious Ezeugwu (✉)
University of Cambridge, Cambridge, UK
e-mail: cre39@cam.ac.uk

A. Achi
The Open University, Milton Keynes, UK
e-mail: awele.achi@open.ac.uk

C. F. Ezeugwu
Enugu State University of Science and Technology, Enugu, Nigeria

have witnessed diverse qualitative and quantitative methods ranging from focused group interviews to self-report measures, with little attention to neuroscientific methods in emerging markets. Although studies exploring neuroscientific methods abound in high-income countries (see Büttner et al., 2014; Hoek et al., 2020; Lapierre, 2019; Lapierre & Rozendaal, 2019; Ohme et al., 2010; Peatfield et al., 2015; Rozendaal et al., 2011; Stipp & Woodard, 2011), the vast consumer environment in emerging markets is yet to witness copious research efforts in this area.

Twenty-first-century consumer behaviour in emerging markets is experiencing changing dynamics, and this is challenging to organisations' efforts to understand how consumers combine their cognition, emotion, and experiences to achieve heuristic decisions that inform their purchasing behaviour (Hsu, 2017; Stanton et al., 2017). New research efforts along this path are centred on how consumers choose between varieties of products and services from the same or different organisations, and this effort has led to a new way of thinking about how to better understand consumers' purchasing behaviour through the application of neuroscientific techniques to marketing (*neuromarketing*). This chapter intends to provide a theoretical linkage between a neuropsychological concept—executive function (EF)—and marketing and then extend this understanding of consumers' buying behaviour when exposed to marketing stimuli. Although rarely discussed, we argue that bringing EF into consumer behaviour and decision-making discourse is essential because of its relevance in understanding how consumers mentally evaluate marketing stimuli. We argue that this will enable organisations to enhance their brand management and develop new marketing campaigns and strategies for consumers in emerging markets.

Prior research suggests that when consumers are faced with choosing from different types of products or services, they completely eradicate available options until they arrive at their final choice (Cherubino et al., 2019; Kahneman et al., 2011; Stasi et al., 2018). This eradication may not be a reflex effort, but an outcome of varying conscious cognitive skills, which, if well understood by organisations, provide an avenue to reduce marketing failures and more consumer-focused campaigns. For instance, in choosing the best pen to buy, a consumer relies on previous information using their *working memory*, resisting the temptation to buy other pens, whether they are cheaper, more expensive, better, or worse (*inhibitory control*), and if their most wanted choice is not available, they *flexibly* satisfice to make their final choice through cognitive manipulations (Argyriou & Melewar, 2011; Diamond, 2013; Peatfield et al., 2015), which are all considered the consequences of EF.

Our chapter contributes to knowledge in two key ways. First, although several studies have examined how neuromarketing affects consumer response to marketing stimuli, few have explored the specific role of EF in successful marketing stimuli. Our chapter extends the neuromarketing and marketing strategy literature by theoretically highlighting the importance of EF in consumer responses to marketing stimuli, especially in emerging markets. Second, the chapter provides key insights into how marketing managers can leverage the distinct dimensions of EF to understand the complex and dynamic process of consumer behaviour in relation to responding to marketing strategies and campaigns.

The rest of our chapter is divided into three sections. We briefly explain the concept of EF and its relation to congruent and incongruent marketing techniques. Next, we discuss the importance of EF to marketing stimuli and show why organisations need to rethink marketing campaigns and strategies in emerging markets. In the final section, we provide a summary and the implications for future research directions.

Executive Function and Its Dimensions

Extant research has reported that EF is a critical factor when considering consumer decision-making (Lapierre, 2019; Peatfield et al., 2015; Wong & Mullan, 2009). Hence, researchers have argued for the need to study the importance of EF in advertising and consumer research (Büttner et al., 2014; Hoek et al., 2020; Lapierre, 2019; Lapierre & Rozendaal, 2019; Rozendaal et al., 2011). In basic terms, EF is an umbrella construct defined as the self-regulatory functions or control that directs and coordinates all emotional responses, overt behaviour, and cognitive activities (Diamond, 2013; Isquith et al., 2005). This definition considers EF as an engine for behaviour that involves conscious efforts, for example, deciding whether to or not buy an item. The EF literature has witnessed a plethora of research that focuses on individuals with cognitive dysfunctions and how this affects their personality and decision-making processes. This idea is obtained from the story of Phineas Gage, whose story set the stage for the neuroscience of decision-making (Doebel, 2020).

Also, past studies have focused on how this construct relates to children's school performance and longitudinally enhances getting and keeping a job (see Gathercole & Pickering, 2000; Gathercole et al., 2004) and adult behavioural dysfunction and decision-making (e.g. Blair et al., 2005). However, the extent to which this construct and its dimensions affect or impede emerging markets' consumer behaviour is still unclear. We explore EF dimensions and how they relate to consumer behaviours next.

Inhibitory Control

One dimension of EF, *Inhibitory control*, refers to the ability to inhibit pre-potent tendencies (Diamond, 2013; Kakoschke et al., 2015). That is, controlling oneself from behaving incongruently with what the individual believes to be the desired behaviour at a particular time. For instance, one may resist the temptation of buying what they never budgeted for even after positive evaluations. This type of behaviour reduces impulse buying, resulting from product information overload (Hausman, 2000; Spiteri Cornish, 2020), and can be detrimental to future buying behaviours.

Although we do not propose that organisations should design marketing campaigns to engage in unethical marketing (Sihem, 2013), we argue that altering a conservative notion of the consumer's beliefs or attitudes about a particular product or service is essential for marketing success (Johnson & Iyamu, 2019; Ndayizigamiye & Khoase, 2018). For instance, migrating from the traditional shopping styles to e-commerce is problematic for emerging market consumers, and one way to effectively initiate a migration process is to understand how their cognition works in initiating inhibitory or self-control when confronted with marketing campaigns introducing un/familiar products or services.

Inhibitory control is important when considering the stop-and-think or go/no go mechanisms underlie consumers' buying or purchase decisions (Büttner et al., 2014). For instance, Rozendaal et al. (2011) argued that most marketing campaigns fail when they cannot neutralise consumers' self-control mechanisms. Effective marketing stimuli will activate the stop-and-think mental processes that enable the consumer to evaluate what is offered against what is known or not known. Therefore, to inhibit one's behaviour towards a marketing campaign or product is to allow passage of the message without engagement (Büttner et al., 2014; Rozendaal et al., 2011). With a high level of inhibitory control, consumers disengage from marketing messages through *mental shifting* and adjust their responses through evaluation of the commercials, making the advertising messages less appealing (Holmberg, 2016). Thus, inhibitory control, which serves as a "cognitive brake", is important when considering driving marketing campaigns, especially in emerging markets (Hoek et al., 2020).

Working Memory

Another dimension of EF, which involves holding information temporarily in the mind while performing other mental activities, is called *working memory* (Alvino et al., 2019; Diamond, 2013). Working memory is central to understanding individual behaviour because it correlates with decision-making processes (Alvino et al., 2019; Diamond, 2013; Gruszka & Nęcka, 2017). Taking a cue from the dual-process theory of cognition, which proposes that humans process information using two distinctive systems—systems 1 and 2. We argue that the dual cognitive system enables and determines how and which information is filtered into the working memory because of its limited capacity.

Accordingly, system 1 involves intuitive and fast processes, while system 2 takes a slow but intuitive pathway (Chaiken & Ledgerwood, 2011; Kahneman et al., 2011). Although the two systems are distinctive, one cannot be used without the other when making decisions (Kahneman et al., 2011; Sanjari et al., 2017). System 1 is used when confronted with less risky information or information that is deemed trustworthy, while system 2 is reserved and used during risky behaviour (Kahneman et al., 2011). Therefore, we argue based on the dual-process assumptions that marketing campaigns that would be allowed into the working memory system by consumers are those they found to be congruent with their mental capacities to avoid cognitive dissonance (Sharma, 2014).

Working memory helps consumers recall a product or service and its features when making a purchasing decision, and this is dependent on whether the consumer is making an outright purchase or making a later decision (Alvino et al., 2019). For instance, after being exposed to an advertisement, the information received by the consumer, depending on which system is activated, is stored for a limited time (Diamond, 2013; Malenka et al., 2009), and then recalled when the product or similar products are encountered (online or offline).

Marketing aims in this regard, especially in emerging markets, will be to understand how consumers perceive the product or service offered. That is, whether it is threatening and not trusted, or welcoming and trusted, which in turn determines the cognitive system that will be activated in favour of or against the advertised products or services. Understanding how consumers perceive and store marketing information and its resultant effect on purchasing behaviour will determine whether a marketing campaign will be successful or not.

Cognitive Flexibility

The third EF dimension, *cognitive flexibility*, refers to the ability to switch between two simultaneous options concurrently (Adams, 2019; Diamond, 2013). For instance, consumers choose another product because they perceive it to be better in the presence or absence of their favourite choice. Cognitive flexibility could take the form of task switching (e.g. consumers picking a physical product over another at sight) or cognitive shifting (unconsciously preferring one product or service over another).

A simple way of explaining cognitive flexibility or shifting is through the A-not-B pathways. That is, what are the neural predictors of consumer purchases in the absence of their favourite choice? The essence of understanding this is to evaluate the processes involved in shifting from one decision to another and how this shifting takes place in the consciousness of the consumer before, during, and after purchases (Knutson et al., 2007). This understanding provides an avenue for marketers on how to shape and direct marketing campaigns in emerging markets.

Congruent and Incongruent Marketing and Executive Function

An influential framework by Mandler (1982) showed that consumers make sense of information (marketing stimuli) after thorough conscious or unconscious evaluation, which affects how they classify such information as congruent or incongruent. According to Mandler's proposition, a congruent campaign will influence positive schematic processing, which will conform to the consumer's expectations, thereby arousing positive feelings. These feelings enhance the working memory storage, lower unfavourable inhibitory control, and create chances for flexible thinking towards making a favourable evaluation of the product.

However, Jhang et al. (2012) suggest that consumers rate brands or services based on the categories congruency, moderately congruent, and extremely incongruent, especially when the brands are new and incompatible with what they are used to, an idea that is entrenched in Halkias and Kokkinaki (2014). We contend that understanding the mechanism of the cognitive processes could determine the framing of advertising messages that would enhance acceptability irrespective of whether the product is familiar or new.

For instance, cognitive flexibility has been reported to increase the possibility of making associative links across categories of information (incongruent and congruent) and to enhance the tendency to have different views about a stimulus (product/service) (De Dreu et al., 2008; Isen, 2001). Hence, we propose that in emerging markets, an organisation that understands that EF (inhibitory control, working memory, and cognitive flexibility) helps the consumer to solve mental incongruity relating to products or marketing messages would have a competitive advantage. This is because most consumers in emerging markets are more conservative and perhaps less receptive to new marketing campaigns, products, or services (Jhang et al., 2012).

Linking Executive Function Studies to Marketing Campaigns in Emerging Economies

As argued earlier, most traditional marketing methods are ineffective due to a lack of understanding of consumers' mental processes before, during, and after being exposed to marketing stimuli (Chaney et al., 2017; Çora, 2019). Accordingly, Shiv et al. (2005) suggest that a neuroscientific approach can address these problems by (a) providing neural-level evidence of consumer behaviours towards marketing stimuli, (b) reconceptualising the operationalisation of consumers' underlying processes for successful marketing campaigns, (c) providing confirmatory evidence about behavioural generalisation through neural exploration, (d) providing more continuous stable data for longitudinal reanalysis and usage, and (e) providing an avenue for robust and rigorous methodological approaches to studying consumer behaviour.

This approach eradicates systematic and methodological limitations common with most traditional means of exploring consumer responses by providing a neural understanding of how consumers will behave when deciding about consumption and what will make them behave or change behaviour in the same, similar, or different circumstances (Agarwal & Xavier, 2015; Shiv et al., 2005). The common variation found in traditional marketing approaches indicates that most obtained results are not ecologically generalisable due to disparity in consumer behavioural intention and actual behaviour. These challenges are often bypassed by a neural-level exploration, which in turn leads to an understanding of consumers' main motives for making a product/service choice (Falk et al., 2012; Walton, 2004).

Although there are arguments that some neuroscientific tools—for example, Electroencephalography, Event-Related Potential, P300, and Functional Magnetic Imaging—are expensive, the rapid dynamic developments in technology have eradicated this challenge, thereby making most of the neuroscientific tools accessible (Falk et al., 2012). Also, investment in these types of marketing techniques provides better marketing dividends than its cost (Agarwal & Xavier, 2015); most EF assessment tools (e.g. Stroop task, dimensional change card sorting) are easily accessible tasks designed to measure cognitive function with evidence showing their ecological validity (Diamond, 2013). Consequently, this provides an efficient and reliable avenue to neuroscientifically explore neural pathways of consumers' decision-making in emerging markets.

Moreover, Ariely and Berns (2010) argued that understanding neuroscientific concepts (e.g. EF) gives organisations a longitudinal advantage when designing or marketing a brand to potential and actual consumers. Therefore, emerging markets that are faced with varying brands can be well understood through mental-level data for marketing maximisation. Accordingly, Ariely and Berns (2010) proposed a framework that incorporates cognitive factors into marketing techniques, and we extend this argument by proposing that after emerging market feasibility choices and analysis, an EF assessment (neural-level measures) is essential to aid product design (prototyping and development), testing, delivery, feedback, and advertising before and after product launch. Our conceptual framework in Fig. 10.1 shows a link between EF and consumers' actual purchasing behaviour.

We draw on this framework to argue that emerging markets need a neural-level marketing approach for a proper understanding of consumers' behaviour, including their mental processes for self-control, storage for recall (working memory), and choosing between similar or contradictory brands (cognitive flexibility). Further, the neural-level processes of EF determine the regulatory processes including covert (unconscious) and overt (conscious) that take place when consumers are faced with brand choices.

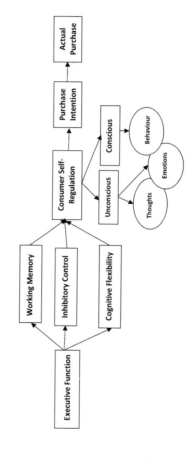

Fig. 10.1 Consumers' cognitive-behavioural processes for brand adoption in emerging markets

The essence of neuromarketing based on this model is to link consumers' thoughts and emotions (unobservable behaviour) and their influences on observable actions of intentional decisions and actual purchase. It is believed that conscious behaviour results from unconscious processes, and actual behaviour occurs when there is congruence between unconscious processes and observable stimuli (brands). For instance, when a consumer sees or hears an advertisement about a product/service, this information, as argued earlier, is stored and later recalled when there is a need to make purchase decisions about the product/service. Although the underlying unconscious processes are invisible to the advertiser or marketer, this plays a crucial role in influencing the actual purchase decision. Hence, our model explains these pathways by emphasising the need to understand and target the unconscious processes for better consumer understanding. The next section discusses why it is important to rethink marketing campaigns in emerging markets.

Rethinking Marketing Campaigns and Implications for Emerging Markets

Several empirically (e.g. Bruce et al., 2014; Lee et al., 2017; Lewinski, 2015; Santos et al., 2012) and conceptually (e.g. Koc & Boz, 2014; Lee et al., 2007) driven reasons exist to argue for the need to rethink how marketing strategies are executed in emerging markets. First, limitations on the use of traditional means of marketing have been accounted for, and researchers have instead advocated for a shift in the marketing approach towards neuromarketing (Ariely & Berns, 2010). However, drawing from Hernández-Fernández et al. (2019), we assert that a blend of these two approaches –

traditional means and neuromarketing—will be beneficial for emerging markets because of their cultural and economic characteristics. That is, data from self-report could be substantiated or refuted when compared to evidence from neuromarketing approaches (Venkatraman et al., 2015). In this case, one strengthens the other and provides robust justifications for marketing campaign decisions.

One core reason to rethink marketing strategies in emerging markets is cultural differences, which inform how the brain develops. This development enhances how campaign messages and brands are sensed and perceived (Sarma & Thomas, 2020). Because these sensations and perceptions are unconscious, it is difficult for marketing researchers adopting traditional techniques to understand how they underlie consumers' decision-making processes and how they switch between decisions. Thus, we postulate that consumers are a fusion of rationality and irrationality, which, when understood as a combination of neural basis and traditional marketing strategies, can provide better results for marketing campaigns in emerging markets.

This understanding provides a logical way of thinking beyond correlational results to ecologically valid experimental evidence that leads to cause-effect explanations of marketing successes and failures. For example, we could use the neural-level analysis to determine how much of the marketing information can be remembered by consumers based on working memory procedures, or how they would react to contradictory or similar products, and/or flexibly switch off or on during a marketing message. This empirical basis helps marketing managers to determine where to focus more on their campaign strategies for organisational growth.

We have argued that neuromarketing provides marketers, managers, and organisations with the opportunity to understand the affect–cognition–behaviour relationship and have drawn insights from EF, a neuropsychological construct. Though our arguments have contrasted with traditional means of marketing campaigns, they offer new insight into how marketing campaigns should be refashioned in emerging markets. Therefore, we rely on supporting neuroscientific evidence to propose a shift in the way emerging market consumers are perceived in the marketing ecosystem for brand acceptance and organisational growth. We predict that this approach will create an avenue for a better marketing intervention for existing and new organisations. To buttress our arguments, we present a case study in the appendix that shows how a company adopted a neuromarketing technique to solve their challenges. We conclude with our views on future research directions.

Conclusion and Future Research Directions

Until recently, organisations and marketing scholars relied on interviews, focus group discussion, and self-report measures to understand the behaviour of consumers. The emergence of neuromarketing has provided the much-needed means for organisations to understand neural-level processes of consumer responses to marketing stimuli.

As indicated in the case presented in the appendix, neuromarketing research has been reported to be useful in consumer research, and we advocate for the need to investigate and understand EF as a neuroscientific concept to leverage for competitive advantage via consumer responses to marketing campaigns. This is because of its advantages in exploring consumers' self-regulation, working memory, and flexible conscious and unconscious behaviour. We argue that researchers, managers, marketers, and the organisation need to acknowledge how important it is to have this insight and then take it further to start applying it in their marketing strategy. Since marketing is essential to business growth, understanding the EF-marketing pathways will provide robust marketing strategies, especially in emerging markets.

Nevertheless, advocating for more ecologically valid marketing measures through neuromarketing studies of EF does not imply that the traditional means should be abandoned. Nor do we argue that it should be condemned. We are aware that organisations use tools they are familiar with, and we recommend that marketing managers relearn the importance of neuromarketing for their campaigns for brand adoption and scaling.

Finally, by identifying cognitive structures and their specific functions related to how they can affect consumers' reaction to marketing campaigns, future research can focus on examining the cognitive processes (EF) and challenges consumers can face in making sense of marketing campaigns for the individual dimensions of EF, as well as how marketing organisations can creatively resolve these obstacles especially in the face of worldwide pandemic recovery. We hope that our chapter is a step in the right direction that can help to spur interest in research examining and documenting the link between cognitive factors, consumer behaviour, and marketing campaigns in an emerging market context.

Appendix

Case Study: Lessons from a Marketing Organisation: How to Understand Consumers' Response Using Neuromarketing
Disclaimer: This hypothetical case study is provided for illustrative and teaching purposes only. The information in the case study does not represent an actual organisation or an actual organisation's experience. It is only meant to stimulate class discussion.

Company Ezy was founded in 1869 and is a leading manufacturer of canned foods in Sub-Saharan Africa and has a presence in other emerging market economies across the world. The company's marketing department had reported that their advertisement campaign for their newly launched canned soup was successful based on feedback obtained from a market research survey. However, this successful campaign did not translate to an increase in sales for the advertised products. Within three years (2005–2008) of product launch, Company Ezy's net sales witnessed a 20% increase with an operating profit of $2,000,000. However, there was a 5.2% decrease in their net sales in the fourth year with a net profit of $780,000, a 61% decrease compared to their previous fiscal year.

Company Ezy's management understood that their brand is a household name because of their history, but they are faced with how to engage consumers to buy their brand. They proposed redesigning their packaging but could not answer whether it was worthwhile since traditional marketing techniques could not tap into how consumers think or monitor their reactions to stimuli in real-time. The company needed an approach that could understand consumers' intent and actual behaviour when faced with the decision of choosing between their brand and other competing brands. They ultimately ended up using neuromarketing techniques.

They consulted a neuromarketing firm whose aim was to understand consumers' physiological and neurological responses when making buying decisions using brain imaging. The firm also aimed to study how long it takes consumers to store product information, resist the urge to pick competing brands, and choose from product ranges of Company Ezy's brand when their favourite is unavailable. The neuromarketing firm utilised breathing rates and heart rates at different levels, stages, and times to understand consumer responses that are transmitted as data. After a series of eye-tracking experiments with 40 consumers, they found that the original packaging invokes an emotional reaction but not enough to induce purchase. Thereafter, the consumers were also interviewed to corroborate the findings. Consumers affirmed that they could identify the company's logo, but the soup label did not look like hot soup, which made them forget it easily and move to buy other brands without hesitation.

The combination of the biometric data with the interview findings revealed that Company Ezy did not need to repackage their soup product but only needed to reduce the size of their company logo and increase the size of the hot soup logo, which would help show their canned soup product as hot rather than an ordinary one. This would help consumers to remember it more easily and to resist the urge to buy other brands. Company Ezy responded by using a smaller company logo and showing a picture of a 3D steamy soup on their label. In the following year, after adopting the recommendations, Company Ezy witnessed a 17% increase in their net sales.

References

Adams, H. (2019). *The role of executive function in impulsive consumer purchasing behavior*. Unpublished Doctoral Thesis. George State University. https://scholarworks.gsu.edu/psych_diss/207/

Agarwal, S., & Xavier, M. J. (2015). *Innovations in consumer science: Applications of neuro-scientific research tools. In Adoption of innovation* (pp. 25–42). Springer.

Alvino, L., van der Lubbe, R., Joosten, R. A., & Constantinides, E. (2019). Which wine do you prefer? An analysis on consumer behaviour and brain activity during a wine tasting experience. *Asia Pacific Journal of Marketing and Logistics, 32*(5), 1149–1170.

Argyriou, E., & Melewar, T. C. (2011). Consumer attitudes revisited: A review of attitude theory in marketing research. *International Journal of Management Reviews, 13*(4), 431–451.

Ariely, D., & Berns, G. S. (2010). Neuromarketing: The hope and hype of neuroimaging in business. *Nature Reviews Neuroscience, 11*(4), 284–292.

Blair, C., Zelazo, P. D., & Greenberg, M. T. (2005). The measurement of executive function in early childhood. *Developmental Neuropsychology, 28*(2), 561–571.

Bruce, A. S., Bruce, J. M., Black, W. R., Lepping, R. J., Henry, J. M., Cherry, J. B. C., ... Savage, C. R. (2014). Branding and a child's brain: An fMRI study of neural responses to logos. *Social Cognitive and Affective Neuroscience, 9*(1), 118–122.

Büttner, O. B., Florack, A., & Serfas, B. G. (2014). A dual-step and dual-process model of advertising effects: Implications for reducing the negative impact of advertising on children's consumption behaviour. *Journal of Consumer Policy, 37*(2), 161–182.

Chaiken, S., & Ledgerwood, A. (2011). A theory of heuristic and systematic information processing. *Handbook of Theories of Social Psychology, 1*, 246–166.

Chaney, D., Touzani, M., & Ben Slimane, K. (2017). Marketing to the (new) generations: Summary and perspectives. *Journal of Strategic Marketing, 25*(3), 179–189.

Cherubino, P., Martinez-Levy, A. C., Caratù, M., Cartocci, G., Di Flumeri, G., Modica, E., ... Trettel, A. (2019). Consumer behaviour through the eyes of neurophysiological measures: State-of-the-art and future trends. *Computational Intelligence and Neuroscience, 2019*, 1–41.

Çora, H. (2019). Strategic perspective in millennium companies. *TURAN-SAM, 11*(41), 335–346.

De Dreu, C. K., Baas, M., & Nijstad, B. A. (2008). Hedonic tone and activation level in the mood-creativity link: Toward a dual pathway to creativity model. *Journal of Personality and Social Psychology, 94*(5), 739.

Diamond, A. (2013). Executive functions. *Annual Review of Psychology, 64*, 135–168.

Doebel, S. (2020). Rethinking executive function and its development. *Perspectives on Psychological Science, 15*(4), 942–956.

Falk, E. B., Berkman, E. T., & Lieberman, M. D. (2012). From neural responses to population behavior: Neural focus group predicts population-level media effects. *Psychological Science, 23*(5), 439–445.

Gathercole, S. E., & Pickering, S. J. (2000). Working memory deficits in children with low achievements in the national curriculum at 7 years of age. *British Journal of Educational Psychology, 70*(2), 177–194.

Gathercole, S. E., Pickering, S. J., Knight, C., & Stegmann, Z. (2004). Working memory skills and educational attainment: Evidence from national curriculum assessments at 7 and 14 years of age. *Applied Cognitive Psychology: The Official Journal of the Society for Applied Research in Memory and Cognition, 18*(1), 1–16.

Gruszka, A., & Nęcka, E. (2017). Limitations of working memory capacity: The cognitive and social consequences. *European Management Journal, 35*(6), 776–784.

Halkias, G., & Kokkinaki, F. (2014). The degree of ad–brand incongruity and the distinction between schema-driven and stimulus-driven attitudes. *Journal of Advertising, 43*(4), 397–409.

Hausman, A. (2000). A multi-method investigation of consumer motivations in impulse buying behavior. *Journal of Consumer Marketing, 17*(5), 403–426.

Hernández-Fernández, A., Mora, E., & Hernández, M. I. V. (2019). When a new technological product launching fails: A multi-method approach of facial recognition and E-WOM sentiment analysis. *Physiology & Behavior, 200*, 130–138.

Hoek, R. W., Rozendaal, E., van Schie, H. T., & Buijzen, M. (2020). Inhibitory control moderates the relation between advertising literacy activation and advertising susceptibility. *Media Psychology, 11*, 1–31.

Holmberg, N. (2016). *Effects of online advertising on children's visual attention and task performance during free and goal-directed internet use: A media psychology approach to children's website interaction and advert distraction.* Lund University. https://doi.org/10.13140/RG.2.2.34031.64168

Hsu, M. (2017). Neuromarketing: Inside the mind of the consumer. *California Management Review, 59*(4), 5–22.

Isen, A. M. (2001). An influence of positive affect on decision making in complex situations: Theoretical issues with practical implications. *Journal of Consumer Psychology, 11*(2), 75–85.

Isquith, P. K., Crawford, J. S., Espy, K. A., & Gioia, G. A. (2005). Assessment of executive function in preschool-aged children. *Mental Retardation and Developmental Disabilities Research Reviews, 11*(3), 209–215.

Jhang, J. H., Grant, S. J., & Campbell, M. C. (2012). Get it? Got it. Good! Enhancing new product acceptance by facilitating resolution of extreme incongruity. *Journal of Marketing Research, 49*(2), 247–259.

Johnson, O., & Iyamu, T. (2019). Framework for the adoption of e-commerce: A case of South African retail grocery sector. *The Electronic Journal of Information Systems in Developing Countries, 85*(5), e12095.

Kahneman, D., Lovallo, D., & Sibony, O. (2011). Before you make that big decision. *Harvard Business Review, 89*(6), 50–60.

Kakoschke, N., Kemps, E., & Tiggemann, M. (2015). Combined effects of cognitive bias for food cues and poor inhibitory control on unhealthy food intake. *Appetite, 87*, 358–364.

Knutson, B., Rick, S., Wimmer, G. E., Prelec, D., & Loewenstein, G. (2007). Neural predictors of purchases. *Neuron, 53*(1), 147–156.

Koc, E., & Boz, H. (2014). Psychoneurobiochemistry of tourism marketing. *Tourism Management, 44*, 140–148.

Lapierre, M. A. (2019). Advertising literacy and executive function: Testing their influence on children's consumer behavior. *Media Psychology, 22*(1), 39–59.

Lapierre, M. A., & Rozendaal, E. (2019). A cross-national study examining the role of executive function and emotion regulation in the relationship between children's television exposure and consumer behavior. *Journal of Youth and Adolescence, 48*(10), 1980–2004.

Lee, N., Brandes, L., Chamberlain, L., & Senior, C. (2017). This is your brain on neuromarketing: Reflections on a decade of research. *Journal of Marketing Management, 33*(11–12), 878–892.

Lee, N., Broderick, A. J., & Chamberlain, L. (2007). What is 'neuromarketing'? A discussion and agenda for future research. *International Journal of Psychophysiology, 63*(2), 199–204.

Lewinski, P. (2015). Don't look blank, happy, or sad: Patterns of facial expressions of speakers in banks' YouTube videos predict video's popularity over time. *Journal of Neuroscience, Psychology, and Economics, 8*(4), 241–249.

Malenka, R. C., Nestler, E. J., & Hyman, S. E. (2009). Higher cognitive function and behavioral control. In *Molecular neuropharmacology: A foundation for clinical neuroscience* (pp. 313–321). McGraw-Hill Medical.

Mandler, G. (1982). The structure of value: Accounting for taste. In M. S. Clarke & S. T. Fiske (Eds.), *Perception, cognition and development: Interactional analysis* (pp. 3–36). Erlbaum.

Mian, G. M., Sharma, P., & Gul, F. A. (2018). Investor sentiment and advertising expenditure. *International Journal of Research in Marketing, 35*(4), 611–627.

Ndayizigamiye, P., & Khoase, R. G. (2018). Inhibitors of the adoption of e-commerce by SMMES in two South African cities. *International Journal of eBusiness and eGovernment Studies, 10*(1), 51–66.

Ohme, R., Reykowska, D., Wiener, D., & Choromanska, A. (2010). Application of frontal EEG asymmetry to advertising research. *Journal of Economic Psychology, 31*(5), 785–793.

Peatfield, N., Caulfield, J., Parkinson, J., & Intriligator, J. (2015). Brands and Inhibition: A Go/No-Go Task Reveals the Power of Brand Influence. *PloS one, 10*(11), e0141787.

Rozendaal, E., Lapierre, M. A., Van Reijmersdal, E. A., & Buijzen, M. (2011). Reconsidering advertising literacy as a defense against advertising effects. *Media Psychology, 14*(4), 333–354.

Sanjari, S. S., Jahn, S., & Boztug, Y. (2017). Dual-process theory and consumer response to front-of-package nutrition label formats. *Nutrition Reviews, 75*(11), 871–882.

Santos, J. P., Seixas, D., Brandão, S., & Moutinho, L. (2012). Neuroscience in branding: A functional magnetic resonance imaging study on brands implicit and explicit impressions. *Journal of Brand Management, 19*(9), 735–757.

Sarma, U. A., & Thomas, M. T. (2020). Breaking the limits of executive functions: Towards a sociocultural perspective. *Culture & Psychology, 26*(3), 358–368.

Sharma, M. K. (2014). The impact on consumer buying behaviour: Cognitive dissonance. *Global Journal of Finance and Management, 6*(9), 833–840.

Shiv, B., Carmon, Z., & Ariely, D. (2005). Placebo effects of marketing actions: Consumers may get what they pay for. *Journal of Marketing Research, 42*(4), 383–393.

Sihem, B. (2013). Marketing mix-an area of unethical practices? *British Journal of Marketing Studies, 1*(4), 20–28.

Spiteri Cornish, L. (2020). Why did I buy this? Consumers' post-impulse-consumption experience and its impact on the propensity for future impulse buying behaviour. *Journal of Consumer Behaviour, 19*(1), 36–46.

Stanton, S. J., Sinnott-Armstrong, W., & Huettel, S. A. (2017). Neuromarketing: Ethical implications of its use and potential misuse. *Journal of Business Ethics, 144*(4), 799–811.

Stasi, A., Songa, G., Mauri, M., Ciceri, A., Diotallevi, F., Nardone, G., & Russo, V. (2018). Neuromarketing empirical approaches and food choice: A systematic review. *Food Research International, 108*, 650–664.

Stipp, H., & Woodard, R. P. (2011). *Uncovering emotion: Using neuromarketing to increase ad effectiveness*. Advertising Research Foundation.

Venkatraman, V., Dimoka, A., Pavlou, P. A., Vo, K., Hampton, W., Bollinger, B., ... Winer, R. S. (2015). Predicting advertising success beyond traditional measures: New insights from neurophysiological methods and market response modeling. *Journal of Marketing Research, 52*(4), 436–452.

Walton, C. (2004, November 19). The brave new world of neuromarketing is here. *B&T Weekly (Australia)*, p. 22.

Wong, C. L., & Mullan, B. A. (2009). Predicting breakfast consumption: An application of the theory of planned behaviour and the investigation of past behaviour and executive function. *British Journal of Health Psychology, 14*(3), 489–504.

11

Advertising in Virtual Reality: A Hierarchy of Effects Paradigm

Ikeola J Bodunde and Eugene Ohu

Introduction

An organisation can achieve its marketing goals to the extent that it does better than its competitors in creating, communicating, and delivering value to its chosen target market, breaking through message and communication clutter (Srivastava & Dorsch, 2020; Kotler, 2000). Marketing communication has long moved beyond merely selling products or services, and instead focuses on using different media and tools to create a lasting impression and meaning in the minds of consumers. Advertising, aimed at increasing awareness about a brand or product, is one of the most prominent and widely used communication tools in marketing. One traditional definition renders it as a paid form of impersonal communication initiated by a known sponsor and deliberately targeted to an individual or a wider audience through the media. Advertising can

---

I. J Bodunde (✉) • E. Ohu
Lagos Business School, Pan-Atlantic University, Lagos, Nigeria
e-mail: ibodunde@lbs.edu.ng; eohu@lbs.edu.ng

© The Author(s), under exclusive license to Springer Nature Switzerland AG 2022
O. Adeola et al. (eds.), *Marketing Communications and Brand Development in Emerging Economies Volume I*, Palgrave Studies of Marketing in Emerging Economies,
https://doi.org/10.1007/978-3-030-88678-3_11

influence the audience through informing or reminding them of a brand's existence, or alternatively, through persuasion, help them differentiate a product or organisation from competitors in the same market (Fill, 2005). The goal of this influence or persuasion is usually to elicit responses, such as attitudinal or behavioural changes, that would result in an intention to purchase the product or service.

Advancements in the information and communication technologies of the Internet and social media have changed how advertisements are served and how consumers respond to them. New spatial computing technologies such as extended reality (XR) (which includes augmented reality-AR, virtual reality-VR, and mixed reality-MR) are growing increasingly popular (Kwok & Koh, 2021; Alcañiz et al., 2019). While VR takes the user into a virtual environment, AR overlays virtual content on the physical world, and MR combines virtual objects and environments with real objects and environments (Alcañiz et al., 2019). The foray of big tech companies like Facebook (with their Oculus Quest VR devices) into extended reality technologies is gradually making these innovative technologies cheaper and more accessible to the wider public. VR is also finding a growing use for entertainment, sports viewing, and training (Lupinek et al., 2021).

A major consideration for advertisers in choosing between one medium or another is how accurately they can measure the effectiveness of a particular campaign in capturing the desired attention. Lack of precision in the measures of effectiveness of some digital advertising has either discouraged or slowed down its adoption (Santoso et al., 2020; Yoo & Baek, 2017; Logan, 2016). Advertisers need detailed metrics of engagement and interest in order to determine the effectiveness of a particular advertising technique or medium. In traditional media such as newspapers, billboards, and television, such metrics include readership and viewer counts, manually or automatically acquired. Advertisers would take more advantage of the more interactive and immersive media technologies, if only they could adequately harness their potential and then, even better, be able to measure how effective they are in engaging consumers.

Extended reality technologies potentially have some superior features, and hence opportunities, that the more traditional advertising media do not have. VR is highly interactive, immersive, and engaging. The immersion is such that users feel almost physically transported into another world such that their participation and interaction in VR becomes almost as real as if it were taking place in their physical environment (Serrano et al., 2013). Furthermore, some VR devices (e.g. the HTC Vive Pro Eye) allow for the tracking and recording of eye movements, enabling advertisers to accurately measure the nature, type, and duration of eye contact with objects and services advertised in the medium.

Unfortunately, many advertisers are still using perspectives and strategies developed for traditional media to understand new media. The Hierarchy of Effects model (Lavidge & Steiner, 1961) describes the process of progression of learning and decision-making that consumers experience in response to an advertising message. Consumers move from the point of initial awareness of a product or service to becoming convinced, deciding whether to purchase or not. The Hierarchy of Effects model has traditionally been used to understand the consumer's decision-making journey, from knowing about the product to the moment of purchase. Studies abound (Powell et al., 2017; Wijaya, 2011; Olson & Thjømøe, 2009) about the application of this model to television and other traditional media, but there are limited studies on its application in virtual reality. Considering the huge potential of emerging technologies like VR, the Hierarchy of Effects model (HoE) can provide the needed framework to best understand the consumer decision-making pathway following their first encounter with a brand or product in this medium (Hazel & Kang, 2018).

The rest of the chapter proceeds as follows. After presenting an overview of advertising and virtual reality definitions, as well as conceptualisations of advertising in emerging markets, we address the traditional medium of advertising and then introduce virtual reality (VR). Against this background, and taking VR as a case study and exemplar of futuristic spatial computing technology for advertising, we suggest how the Hierarchy of Effects model offers a lens to understand better how consumers might be brought to interact with a brand presented through it. We believe that lessons drawn from applying HoE to VR suggest a pattern that can, to a great extent, be generalised to many emerging technologies (especially extended realities). The chapter concludes with some recommendations for organisations deploying virtual reality.

Advertising in an Emerging Market (the African Context)

Africa is an emerging but fast-growing market, and advertising is hugely important in reaching the continent's vast population of 1.3 billion people. From a general market or an economic perspective, emerging markets have one unique characteristic: their economy is growing rapidly, a fact shown by rising Gross Domestic Product (GDP), increased trade, as well as increased foreign reserves (Paul, 2020; Techo, 2018). Market size is an important determinant of economic progress, as shown by the BRICS (Brazil, Russia, India, China, and South Africa), which has seen growth spurred by market size. The aggregate GDP in emerging markets and developing economies including China is expected to grow by 5% in 2021 after a contraction of 2.6% in 2020. During the same period, some poorer economies are expected to experience a 3.3% increase in activities, after a contraction of 0.9% in 2020 (World Bank, 2021).

In spite of this growth in various economies, many brands still find it hard to succeed, and advertisers are having a hard time working in such markets. An increasingly diverse and complex world is a challenge for advertisers, who have to contend with multiple economic models, different types and sizes of social structures, firms, and marketing systems, as well as various purchasing habits and abilities (Makhlouf, 2019). Now that competitive advantage is shifting from low resource cost to technological capability, the survival of organisations will depend more and more on technological capabilities.

Advertising is a form of communication that continuously and subtly affects our daily lives, and in its pervasiveness, which we may be unaware of, reflects and sometimes manipulates our culture and influences our decisions (Swami & Dutta, 2010; Dyer, 2008). Various authors have suggested that we are each exposed to about 3500 advertisements daily (Dahlén & Edenius, 2007; Godin, 1999 in Richards & Curran, 2002), a number that varies depending on what is classified as advertising. "Advertising" has for a long time been described as every form of commercial, promotional activity, from sponsorship to email marketing (Schultz, 1995). Others (e.g. Osama Mohamed Abdelaziz, 2021; van der

Lans et al., 2021; Zgheib, 2017) view advertising as a way to differentiate one brand from the competition, while some consider it as a way to manipulate an audience (Kulikova et al., 2021; Katermina & Buyanova, 2020; Susser et al., 2019).

Each viewpoint presents only some aspects of the reality of "advertising". A single definition therefore lacks the required precision to distinguish advertising from other forms of marketing communication (Schultz, 2016; Bergkvist & Langner, 2017; Richards & Curran, 2002; Rust & Oliver, 1994). There is, however, one common "denominator" among these perspectives, which is that advertising is paid for and non-personal, there is a known sponsor, and it is disseminated through the mass media with a view to persuade or influence consumers or target audiences (Lamb Jr. et al., 2000; O'Guinn et al., 2000; Vanden Bergh & Katz, 1999). This is the definition of advertising adopted for the current study: a paid, non-personal communication by an identified sponsor, through the mass media to persuade or influence someone.

The technology frontier is becoming more sophisticated very fast. Extended reality (XR) is able to reproduce and render high-quality virtual environments and objects, making it a potential tool that can be used to generate, in consumers, experiences similar to what they would experience in the real world. By 2015, three three-year global projection of the number of VR users was 171 million people, with about 28 million of them estimated to be prepared to pay for the VR content they consume (Grudzewski et al., 2018).

Facebook is one of the big technology companies leading the way in extended reality innovations. As at 2020, the number of Facebook users in Africa was pegged at above 250 million subscribers (Internet World Stats, 2020). Another 2020 estimate put the number of Nigerian users of Facebook at 23 million (Statista, 2021). However, to date, Facebook does not have an office in Nigeria, the country with the largest population in Africa. Despite this, many Nigerians have Facebook's VR headset Oculus Quest (a virtual reality headset developed by Oculus, a division of Facebook), and the developer community around extended reality is growing. Facebook is currently experimenting with how to place advertising in VR games. The attempt has been met with varying degrees of success and acceptability by the public (BBC, 2021). It is therefore expected that a country with the highest population in Africa presents a huge advertising market for such big tech companies in VR. Highlighting some differences between a virtual experience and an "indirect" one offered by traditional advertising may further illustrate the exciting and richer advantages that the former offers.

Traditional Advertising Media

Traditional advertising began with the development of printing in the fifteenth and sixteenth centuries. A century later, weekly newspapers in London began publishing advertisements, a trend that reached its peak in the eighteenth century (Britannica, 2021). Television and radio became the most pervasive media in western industrialised nations. When in 1941 the first TV ad appeared by a company selling the Bulova wristwatch for four to nine dollars, it did not seem much like a revolution because only the 4000 people who had a TV in New York at that time were able to see it. The 10-second ad, which had a voiceover saying "Americans run on Bulova time", ran on the eve of the entry of the United States into World War II. The setting and timing made America stand out as a technology forerunner (Mertes, 2021). The Internet has now revolutionised advertising in a most dramatic and revolutionary way, changing how advertisements are broadcast and increasing exponentially the number of people who can see ads. It has also changed how consumers interact with ads, influencing how they are affected as a result.

Traditional media has been used to gather and disseminate news and information to a heterogeneous and dispersed audience, to set agendas and frames for conversations. Also, because traditional media are easily accessible, advertisers have continued to patronise them in order to reach as many people as possible within the shortest time.

Radio, television, and newspapers, among others, have been the traditional media platforms used by advertisers to make their goods and services known to a heterogeneous mass audience. However, traditional media is not able to connect more intimately and more directly with the target, but is rather more adept at delivering information. For this reason, it cannot be solely relied upon to reach the desired advertising target audience all the time (Papasolomou & Melanthiou, 2012). Traditional media also lacks interactivity as it is usually linear or uni-directional. Consumers are thus mostly at the receiving end of the information, with little input into what they receive. Product advertising is thus often linear, with one ad following the other and consumers viewing information in a predetermined sequence beyond their control.

The linear flow of information in traditional advertising media such as TV and newspapers stands in sharp contrast to more interactive media (Bezjian-Avery et al., 1998). Although we suggest that non-traditional advertising media would be richer and more persuasive, not all authors agree. Dahlén and Edenius (2007) argue that non-traditional adverts are not persuasive enough to make experimental subjects take action. Respondents in the Dahlén and Edenius (2007) study stated that they did not as readily form a mental representation of them as advertising. The authors argue that when the audience sees an advert, say on social media, it is less persuasive, as they do not consider it an advert but rather perceive it as publicity or mere information. However, when they see the same ad on TV, it feels more like an advertisement. Alcañiz et al. (2019) argue the opposite: that non-traditional advertising media provide a richer experience. According to them, a virtual environment provides a richer experience than traditional advertising and viewers tend to equate the advert with a direct experience. In other words, consumers may learn better in a virtual experience than in a direct experience. Therefore, both traditional and non-traditional advertisements should be seen as complementary and not in competition, as both contribute to actualising the advertising goals set by a brand.

Many people are distracted when they watch entertainment programmes on television. A study by Edelman Global Survey (2013) found that 96% of respondents simultaneously use a device while viewing entertainment on another device, and that of those, 51% do so regularly. Other factors that determine how people consume and their level of engagement with the advertised brand include their personality traits. Another is the "distance" between the viewer and the device. The more physically near the person is to the advertising image, the closer they are likely to feel towards it. This is greater with VR than with traditional media.

Virtual Reality

Virtual reality (VR), though in its early stages, is fast gaining ground and also attracting increasing attention in the mainstream media. VR is a virtual, three-dimensional, highly interactive, simulated, computer-generated environment where a real person can play an active agent role (Onyesolu & Eze, 2011; Mazuryk & Gervautz, 1999), depending on whether they are *observing* or *embodying* a character. The realism of the three-dimensional virtual environment is often enhanced with spatial sound, and sometimes with haptic feedback. Experiments are even under way to add smell to the VR experience (Wang et al., 2021; Munyan et al., 2016). VR may allow users to be brought in contact with virtual representations of other people, past and present, real or imaginary (Onyesolu & Eze, 2011; Isdale, 1998; Baieier, 1993). This multimedia environment is a virtually rendered digital space that the user sees, usually by wearing a VR "headset" designed as a head-mounted display (HMD). This has sensors that track the movements of the user's body and hands, which in turn can be used to move objects inside the virtual environment or to control the "movement" of the user's virtual representation (avatar) in VR. Thus, the virtual movements respond to the real-world movements of the user. A virtual environment in VR attempts to replace the elements and cues of the physical world with digital equivalents. In this way, VR is potentially more immersive and engaging than the physical world, which, in the best representation of VR, is completely blocked out (Fox et al., 2009).

VR simulates the natural stereoscopic viewing mechanism by digitally generating right-eye and left-eye images of any given object or scene in 3D. The information provided from both eyes helps the viewer's brain integrate the information to create the perception of 3D space (Ye et al., 2007; Wann et al., 1995;). Thus, VR technology creates the illusion in the mind of the user that the images shown on-screen have depth and presence, rather than being a flat image projected onto the screen. With this, they are able to perceive the objects projected more accurately, realistically, and precisely. VR affords a greater level of interactivity than traditional media. In VR, a user in a virtual space is able to engage within the environment and each action taken has an immediate and observable effect that the user can more tangibly relate to. The interactivity of VR keeps the user engaged cognitively and actively, unlike other passive media like television (Kim et al., 2021).

Advertising has continued to evolve along with technological innovations. Compared with traditional media, VR allows higher levels of interactivity and realism, which results in visual richness (Grudzewski et al., 2018; Van Kerrebroeck et al., 2017; Choi & Taylor, 2014). To achieve a more realistic presentation of products and services, image richness is an important factor to consider in marketing communication. Cheng, Chieng, and Chieng (2014) suggest that the richness of imagery can be affected by sound or animation. The realism of VR content can also positively affect consumers' attitudes towards the advertised brand and even stimulate purchase intentions.

The possibilities of VR are almost limitless. It is expected to herald several innovations that would impact human life and work in several different ways. Over 15 years ago, Cline predicted that VR would find its way into various aspects of human activity, with notable impacts on behaviour, cognition, and communication (Cline, 2005).

VR technology can change our daily lives—from how we communicate to how we spend our leisure time. VR is finding increasing use in sectors such as education, training, engineering, medicine, manufacturing, design evaluation, architecture and architectural walk-through, behavioural and clinical studies, physiotherapeutic treatment of psychological disorders, and entertainment and gaming (Halabi, 2020; Solmaz & Van Gerven, 2021; Safikhani et al., 2021; Brady et al., 2021; Teoh et al., 2021). VR technology is now widely recognised as a major breakthrough in technological advancement in science. Though still early days, many big tech companies (Facebook, Google, Apple, HTC, and Amazon) are injecting huge human and material resources into extended reality research and development. The billions of dollars expended thus far provide a glimpse of the projections they are making for the future of VR and other extended realities.

Features of VR that Support Advertising

4.1.1 Eye tracking. This feature (present in VR HMDs such as the HTC Vive Pro Eye or the Varjo VR-2 Pro) tracks the movement of the eye, recording its coordinates throughout the experience to indicate exactly what the viewer is seeing. For businesses and advertisers, determining the effectiveness of digital advertising has remained a key issue so that they can accurately determine how successful a medium is (Hall, 2020). Since eye movements have been linked to cognition, this feature would allow for the collation of more in-depth information about the user. It would also allow for more granular and precise monitoring and measurement of engagement with the object of advertising.

4.1.2 Immersion. VR is immersive. Users enter a virtual space, somewhat cut off from the physical world. The VR Head Mounted Display (HMD) covers their entire face, with headphones blocking out external sound, fully immersing the user in the VR world.

4.1.3 Physical Tracking and Live Rendering. During VR use, the device tracks the external and internal environment. By tracking the physical position and movement of the user, it is able to position the physical user within a defined virtual space. The computer continuously renders the digital images in accordance with the changes in the user's physical position around the play area. Thus, moving the physical head or body gives the illusion that one is actually moving in the virtual world. This synchronous and high-fidelity rendering of virtual imagery contributes to the experience of "presence" in VR, thus increasing the user's engagement with the advertised brand.

4.1.4 Interactivity. In VR, users can interact with digital objects the same way they do in real life (Kim et al., 2021; Vergari et al., 2021). They can "touch" digital objects, throw or lift them. Through the implementation of "physics" in VR, some of these motions respond appropriately to the amount of force exerted by the user, respecting the laws of physics (e.g. heavier objects move more slowly, or require both hands to lift). An example of this physics implementation can be found in the VR game *Boneworks* (Cameron, 2020).

Advertisements and Virtual Reality

In the field of cognitive and social psychology, VR has been dubbed the "empathy machine" (Hassan, 2020; Bujić et al., 2020). This is due to its ability (through transporting the user to a different virtual world) to take the perspective of people in some distant and remote place. Perspective-taking is possible by observing (in VR) other circumstances, or taking up the virtual body (embodying) of the within-VR character. Either way, perspective-taking illustrates virtual reality's visual power, which can be taken advantage of to increase a user's affinity and closeness to a product or brand. VR allows people to "escape" from the real world to a virtual one, thus finding application in industries like real estate, medicine, entertainment, and sports (Hassouneh & Brengman, 2015).

Due to its unique features, VR performs in a superior way some traditional advertising functions, such as informing, persuading, entertaining, educating, and providing social inspiration (Hamilton et al., 2021; Ahn, 2021; Spielmann & Orth, 2021). Using VR to create lasting impressions while achieving all the uses mentioned above can build a sense of value and loyalty to a brand.

A virtual world such as exists in VR allows for a flexible combination of different advertising methods in a single channel. Products can be "placed" as digital three-dimensional objects in VR, thus mimicking what happens in the real world with billboards or television. Advertising can also be placed as mini-games within a VR experience (Vedrashko, 2006).

A number of advertising agencies are now experimenting with VR In-Game Advertising (IGA), which is the placement of advertising in virtual reality experiences (Lupinek et al., 2021). One expected benefit of IGA over traditional advertisements is that consumers are less likely to multitask during game play. Apart from the long development cycle of video games, advertisers are still hesitant about embracing video games as an advertising platform due to the uncertainties surrounding accurate measures of advertising effectiveness in VR.

Another concern advertisers have with regard to integrating IGA into games is how to do this effectively without distracting the players and affecting their enjoyment of the game, which may alienate them from the advertised brand. Studies are still ongoing in search of empirical support for the influence that virtual reality communication has on message perception and attitude towards a brand (Grudzewski et al., 2018).

The interactive nature of VR allows users to relate to objects representing brands in novel ways. In VR, users (consumers) can pick up products and examine them from different angles in a more realistic manner using one or two hand-held controllers. Highly realistic images and videos are easily integrated into VR applications, allowing players to interact with a "hyper-realistic" model of a product virtually (Petit et al., 2019). This type of interaction mimics real-world interaction and facilitates consumer learning of the product and improved familiarity with the product. Virtual reality thus holds promise as a new medium for rich, varied advertising methods that are more immersive, more absorbing, and more interactive. VR ads can take the form of "placement" of the 3D depictions of a product within an educational experience, on billboards, during musical performances, in movies, as 360-degree videos, short video clips, and games, and through cross-promotional offers and activities.

Some VR Ad Placement Techniques

Advertisers are still experimenting to find the most effective ways to place ads within VR, while causing minimal disruption to the user. The less disruptive an ad is, the greater the chance that the user will not feel any aversion towards the brand represented. Three of the methods for placing ads in VR are:

- Playing a one-time video at the beginning of the VR experience (Lee & Faber, 2007).
- Embedding the brand or product in the VR experience so that participants interact actively with it as a natural part of the experience (Redondo, 2012).
- Having the user "enter" a VR "virtual room" in the course of the experience. A virtual room (a sub-app within a VR experience) may contain an environment, an object (representing the brand), and the interactions. Users will be encouraged to visit the room, usually in

exchange for some reward, such as game points if the VR experience is a gamified one.

Here is how the cross-platform game engine owners Unity Technologies describe an attempt at IGA: "The Ad appears in a natural part of the game's storyline. Never forced, the player has the ability to choose to enter into the room, in which they then become fully immersed in the brand's experience for 30-60 seconds. Upon completion, they receive some sort of reward or gift for viewing, creating a memorable experience" (Unity3D, 2019).

Hierarchy of Effects Model

The Hierarchy of Effects model describes how advertising influences a consumer's decision to purchase or not purchase a product or service. Determining the hierarchical processes in marketing allows us to predict behaviour and obtain information on what advertising strategy to adopt. This process should aid the organization and execution of tasks and the exercise of different functions (physical or conceptual) within a firm (Preston & Thorson, 1983; Barry & Howard, 1990). It was conceived by Lavidge and Steiner (1961) and is one of the leading theories in the marketing communication framework (Kucuk, 2017). This hierarchy depicts the sequence of consumer learning and decision-making experiences when they have come in contact with an advertisement. It is structuring of a product or service's advertising message objectives, such that a sale is made at the end. With the Hierarchy of Effects model, the advertising campaign objectives include awareness, knowledge, liking, preference, conviction, and purchase (Fig. 11.1).

Lavidge and Steiner (1961) represented the communication process in their hierarchy models. They saw advertising as a long-term investment that moves the consumer through various steps and stages over time, beginning with product awareness to the "knowledge", 'liking', and 'preference' and moving ultimately to actual purchase (Barry & Howard, 1990; Wijaya, 2015; Augustin & Liaw, 2020).

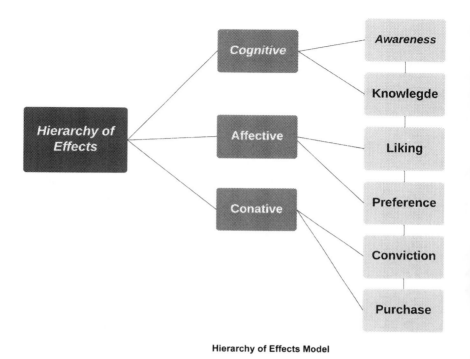

Fig. 11.1 Hierarchy of Effects models; Source: Adapted from Lavidge and Steiner

The model tries to explain the process through which advertising messages create an impact on the consumer. According to the model, the stages are grouped into three main processes. These are the cognitive, affective, and conative processes (Wensley, 2016). Cognitive implies that consumers have received the message and are aware of it. Message strategy in this area is used to create influence on customers' minds, beliefs, and knowledge. The affective process refers to consumers' attitudes and their reactions to the advertising messages. Message strategies invoke the feelings of customers, enhancing product likeability. The final process, conative, represents the actual purchase of the advertised product or service (Wijaya, 2015; Clow & Baack, 2007; Kerin & Hartley, 2015).

VR, Advertisement, and Hierarchy of Effects Model

The Hierarchy of Effects model (HoE) affords, through VR, a potentially better understanding of the customer through some unique features of the technology. According to the HoE, following an initial "meeting" with a brand, the customer follows six steps that should result in purchase or alienation. The steps are, chronologically: awareness, knowledge, liking, preference, conviction, and purchase (each successive pair representing respectively cognition, affection, and conation) (Miraki et al., 2021; Augustin & Liaw, 2020; Wijaya, 2015).

Compared to other technologies, such as TV, VR is potentially more immersive and interactive. A greater immersion, as is found in VR, means that the user feels more "present" in the virtual environment, resulting in an increased awareness of both the environment and the objects therein. Through subjective measures (surveys or interviews), or objective measures (eye-tracking features of high-end VR devices), advertisers are able to measure the degree of awareness attained by the user during the VR experience.

VR is also more interactive. Rather than passively "watching" the scenarios, users can more actively interact with the environment and objects as if in the physical world. Combined with the immersive property, such interactivity can potentially increase the user's theoretical and practical understanding of the brand within VR (knowledge). Like awareness, this knowledge can be captured through both subjective and objective measures, providing the second dimension of the Hierarchy of Effects model.

The realism of VR provided by a greater immersion and interactivity should increase the chances that a user will return to such VR experiences (Al-Ghamdi et al., 2020; Farah et al., 2019), with the result that they encounter the advertised brand more frequently. In the presence of alternatives, a user's decision to repeatedly interact with a particular VR experience may connote a greater liking and preference. This can provide measures of the third and fourth dimensions of the HoE, respectively. A greater liking and preference ought naturally to result in a greater conviction about a brand or product and ultimately purchase.

In one case of marketing communication in a more developed market, OREO, the largest brand owned by Mondelēz International in the United States, in 2016 ran a VR advertising campaign called "Wonder Vault" to launch a new product. The VR experience transported viewers into a magical land of milk rivers and cupcake-flavored Oreo biscuits. This phantasmagorical 360-degree experience was viewed with a cheap VR device made from cardboard (the Google VR Cardboard). This marked Oreo's first venture into VR (Sharma, 2020). Even though the VR viewer was not sophisticated, it still resulted in an increased awareness and knowledge about the new product, more people got to develop a liking for the product, and there was an increase in audience engagement. Ultimately, more than 3.6 million people who viewed it were enticed (Harwell, 2016).

HoE in VR

We illustrate HoE in VR with a hypothetical case. A game called *VR Sports Challenge* playable in the Oculus Rift allows a player the use of his virtual hands to play one of four sports: baseball, basketball, hockey, or American football. In the (virtual) playing field of the American football game, for example, the player sees an environment that looks like the real-life equivalent. Although the game has no VR advertisement, an advert could be placed across the stadium/arena advertising boards. To thus create awareness about a brand, the advert has to be engaging but simple. The realism of the VR experience already makes objects appear life-size and close, which positions the brand to be properly seen, thus ensuring awareness and knowledge—the *cognitive* process.

The *affective* stage is where the consumer builds a liking for what is being advertised and begins to consider the product's benefits. The uniqueness of the product and how it differs from others is also considered, helping the consumer make a choice. One feature of VR is the simulation of "presence", which is here influenced by an absorption of the user in the experience (Barnes, 2016). It can facilitate the *affective* stage where the total attention of the user is in the experience.

The *conative* stage is the behaviour or action stage of the process. This is when the consumer, after considering the benefits and costs, and having made a decision about their preference, then buys the real product after "coming out" of the virtual experience.

VR provides advertisers a further ability to arouse the player's desire towards increasing their conviction about purchasing the advertised product. One way to do this would be to allow the consumer to "test" or "feel" the product, both of which can be simulated in virtual reality, thus improving their confidence in their purchase decision-making.

Recommendations

Virtual reality promises to be a major component of a digital technology advertising future, and advertisers should therefore include it in their marketing plans. However, the novelty of the technology requires adequate skills and knowledge to enable advertisers to design and deploy it appropriately. This would require planning for the needed training and education of talents. For the HoE model, the advertisers deploying it in VR need to understand the right persuasive skills and deploy it for success.

VR experiences work well with storytelling. Advertisers using VR to increase brand awareness and affinity should consider embedding these within stories, which may have a greater chance of appealing to varied audiences, leading the consumer to thinking, feeling for the product, and then acting towards purchase.

VR can potentially be so real that users think they are in the physical world. Advertisers can take advantage of this by deliberately designing VR experiences that are as similar to the real brands as possible. This should increase brand recognition and potentially grow affinity.

Users' preferences often depend on their characteristics, such as demographic uniqueness. Advertisers in VR should invest in user-centric research in order to better adapt VR experiences to their uniqueness.

A device that is as immersive and interactive as VR potentially collects a huge amount of personal information of the users, often in real time. Adequate consideration should therefore be given to the privacy and security of user information, as well as protection of their right to privacy, especially among more vulnerable users, such as children.

Conclusion

Virtual reality (an expression of extended reality) presents a novel and potentially more engaging digital advertising medium. This chapter applies the Hierarchy of Effects model in a novel way to VR. We suggest that VR's inherent abilities to induce a more immersive perspective-taking and the more realistic interaction made possible with digital objects affords advertisers a better understanding of the cognitive, affective, and conative processes involved in users' interaction with a brand. This improved understanding should also cover the steps of awareness, knowledge, liking, preference, and conviction about the brand or product, hopefully leading to taking action: purchase.

Africa possesses one of the fastest-growing populations and markets. Its relatively young population is also one of the fastest adopters of digital technology, evidenced by many technology startups. The cost of consumer-grade VR is falling and, although it is still an innovative technology in Africa as in the rest of the world, since technology democratises digital access, the continent should prepare to *leapfrog* development by taking advantage of VR.

References

Ahn, S. J. (2021). 9 designing for persuasion through embodied experiences in virtual reality. In *Persuasive gaming in context* (pp. 163–180). Amsterdam University Press.

Alcañiz, M., Bigné, E., & Guixeres, J. (2019). Virtual reality in marketing: A framework, review, and research agenda. *Frontiers in Psychology, 10*, 1530.

Al-Ghamdi, N. A., Meyer, W. J., III, Atzori, B., Alhalabi, W., Seibel, C. C., Ullman, D., & Hoffman, H. G. (2020). Virtual reality analgesia with interactive eye tracking during brief thermal pain stimuli: A randomized controlled trial (crossover design). *Frontiers in Human Neuroscience, 13*, 467.

Augustin, J. L. P. M., & Liaw, S. Y. (2020). Exploring the relationship between perceived big data advantages and online consumers' behavior: An extended hierarchy of effects model. *International Business Research, 13*(6), 73–85.

Baieier, K. P. (1993). Virtual reality: Short introduction.

Barnes, S. (November 3, 2016). *Understanding virtual reality in marketing: Nature, implications and potential. Implications and Potential.* Retrieved from https://papers.ssrn.com/sol3/papers.cfm?abstract_id=2909100

BBC. (2021, June 18). Facebook tests ads in virtual reality headsets. Retrieved from https://www.bbc.com/news/technology-57526135

Bergkvist, L., & Langner, T. (2017). Construct measurement in advertising research. *Journal of Advertising, 46*(1), 129–140.

Bezjian-Avery, A., Calder, B., & Iacobucci, D. (1998). New media interactive advertising vs. traditional advertising. *Journal of Advertising Research, 38*, 23–32.

Brady, N., Lewis, J., McCreesh, K., Dejaco, B., & McVeigh, J. G. (2021). Physiotherapist beliefs and perspectives on virtual reality–supported rehabilitation for the assessment and management of musculoskeletal shoulder pain: A focus group study protocol. *HRB Open Research, 4*, 40.

Britannica, T. Editors of Encyclopaedia (2021, June 8). advertising. Encyclopedia Britannica. https://www.britannica.com/topic/advertising

Bujić, M., Salminen, M., Macey, J., & Hamari, J. (2020). "Empathy machine": how virtual reality affects human rights attitudes. Internet Research.

Cameron, P., (March 6, 2020). How "Classical Game Mechanics" and Physics Converge in VR Hit *Boneworks. Game Developer.* Retrieved from https://www.gamedeveloper.com/design/how-classical-game-mechanics-and-physics-converge-in-vr-hit-i-boneworks-i-

Choi, Y. K., & Taylor, C. R. (2014). How do 3-dimensional images promote products on the internet? *Journal of Business Research, 67*(10), 2164–2170.

Dahlén, M., & Edenius, M. (2007). When is advertising advertising? Comparing responses to non-traditional and traditional advertising media. *Journal of Current Issues & Research in Advertising, 29*(1), 33–42.

Dyer, G. (2008). *Advertising as communication.* Routledge.

Farah, M. F., Ramadan, Z. B., & Harb, D. H. (2019). The examination of virtual reality at the intersection of consumer experience, shopping journey and physical retailing. *Journal of Retailing and Consumer Services, 48*, 136–143.

Fill, C. (2005). *Marketing communications: Engagements, strategies and practice.* Pearson Education.

Fox, J., Arena, D., & Bailenson, J. N. (2009). Virtual reality: A survival guide for the social scientist. *Journal of Media Psychology, 21*(3), 95–113. https://adespresso.com/blog/virtual-reality-marketing/

Grudzewski, F., Awdziej, M., Mazurek, G., & Piotrowska, K. (2018). Virtual reality in marketing communication–the impact on the message, technology and offer perception–empirical study. *Economics and Business Review, 4*(3), 36–50.

Halabi, O. (2020). Immersive virtual reality to enforce teaching in engineering education. *Multimedia Tools and Applications, 79*(3), 2987–3004.

Hamilton, D., McKechnie, J., Edgerton, E., & Wilson, C. (2021). Immersive virtual reality as a pedagogical tool in education: A systematic literature review of quantitative learning outcomes and experimental design. *Journal of Computers in Education, 8*(1), 1–32.

Harwell, D. (2016, March 10). The creepy, inescapable advertisements that could define virtual reality https://www.washingtonpost.com/news/the-switch/wp/2016/03/10/the-creepy-inescapable-advertisements-that-could-define-virtual-reality/

Hassan, R. (2020). Digitality, virtual reality and the 'empathy machine'. *Digital Journalism, 8*(2), 195–212.

Hazel, D., & Kang, J. (2018). The contributions of perceived CSR information substantiality toward consumers' cognitive, affective, and conative responses: The hierarchy of effects model approach. *Clothing and Textiles Research Journal, 36*(2), 62–77.

Internet World Stats (March 31, 2020). *Internet Penetration in Africa.* Retrieved from https://www.internetworldstats.com/stats1.htm

Isdale, J. (1998). What is virtual reality. Virtual Reality Information Resources http://www.isx.com/~jisdale/WhatIsVr.html,4.

Katermina, V. V., & Buyanova, L. Y. (2020). Modern Russian Advertising Discourse: Semiotics, Mentality, Manipulation. In Proceedings of the Philological Readings (PhR 2019) (pp. 438–446).

Kim, J. H., Kim, M., Park, M., & Yoo, J. (2021). How interactivity and vividness influence consumer virtual reality shopping experience: The mediating role of telepresence. *Journal of Research in Interactive Marketing.*

Kotler, P. (2000). *Marketing management: The millennium edition* (Vol. 199). Prentice Hall.

Kulikova, E., Brusenskaya, L., & Yu, K. (2021). Linguolegal Expertise of Advertising and Media Criticism as a Means of Manipulation Countermeasure in the Media Space (in the Light of Laws" On Advertising" and" On Protection of Consumer Rights"). Медиаобразование (1).

Kwok, A. O., & Koh, S. G. (2021). COVID-19 and extended reality (XR). *Current Issues in Tourism, 24*(14), 1.

Lamb, C., Jr., Hair, J. F., Jr., & McDaniel, C. (2000). *Marketing* (5th ed.). South-Western College Publishing.

van der Lans, R., Pieters, R., & Wedel, M. (2021). Online Advertising Suppresses Visual Competition during Planned Purchases. Journal of Consumer Research.

Lavidge, R. J., & Steiner, G. A. (1961). A model for predictive measurements of advertising effectiveness. *Journal of Marketing, 25*(6), 59–62.

Lee, M., & Faber, R. J. (2007). Effects of product placement in on-line games on brand memory: A perspective of the limited-capacity model of attention. *Journal of Advertising, 36*(4), 75–90.

Logan, K. (2016). Have perceptions of internet advertising value changed over time? In American Academy of Advertising. Conference. Proceedings (Online) (p. 18). *American Academy of Advertising.*

Lupinek, J. M., Yoo, J., Ohu, E. A., & Bownlee, E. (2021). Congruity of virtual reality in-game advertising. *Front. Sports Act. Living, 3*, 728749. https://doi.org/10.3389/fspor.2021.728749

Makhlouf, H. H. (2019). Global advertising issues and challenges. *American International Journal of Business Management, 2*(6), 86–91.

Mazuryk, Tomasz, & Gervautz, Michael. (1999). Virtual Reality—History, Applications, Technology and Future. https://www.researchgate.net/publication/2617390_Virtual_Reality_-_History_Applications_Technology_and_Future

Miraki, M., Yektayar, M., & Esmaeily, N. (2021). Prioritization of Indicators and Integrated Marketing Communication Tools in The Iranian Clothing and Sports Equipment Industry Based On The Hierarchy Of Effects Model. *Communication Management in Sport Media.*

Munyan, B. G., Neer, S. M., Beidel, D. C., & Jentsch, F. (2016). Olfactory stimuli increase presence in virtual environments. *PLoS One, 11*(6), 1–19.

O'Guinn, T. C., Allen, C. T., & Semenik, R. J. (2000). *Advertising* (2nd ed.). South-Western.

Olson, E. L., & Thjømøe, H. M. (2009). Sponsorship effect metric: Assessing the financial value of sponsoring by comparisons to television advertising. *Journal of the Academy of Marketing Science, 37*(4), 504.

Onyesolu, Moses & Eze, Udoka. (2011). Understanding Virtual Reality Technology: Advances and Applications. https://doi.org/10.5772/15529. In book: *Advances in Computer Science and Engineering.*

Osama Mohamed Abdelaziz, A. (2021). Comparative advertising as a competitive tool for advertising institutions. *Journal of Intellectual Property and Innovation Management, 2*(2), 98–130.

Papasolomou, I., & Melanthiou, Y. (2012). Social media: Marketing public relations' new best friend. *Journal of Promotion Management, 18*(3), 319–328.

Paul, J. (2020). Marketing in emerging markets: A review, theoretical synthesis and extension. *International Journal of Emerging Markets, 15*(3), 446–468.

Petit, O., Velasco, C., & Spence, C. (2019). Digital sensory marketing: Integrating new technologies into multisensory online experience. *Journal of Interactive Marketing, 45*, 42–61.

Powell, L. M., Wada, R., Khan, T., & Emery, S. L. (2017). Food and beverage television advertising exposure and youth consumption, body mass index and adiposity outcomes. *Canadian Journal of Economics/Revue canadienne d'économique, 50*(2), 345–364.

Redondo, I. (2012). The effectiveness of casual advergames on adolescents' brand attitudes. *European Journal of Marketing, 46*(11/12), 1671–1688.

Richards, J. I., & Curran, C. M. (2002). Oracles on "advertising": Searching for a definition. *Journal of Advertising, 31*(2), 63–77.

Rust, R. T., & Oliver, R. W. (1994). The death of advertising. *Journal of Advertising, 23*(4), 71–77.

Safikhani, S., Pirker, J., & Wriessnegger, S. C. (2021, May). Virtual Reality Applications for the Treatment of Anxiety and Mental Disorders. In *2021 7th International Conference of the Immersive Learning Research Network (iLRN)* (pp. 1–8). IEEE.

Santoso, I., Wright, M., Trinh, G., & Avis, M. (2020). Is digital advertising effective under conditions of low attention? *Journal of Marketing Management, 36*(17–18), 1707–1730.

Schultz, D. E. (1995). From the editor. Understanding the new research needs.

Schultz, D. (2016). The future of advertising or whatever we're going to call it. *Journal of Advertising, 45*(3), 276–285.

Serrano, B., Botella, C., Baños, R. M., & Alcañiz, M. (2013). Using virtual reality and mood-induction procedures to test products with consumers of ceramic tiles. *Computers in Human Behavior, 29*(3), 648–653.

Sharma, A. (2020, November 3). *6 Virtual Reality Use Cases Every Business Should Know*. Geekflare. Retrieved from https://geekflare.com/virtual-reality-use-cases/

Solmaz, S., & Van Gerven, T. (2021). Automated integration of extract-based CFD results with AR/VR in engineering education for practitioners. *Multimedia Tools and Applications, 1,* 1–23.

Spielmann, N., & Orth, U. R. (2021). Can advertisers overcome consumer qualms with virtual reality?: Increasing operational transparency through self-guided 360-degree tours. *Journal of Advertising Research, 61*(2), 147–163.

Srivastava, R. K., & Dorsch, M. J. (2020). Understanding the viability of three types of approach of advertising in emerging markets. *Journal of Marketing Communications, 26*(8), 799–812.

Statista. (2021, August 23). Number of Facebook users in Nigeria from 2017 to 2026. Retrieved from https://www.statista.com/statistics/972927/number-of-facebook-users-nigeria/

Susser, D., Roessler, B., & Nissenbaum, H. (2019). Technology, autonomy, and manipulation. *Internet Policy Review, 8*(2).

Swami, S., & Dutta, A. (2010). Advertising strategies for new product diffusion in emerging markets: Propositions and analysis. *European Journal of Operational Research, 204*(3), 648–661.

Techo, V. (2018). Introduction to Emerging International Markets. https://doi.org/10.13140/RG.2.2.18491.72482. https://www.i-scoop.eu/evolutions-preferences-entertainment-content/

Teoh, S. E. M., Cao, Q., & Cai, Y. (2021). Learning to Take a Shower Through VR Serious Gaming. When VR Serious Games Meet Special Needs Education: Research, Development and Their Applications, 3–29.

Unity3D. (2019). Unity Ads. Retrieved August 25, 2020, from https://unity.com/solutions/unity-ads.

Van Kerrebroeck, H., Brengman, M., & Willems, K. (2017). Escaping the crowd: An experimental study on the impact of a virtual reality experience in a shopping mall. *Computers in Human Behavior, 77,* 437–450.

Vedrashko, I. (2006). Advertising in computer games (Doctoral dissertation, Massachusetts Institute of Technology).

Vergari, M., Kojić, T., Vona, F., Garzotto, F., Möller, S., & Voigt-Antons, J. N. (2021, March). Influence of Interactivity and Social Environments on User Experience and Social Acceptability in Virtual Reality. In *2021 IEEE Virtual Reality and 3D User Interfaces (VR)* (pp. 695–704). IEEE.

Wang, Q. J., Escobar, F. B., Da Mota, P. A., & Velasco, C. (2021). Getting started with virtual reality for sensory and consumer science: Current practices and future perspectives. *Food Research International, 145,* 110410.

Wann, J. P., Rushton, S., & Mon-Williams, M. (1995). Natural problems for stereoscopic depth perception in virtual environments. *Vision Research, 35*(19), 2731–2736.

Wijaya, B. S. (2011). New model of hierarchy of effects in advertising. *ISSIT 2011, 1*(1), 5–15.

Wijaya, B. S. (2015). The development of hierarchy of effects models in advertising. *International Research Journal of Business Studies, 5*(1), 1.

World Bank. (January 5, 2021). United States : Global Economy to Expand by 4% in 2021; Vaccine Deployment and Investment Key to Sustaining the Recovery. MENA Report, Albawaba (London) Ltd., Jan. 2021. Retrieved from https://www.worldbank.org/en/news/press-release/2021/01/05/global-economy-to-expand-by-4-percent-in-2021-vaccine-deployment-and-investment-key-to-sustaining-the-recovery

Ye, J., Badiyani, S., Raja, V., & Schlegel, T. (2007). Applications of virtual reality in product design evaluation. In *The international conference on human-computer interaction* (pp. 1190–1199). Springer / Heidelberg.

Yoo, C. Y., & Baek, T. H. (2017). Assessing the Financial Value of Digital Advertising. *Digital Advertising: Theory and Research*, 222.

Zgheib, P. W. (2017). Advertising deceit: Manipulation of information, false advertising, and promotion. In *Advertising and branding: Concepts, methodologies, tools, and applications* (pp. 1482–1494). IGI Global.

12

The Future of Marketing: Artificial Intelligence, Virtual Reality, and Neuromarketing

Ogechi Adeola, Olaniyi Evans, Jude Ndubuisi Edeh, and Isaiah Adisa

Introduction

"We always overestimate the change that will occur in the next two years and underestimate the change that will occur in the next ten. Don't let yourself be lulled into inaction."

O. Adeola (✉)
Lagos Business School, Pan-Atlantic University, Lagos, Nigeria
e-mail: oadeola@lbs.edu.ng

O. Evans
School of Management and Social Sciences, Pan-Atlantic University, Lagos, Nigeria

J. Ndubuisi Edeh
Kedge Business School Marseille, Marseille, France
e-mail: judede@alum.us.es

I. Adisa
Olabisi Onabajo University, Ago-Iwoye, Nigeria

In this often-cited quote, Microsoft founder Bill Gates encourages organisations to be more proactive and future-oriented in their strategies for technology adoption. These viewpoints are particularly relevant to marketing, as planning for future change has been acknowledged as the main challenge in both marketing research and practice, particularly in relation to new technologies (Shankar et al., 2011).

According to Stone et al. (2020), marketing has undergone several transformations over the decades and is likely to experience more phenomenal changes in the future. Consequently, the scope of the application of technologies in marketing will grow over time. Contemporary marketing research shows that the future of marketing will focus on artificial intelligence (AI), virtual reality (VR), and neuromarketing (e.g. Huang & Rust, 2021). This chapter contributes to knowledge first by reviewing literature on marketing-related AI, VR, and neuromarketing issues. Second, it provides guidance on how enhanced marketing outcomes can be achieved through the applications of these new technologies and tools. Finally, it draws on Stone et al.'s (2020) suggestion to integrate marketing literature into marketing-technology prediction.

Definitions of Key Concepts

Artificial Intelligence

Artificial intelligence (AI) is a form of intelligence displayed by machines (Wirth, 2018) using multiple technologies to enable computers to sense, comprehend, learn, and act, including procedures such as computational intelligence, natural language processing, machine learning, and knowledge representation (Awalegaonkar et al., 2019). The fact that AI is increasingly replacing and improving human thinking capability can be regarded as disruptive. Because AI can identify, merge, and analyse large, varied data types, it represents a remarkable revolution in marketing's capability to target individual customers.

Marketing tasks rely on intelligence, and AI is capable of analysing customers' buying patterns, designing advertisements to suit target customers, and setting proper pricing to maximise revenues generated from individual customers (Marinchak et al., 2018). AI deployment in marketing has gained importance due to increased computing power, reduced computing costs, the accessibility of big data, and the spread of machine learning algorithms. There are broad applications of AI in many areas of marketing. For instance, Amazon.com's Prime Air deploys drones to automate shipping and delivery. Lexus uses IBM Watson to script its TV commercial "Driven by Intuition". Considering its applications, it is believed that AI will change the future of marketing (Eriksson et al., 2020).

Virtual Reality

According to Craig, Sherman and Will (2009, p. 11), virtual reality (VR) is a "media comprising interactive 3D computer simulations that sense the participant's position and actions, provide synthetic feedback to one or more senses, [and yield] feeling immersed in the simulation". VR represents an important marketing tool, with many applications ranging from VR-based offerings (e.g. Disney Movies VR) and promotional tools (e.g. Coca-Cola's Virtual Locker Room), to distribution channels (e.g. Wayfair IdeaSpace). According to Hollebeek et al. (2020), VR can help potential customers better assess brands, especially where the customers are remote from the offering (e.g. e-commerce) or where 2D models fall short (e.g. tourism). VR can make traditional brand communications more experiential, providing a desirable "pre-consumption experience" that can boost consumers' attitudes towards brands. In a review of the VR-marketing literature, Alcañiz et al. (2019) suggest that VR marketing is an effective tool because of its capability to deepen consumer experiences. Therefore, by complementing or substituting with other marketing tools, VR can enrich customers' experiences, thereby providing key advantages to marketers (Dobrowolski et al., 2014).

Companies are increasingly using VR marketing practices (e.g. branded VR games) to promote their business (Jung & tom Dieck, 2017). Flavián et al. (2019) further conceptualise the importance of VR in marketing by incorporating it into the consumer hierarchy framework. These authors posit that technology can enhance consumer core experiences (e.g. product appraisal), making the experiences more valuable. For example, VR headsets allow users to interact with objects at a 360° angle in virtual space, a real-world simulation that enriches consumers' experience with the product (van Berlo et al., 2021).

Neuromarketing

Neuromarketing refers to an application of neuropsychology to market research, with the goal of studying consumers' cognitive responses to marketing stimuli (Sebastian, 2014). This psychosocial approach is increasingly shaping marketing research and practice. For example, conventional marketing tools for collecting and analysing consumer feedback are time-consuming, carry a high cost, and often yield inaccurate results (Malhotra & Dash, 2016). Compared to conventional techniques, neuromarketing can capture consumers' tacit cognitive and emotional responses to marketing stimuli, useful for the prediction of consumers' purchase decisions (Rawnaque et al., 2020).

Neuromarketing employs non-invasive brain signal recording techniques to gauge the response of a customer's brain to marketing stimuli, thus surpassing conventional survey methods (Vecchiato et al., 2011). Examples of neural recording devices commonly used in neuromarketing research are electroencephalography (EEG), functional magnetic resonance (fMRI), magnetoencephalography (MEG), positron emission tomography, transcranial magnetic stimulator, and functional near-infrared spectroscopy (fNIRS). Customers' cognitive and emotional responses (i.e. like/dislike, approach/withdrawal) can be examined by obtaining neuronal activity from the brain using these devices. Different stimuli activate associated responses in the human brain, and these responses can be tracked by observing the changes in neuronal signals (or brainwaves).

Contemporary Marketing Discourse

Artificial Intelligence

The marketing literature has delved into the general applications of AI (De Bruyn et al., 2020; Jarek & Mazurek, 2019; Ma & Sun, 2020; Wirth,

2018), the application of AI in strategic marketing decision-making (Eriksson et al., 2020; Stone et al., 2020), AI and branding (Jones, 2018; West et al., 2018), and development of a strategic framework for AI in marketing (Huang & Rust, 2021). Kiron and Schrage (2019) highlighted that the majority of the extant literature focuses on the strategic extension of AI in organisations, particularly in operational areas.

There are three main phases in the studies on AI. The first phase focuses on basic understanding of AI in marketing (e.g. Martínez-López & Casillas, 2013; Wierenga, 2010); the second phase considers the applications of AI in various marketing contexts (e.g. Rekha et al., 2016; Stone et al., 2017); the third phase addresses issues related to emerging technologies for predictive analytics, such as neural networks, big data, and machine learning (e.g. Chi-Hsien & Nagasawa, 2019; Liu, 2020). Table 12.1 offers summaries of recent studies on AI in marketing research.

Virtual Reality

Virtual reality is a useful tool for the prediction of consumer behaviour in real stores (Bigné et al., 2016; Vrechopoulos et al., 2009). Recent studies used a 3D web-based virtual supermarket to explore consumer behaviour (Waterlander et al., 2015) and high-immersive visual interfaces (based on head-mounted displays, HMDs) to examine consumer perceptions and purchasing behaviour (e.g. Bigné et al., 2018; Castellanos et al., 2018; Verhulst et al., 2017). The empirical evidence from recent VR marketing research suggests that VR marketing is largely effective at closing the gap between action and experience. For example, Tussyadiah et al. (2018) found positive effects of the use of VR marketing in a tourism context on consumers' attitudes and behavioural intentions. Comparable results were highlighted by Wang and Chen (2019), who suggest that product placements in VR videos foster interest in the products' brands and purchase intentions. In another study, Martínez-Navarro et al. (2019) showed the positive effect of VR in an e-commerce context on brand recall and purchase intention.

Table 12.2 summarises recent research on VR in marketing. These studies investigated strategies for marketing using VR games (Ho &

Table 12.1 Recent literature on AI in marketing

Authors	Focus/title	Findings	Comments/suggestions for future research
Wirth (2018)	Hello, marketing: What can artificial intelligence help you with?	It is time to embrace artificial intelligence. Marketing and data scientists can leverage a rich toolbox of predictive models and machine learning approaches.	Recent developments are calling for a more granular terminology than the two extremes of narrow artificial intelligence and full artificial intelligence.
Jones (2018)	Voice-activated change: Marketing in the age of artificial intelligence and virtual assistants	The focus for brands must be on the audience. This is something marketers ought to know, but it becomes important in the case of voice-activated assistants.	With the growth of AI and increasingly connected homes, users' decisions may be replaced with devices making decisions, providing curated answers, talking to each other, and employing machine learning to become more personalised. Marketers may find themselves marketing to these devices instead.
West et al. (2018)	"Alexa, Build me a Brand" An investigation into the impact of artificial intelligence on branding	AI can improve operational efficiency by improving the consistency with which a brand delivers its promise. Natural Language Processing can improve many elements of customer service. Machine learning enables personalised offerings, but organisations are constrained by data quality and quantity, and knowledge of the application of the technologies.	Future research should investigate the effect of AI technologies (automation, machine vision) and examine their effects on a broader range of brand elements (communications, loyalty, pricing) to establish other ways AI can be deployed to build brand value.

(continued)

Table 12.1 (continued)

Authors	Focus/title	Findings	Comments/suggestions for future research
Jarek and Mazurek (2019)	Marketing and artificial intelligence	AI is extensively introduced into the marketing domain, even though the applications are still at the operational level. AI affects all aspects of marketing mix, influencing both consumer value delivery and the marketing organisation (including the management).	There is a need for future research to examine the effect of AI on marketing, particularly the business effect.
Huang and Rust (2021)	A strategic framework for artificial intelligence in marketing	AI can be used for marketing research, strategic planning (segmentation, targeting, and positioning—STP), and actions.	N/A
Eriksson et al. (2020)	Think with me, or think for me? On the future role of artificial intelligence in marketing strategy formulation	AI can be deployed as an effective response to the external contingencies of large volumes of data and uncertain environmental conditions. It is, as well, an effective response to the external contingencies of constrained managerial cognition.	The barriers to use of AI (i.e. business culture, digital readiness) are worthy of further inquiry. It is necessary that future studies explore the contingencies of firms benefitting from deploying AI, thereby carrying out a cost-benefit analysis. Another important future consideration is a "creative-possibility perspective".

(continued)

Table 12.1 (continued)

Authors	Focus/title	Findings	Comments/suggestions for future research
Stone et al. (2020)	Artificial intelligence (AI) in strategic marketing decision-making: A research agenda	There is a critical need for more research, both to pilot how marketing academics train their students and prepare them for the marketing field, and to guide marketing, information technology, and strategy decision-makers on artificial intelligence investments, deployment and exploitation.	Other areas that require more research include how to maintain innovativeness in strategic marketing decision-making and planning in an AI-driven world.
De Bruyn et al. (2020)	Artificial intelligence and marketing: pitfalls and opportunities	AI will have a profound impact on predictive tasks that can be automated and demand little explanation.	AI will fall short of its promises in many respects in marketing domains if the challenges of tacit knowledge transfer between AI models and marketing organisations are not resolved.
Ma and Sun (2020)	Machine learning and AI in marketing–connecting computing power to human insights	The coming decades will witness the proliferation of automated AI agents powered by machine learning methods in every aspect of marketing, driven by big data, technology, and competition.	It is imperative to take advantage of the rich digital information to expand the understanding of firms and consumers, to address emerging issues in the marketing field, and to create scalable and automated decision support capacities that will be vital to business managers.

Source: Authors' compilation

Table 12.2 Recent literature on VR in marketing

Authors	Focus	Findings	Comments/ suggestions for future research
Ho and Zhang (2020)	Strategies for marketing really new products to the mass market: A text mining-based case study of virtual reality games	The marketing of a class of "really new products" may focus on its uniqueness upon initial introduction. It may shift from uniqueness to the new elements of each individual product as the newness of the class of "really new products" fades over time. In addition, the marketing strategies of "really new products" may experience an exploratory process after months (or years) of their initial launch.	Future research could expand the input to incorporate VR game screenshots and trailers.
Kong et al. (2020)	VR technology in marketing from the perspective of customer experience	The most direct impact factors of VR on the operation of strategic marketing models are immersion, conception, and customer buying behaviour. Product added value and brand design are indirect impact factors. Corporate profitability is the most important factor influencing the operation of marketing models.	N/A

(continued)

Table 12.2 (continued)

Authors	Focus	Findings	Comments/ suggestions for future research
van Berlo et al. (2021)	Brands in virtual reality games: Affective processes within computer-mediated consumer experiences	Virtual product appeal reinforces the influence of brands in VR games on brand attitude. Additionally, brands in VR games show emotional responses, which subsequently drive brand attitude and purchase intention.	Future research might manipulate specific attributes of an embedded virtual product (e.g. the image quality of the virtual product). It should explore whether the findings of van Berlo et al. (2021) corroborate different consumer learning situations as simulated in HMD VR.
Subawa et al. (2021)	The practices of virtual reality marketing in the tourism sector, a case study of Bali, Indonesia	There is hegemony in the practice of VR marketing to tourists and potential consumers, using major technology. The marketers practise the hegemony of VR marketing on tourists and potential customers. Tourism capitalism, as a chain link in the tourism industry, can be integrated into marketing through VR.	Subsequent studies are encouraged to perform a review of VR marketing in various regions so as to obtain a robust comparison, and there is a need to emphasise the readiness of government regulations that adopt VR marketing.
Zheng (2021)	Application of virtual reality technology in marketing training	The deployment of proper algorithms can foster the application of virtual reality technology in marketing training.	N/A

(continued)

Table 12.2 (continued)

Authors	Focus	Findings	Comments/ suggestions for future research
Sung et al. (2021)	The effectiveness of a marketing virtual reality learning simulation: A quantitative survey with psychophysiological measures	VR leads to a higher experience of immersion, learning attitude, and enjoyment. Further, immersion was found to mediate the positive effects of VR simulation on learning attitude, but not on enjoyment. Remarkably, students in the video performed better on the knowledge-based test than those in the VR.	The current prototype of VR simulations could be used as a supplementary resource to improve the learning attitude and enjoyment, but not as the major teaching material to foster knowledge-based performance in marketing.

Source: Authors' compilation

Zhang, 2020;), algorithms of VR technology in marketing training (van Berlo et al., 2021; Zheng, 2021), VR marketing from the perspective of the customer (Hollebeek et al., 2020; Kong et al., 2020), VR marketing in the tourism sector (Subawa et al., 2021), and marketing VR learning simulation (Sung et al., 2021). In the early 2000s, research into VR explored virtual worlds (which allowed navigation in virtual stores). Studies analysed the role of *Second Life*, launched in 2003, as a tool for virtual product sales (Jin & Bolebruch, 2009) and marketing research (Kaplan & Haenlein, 2009).

Neuromarketing

As technologies continue to advance, marketing stimuli are becoming more oriented towards TV commercials or images of the product (rather than the real product) (Boccia et al., 2019; Çakir et al., 2018; Shen et al., 2018). Three-dimensional images of products, especially e-commerce products, have contributed to virtual product purchase decision-making and have gained interest in the neuromarketing discourse (Çakar et al., 2017; Chew et al., 2015). Aside from marketing-focused stimuli, some studies (e.g. Ariely & Berns, 2010; Redcay & Schilbach, 2019; Shen & Morris, 2016) focused on social advertisements using neuroimaging and neural signal decoding techniques to examine and predict the success of their message. Analysis of consumers' emotional responses, an emphasis in recent neuromarketing research, utilises Frontal Alpha Asymmetry theory for right and left frontal channel as well as alpha, beta, and theta bands (to identify the cognitive and emotional response of the consumers).

Table 12.3 summarises recent research into the technological advancements and opportunities in neuromarketing (Dapkevičius & Melnikas, 2009; Rawnaque et al., 2020; Roth, 2014), neuromarketing in branding and advertisement (Hafez, 2019), neuromarketing applied to packaging (Juarez et al., 2020), neuromarketing in subliminal advertising (Hsu & Chen, 2020), and the decision to adopt neuromarketing techniques (Nilashi et al., 2020).

In the last half-decade of consumer neuroscience research, the use of EEG devices has become more prevalent than fMRI scanners. Whilst EEG is particularly employed in TV ad evaluation (where high resolution is needed to explore the dynamic effects of commercials), fMRI is used in the display of product images to explore consumers' purchase decisions. In fMRI-based neuromarketing research, the merit of using product images as marketing stimuli is that fMRI can identify the activated brain region the moment a consumer experiences a marketing stimulus. fNIRS has the advantage of mobility and is used in consumer reaction examination and purchase behaviour correlation (Çakir et al., 2018; Krampe et al., 2018). fNIRS is claimed to have an accuracy of over 70% and a reliability scale of 0.7 out of 1 (Çakir et al., 2018). fNIRS is therefore believed to have great potential in neural recording for future experiments in neuromarketing (Rawnaque et al., 2020).

Most of the EEG devices used in academic research are Emotiv Epoc, Emotive Epoc+, BrainAmp, eego Sports and NeuroSky MindWave. Over the last few years, fMRI-based neuromarketing research has employed 3-Tesla fMRI scanner Magnetom Trio, SIEMENS, and Siemens Verio scanner for experiments (Hubert et al., 2018). In most studies, signal pre-processing was

Table 12.3 Recent literature on neuromarketing

Authors	Focus	Findings	Comments/suggestions for future research
Dapkevičius and Melnikas (2009)	Influence of price and quality to customer satisfaction: neuromarketing approach	Neuromarketing is increasingly used and has future prospects in marketing research to enhance marketing strategies, ad campaigns, and brand building.	Some scholars believe that neuromarketing could lead to invasion of privacy and influence customers' purchase choices. Nevertheless, many companies will still utilise it in their marketing campaigns.
Hafez (2019)	Neuromarketing: a new avatar in branding and advertisement	If a stimuli-related brand or advertisement triggers the hippocampus, dorsolateral prefrontal cortex, and midbrain, customers will definitely purchase the brand. Ads should include deep emotional context so as to activate the emotional brain, which, in turn, can lead to a purchase decision.	Sometimes consumers cannot describe their true feelings and emotions for a particular brand or ad, which can be explored by neuromarketing.
Juarez et al. (2020)	Neuromarketing Applied to Educational Toy Packaging	The motivations in the process of buying educational toys are the graphic details of the packaging. Further, there is a significant social component when the product is bought as a gift for a third party.	It is considered necessary to examine other types of educational toys, in order for the results to be generalisable.

(continued)

Table 12.3 (continued)

Authors	Focus	Findings	Comments/suggestions for future research
Hsu and Chen (2020)	Neuromarketing, subliminal advertising, and hotel selection: An EEG study	Subliminal advertising significantly influences consumers' selection of hotels. An emoji smiling face (as a subliminal message) affects consumers' hotel choice. A consumer's theta band significantly increases while watching hotel videos with subliminal messages. A consumer's beta brainwave significantly decreases when videos are viewed with a smiling face emoji (as subliminal stimulus in the hotel video).	Future research utilising EEG on event-related potential (in the field of tourism and hospitality) can gain insights into the consumer's mind right from the moment they push the buy-button in their brain, as 80% of buying behaviours are determined on a subconscious or unconscious level.
Nilashi et al. (2020)	Decision to adopt neuromarketing techniques for sustainable product marketing: a fuzzy decision-making approach	The cost, usefulness, accuracy, time-saving, bias, deep probing of memory, quality of information, and emotions are neuromarketing advantages that significantly influence its adoption. Accuracy and bias are two factors that significantly influence green product suppliers in using neuromarketing advertising and branding.	Future studies should explore the relation between the techniques (i.e. fMRI, EEG, and MEG), neuromarketing factors, and neuromarketing contributions in the use of neuromarketing in green product marketing.

(continued)

Table 12.3 (continued)

Authors	Focus	Findings	Comments/suggestions for future research
Rawnaque et al. (2020)	Technological advancements and opportunities in Neuromarketing: a systematic review	Consumer goods are the prevalent marketing stimuli employed in both product and promotion forms in the literature. The trend in consumer emotion recognition-based experiments is to analyse frontal and prefrontal alpha band signals. EEG usage is favoured by researchers over fMRI in video advertisement-based neuromarketing experiments (this is perhaps attributable to its low cost and high time-resolution). Found in most of the studies are physiological response measuring techniques (e.g. eye tracking, heart rate monitoring), independent component analysis (e.g. artefact removal from neural signal), and consumer response prediction and classification (e.g. Artificial Neural Network, Support Vector Machine, and Linear Discriminant Analysis).	Among the brain signal recording devices, EEG is increasingly more popular in neuromarketing experiments (especially with television commercials analysis because of its high temporal resolution). However, EEG devices possess diverse sampling rates, leading to a limit for the highest analysable frequency. Future research should investigate this.

Source: Authors' compilation

performed via MATLAB and EEGLAB. A number of research experiments utilised AI algorithms for prediction and classification.

Discussion and Implications for Marketing Managers

Artificial Intelligence

The benefits of AI application to marketing managers' strategic decision-making in emerging markets are expected to include the following (Stone et al., 2020):

- Accelerated decision-making, particularly in the face of availability of new data or emergence of competitive threats, enabling companies to seize the benefits of stronger market positions ahead
- Detection of missing data
- Improved rationality, especially in the form of removal (or reduction) of cognitive bias by decision-makers
- A common basis for decision-making
- Learning from experience
- Improved quality management of marketing projects

The growth of AI applications in marketing can be said to be synchronous with the rapid advance of marketing technology, be it front-line marketing operations (e.g. contact centres) or the management of marketing resources. This development helps in the application and support of AI in marketing as it automates other aspects of marketing and generates usable data (Stone et al., 2020). The implication is that AI deployment can be integrated into various applications by taking data feeds automatically and providing feedback to those applications.

Early thinking on business-to-business marketing arose from companies who kept contact with customers via sales forces and then contact centres. However, the data richness of the current consumer market has led to marketing automation focused on consumer markets (Stone et al.,

2020). A larger part of business-to-business marketing is also becoming widely digitalised given its similarity to consumer marketing (especially where it entails marketing to small businesses). The implication is that advanced content management systems can be deployed to target content to suitable prospects and customers; then, the download and engagement of the content is tracked. By so doing, suppliers can prioritise customers who have shown interest in their service.

AI is driven by the availability of data. For example, giant web retailers (e.g. Amazon, eBay) and advertising platforms (e.g. Bing ads, YouTube) generate rich data regarding product and service purchasing. In contemporary markets, the larger percentage of consumer (and government) expenditure is on services. Depending on the degree of digitalisation, services yield richer data flows regarding consumer behaviour: "usage, not just purchase, can be or is tracked" (Stone et al., 2020, p. 5). Data richness is expanding (e.g. some motor insurance policies feature tracking devices which measure frequency and mode of usage), and marketers must take advantage of the opportunities.

In the future, it is expected that AI will be used in strategic decision-making concerning the markets to target, the type of products to market, the channels of communication and distribution to utilise, and the form of pricing and competitive positioning. According to Stone et al. (2020), the current focus is not primarily on the replacement of human decision-making in strategic decisions, but on the creation of higher-quality decision-making mechanisms, using AI, to more quickly provide marketers with more comprehensive information and options.

AI will fall short of its promises in many respects in marketing domains if the challenges of tacit knowledge transfer between AI models and marketing organisations are not resolved (De Bruyn et al., 2020). With the growth of AI and increasingly internet-connected homes, user decisions may be replaced by devices that employ machine learning for personalisation and curated answers. As a result, marketers may find themselves marketing to these devices instead of the users (Jones, 2018). It is therefore imperative to take advantage of the rich digital information to expand the understanding of firms and consumers, address emerging issues in the marketing field, and create scalable and automated decision support capacities vital to business managers (Ma & Sun, 2020).

Virtual Reality

One of the most important advantages of VR is that it can develop "consumer-product and consumer-context interactions that are not possible in the real world" (Alcañiz et al., 2019, p. 5). Virtual reality can be a perfect platform for experiential marketing (Loureiro et al., 2019), given the related technology that enhances consumer experiences (Jung et al., 2016). Managers, especially in emerging markets, should set up virtual flagship stores for promotion purposes. VR provides richer communication between the consumer and the product when compared to traditional advertising. Since VR enhances customer experiences from evaluation to the actual purchase, companies can obtain valuable insights from their actions. The virtual world is more interactive than traditional marketing communication tools and inspires customer engagement with the brand and the company. For example, SMEs in emerging markets can take advantage of VR by using virtual magazines as an alternative to the paper press.

In digital marketing, VR is identified as a critical digital technology that will lead to novel marketing prospects. In the future, the use of interactive immersive 3D virtual stores will become more popular. Two purchase channels will coexist: first, virtual stores where consumers can interact virtually with products and, second, physical stores where consumers can interact with real products (Alcañiz et al., 2019). The two complementary channels will shore up the new concept of omnichannel retailing (Verhoef et al., 2015). For example, tourism organisations can be more active in virtual worlds through the utilisation of 3D cities, hotels simulations to the real world's destinations.

Neuromarketing

Sometimes consumers cannot describe their true feelings about a particular brand or advert, but those emotions can be explored by neuromarketing (Hafez, 2019). Neuromarketing uses physiological signals (i.e. heart rate, eye tracking, and skin conductance measurements) to garner insights into audiences' physiological responses to stimuli. These neurophysiological signals can provide accurate portrayals of consumers' preferences (and likes/dislikes) using machine learning algorithms and advanced spectral analysis (Kroupi et al., 2014). Marketing managers, especially in emerging markets, can use neuromarketing to capture consumers' tacit cognitive and emotional responses to marketing stimuli and thus predict consumers' purchase decisions.

Some scholars argue that neuromarketing could lead to invasion of privacy and confuse customers' purchase choices. Nevertheless, many companies in emerging markets can still utilise it in their marketing campaigns (Dapkevičius & Melnikas, 2009) to measure and analyse the meanings of brainwaves using machine learning algorithms as well as signal and image processing techniques. The implication is that the buying behaviour can be detected, analysed, and predicted in marketing with the aid of brain–computer interface technologies that explore consumers' mental states (i.e. engagement, excitement, withdrawal) while experiencing the marketing stimuli (Izhikevich, 2003).

Direction for Future Research in Marketing Communications

Artificial Intelligence: Research into the deployment of AI in marketing has four main themes: (1) technical AI algorithms for the resolution of particular marketing problems (Capatina et al., 2020; Mogaji et al., 2020); (2) customers' reactions to AI (Gursoy et al., 2019; Xu et al., 2020); (3) effects of AI on society (Agrawal et al., 2019; Bag et al., 2021); and (4) managerial and strategic issues associated with AI (Eriksson et al., 2020; Huang & Rust, 2021). The fourth theme—managerial and strategic issues associated with AI—lacks a robust academic basis, even though some recent studies endeavour to address strategic marketing issues. Some examples include the deployment of machine learning for the prediction of mobile marketing personalisation (Tong et al., 2020) and AI for personalised customer engagement (Eriksson et al., 2020; Kumar et al., 2019; Overgoor et al., 2019).

In addition, recent research calls for more terminologies other than the two extremes of narrow artificial intelligence and full artificial intelligence (Wirth, 2018). Other areas that need further investigation include how to maintain innovativeness in strategic marketing decision-making and planning in an AI-driven world (Stone et al., 2020). Future research should investigate the effect of other AI technologies (e.g. automation, machine vision) and examine their effects on a broader range of brand elements (e.g. communications, loyalty, pricing) to establish other ways AI can be deployed to build brand value (West et al., 2018). The barriers to the use of AI (i.e. business culture, digital readiness) are worthy of further inquiry. Also, future research can explore contingencies for firms to benefit from using AI, and if its cost and required efforts are worth the advantages.

Virtual Reality: The literature regarding the use of VR in marketing is quite fragmented: "Perhaps this is due, in part, to the fact that it is a multidisciplinary field combining several research areas, such as social and technological sciences, with profound methodological differences" (Alcañiz et al., 2019, p. 11). Thus, it is vital to define a rigorous methodological framework that allows the classification of research activities in the field. In addition, most of the studies to date lack a certain level of methodological rigour in either their characterisation of VR technologies or the techniques used to characterise the consumer experience. This limits the generalisation of results in the literature.

The capacity of VR to produce new virtual realities will enable controlled laboratory experiments to study the factors that influence the acceptability of new products and the influence of the various attributes (e.g. age, gender, education, and location) of consumers on their purchase decisions. The current prototype of VR simulations could be used as a supplementary resource to improve learning attitudes and enjoyment, but not as the major teaching material to foster knowledge-based performance in marketing (Sung et al., 2021). Future research could expand the input to incorporate VR game screenshots and trailers (Ho & Zhang, 2020) or ways to manipulate specific attributes of an embedded virtual product (e.g. the image quality of the virtual product). Scholars should explore whether the findings of van Berlo et al. (2021) corroborate different consumer learning situations as simulated in HMD VR. Moreover, subsequent studies are encouraged to review VR marketing in various regions to obtain a robust comparison, and research is needed into the status of government regulations related to VR marketing (Subawa et al., 2021).

Neuromarketing: Research into neuromarketing implications involving product assessment and product purchase decision-making uses functional MRI to identify the activated region in the brain to predict interest in a product. To diagnose consumer engagement with a product, it will be worthwhile to employ EEG devices with high temporal resolution. While neuromarketing experiments using EEG devices of 32 channels and 14 channels have topped the research performance, data availability should be kept in mind in the selection of an EEG device. According to Rawnaque et al. (2020, p. 16), future research should consider the availability of "bilateral EEG electrodes if they would like to utilise frontal alpha asymmetry theory. Accompanying EEG, eye tracking has also shown high performance in attention and arousal locating". Eye trackers, galvanic skin response devices, and heart rate monitors can be used together with brain signals to confirm the experimental findings.

Future research using EEG on event-related potential (in the field of tourism and hospitality) should gain insights into the consumer's mind right at the moment they push the mental buy-button, as 80% of buying behaviours are determined on a subconscious level (Hsu & Chen, 2020). More studies can advance knowledge by exploring the relation between the techniques (i.e. fMRI, EEG, and MEG), neuromarketing factors, and neuromarketing contributions in areas such as green product marketing (Nilashi et al., 2020). For instance, EEG is increasingly becoming more popular among brain signal recording devices in neuromarketing experiments, particularly television commercials analysis, due to its high temporal resolution (Rawnaque et al., 2020). However, Rawnaque et al. suggest that as EEG devices possess diverse sampling rates, which can cause a limitation for the highest analysable frequency, this should be further investigated (Rawnaque et al., 2020). In addition, in-depth elaboration of a code of ethics for neuromarketing research is considered essential since this represents the main criticism of neuromarketing (Roth, 2014). Finally, studies can propose how firms in emerging markets can respond to the future realities of marketing communications by leveraging contemporary tools of artificial intelligence, virtual reality, and neuromarketing.

Conclusion

The chapter concludes that there are emerging trends in marketing communications that organisations must be aware of, and they must put in place strategic plans to take advantage of them. Several organisations are adopting artificial intelligence, virtual reality, and neuromarketing to make informed marketing decisions that will enhance the understanding of consumers' needs and behaviour and achieve competitive advantage. Organisations seeking market share in the emerging markets must not ignore the contemporary issues, future trends and technology-driven innovations in marketing communications.

References

Agrawal, A., Gans, J. S., & Goldfarb, A. (2019). Artificial intelligence: The ambiguous labor market impact of automating prediction. *Journal of Economic Perspectives, 33*(2), 31–50.

Alcañiz, M., Bigné, E., & Guixeres, J. (2019). Virtual reality in marketing: A framework, review, and research agenda. *Frontiers in Psychology, 10*, 1530.

Ariely, D., & Berns, G. S. (2010). Neuromarketing: The hope and hype of neuroimaging in business. *Nature Reviews Neuroscience, 11*(4), 284–292.

Awalegaonkar, K., Berkey, R., Douglass, G., & Reilly, A. (2019). AI: Built to scale. *Accenture.* www.accenture.com/gb-en/insights/artificial-intelligence/ai-investments

Bag, S., Gupta, S., Kumar, A., & Sivarajah, U. (2021). An integrated artificial intelligence framework for knowledge creation and B2B marketing rational decision making for improving firm performance. *Industrial Marketing Management, 92*, 178–189.

Bigné, E., Alcañiz, M., & Guixeres, J. (2018). *Visual attention in virtual reality settings*. World Marketing Congress.

Bigné, E., Llinares, C., & Torrecilla, C. (2016). Elapsed time on first buying triggers brand choices within a category: A virtual reality-based study. *J. Bus. Res., 69*, 1423–1427. https://doi.org/10.1016/j.jbusres.2015.10.119

Boccia, F., Malgeri Manzo, R., & Covino, D. (2019). Consumer behavior and corporate social responsibility: An evaluation by a choice experiment.

Corporate Social Responsibility and Environmental Management, 26, 97–105. https://doi.org/10.1002/csr.1661

Çakar, T., Rızvanoğlu, K., Öztürk, Ö., Çelik, D. Z., & Gürvardar, İ. (2017). The use of neurometric and biometric research methods in understanding the user experience during product search of first-time buyers in E-commerce. In *International conference of design, user experience, and usability* (pp. 342–362). Springer.

Çakir, M. P., Çakar, T., Girisken, Y., & Yurdakul, D. (2018). An investigation of the neural correlates of purchase behavior through fNIRS. *Eur J Mark, 52*(1/2), 224–243. https://doi.org/10.1108/EJM-12-2016-0864

Capatina, A., Kachour, M., Lichy, J., Micu, A., Micu, A. E., & Codignola, F. (2020). Matching the future capabilities of an artificial intelligence-based software for social media marketing with potential users' expectations. *Technological Forecasting and Social Change, 151,* 119794.

Castellanos, M. C., Ausin, J. M., Guixeres, J., & Bigné, E. (2018). Emotion in a 360-degree vs. traditional format through EDA, EEG and facial expressions. In V. Cauberghe, L. Hudders, & M. Eisend (Eds.), *Advances in Advertising Research IX* (pp. 3–15). Springer Gabler). https://doi.org/10.1007/978-3-658-22681-7_1

Chew, L. H., Teo, J., & Mountstephens, J. (2015). Aesthetic preference recognition of 3D shapes using EEG. *Cognit Neurodynamics, 10*(2), 165–173.

Chi-Hsien, K., & Nagasawa, S. (2019). Applying machine learning to market analysis: Knowing your luxury consumer. *Journal of Management Analytics, 6*(4), 404–419.

Craig, A., Sherman, W., & Will, J. (2009). *Developing virtual reality applications: Foundations of effective design.* Morgan-Kaufman.

Dapkevičius, A., & Melnikas, B. (2009). Influence of price and quality to customer satisfaction: Neuromarketing approach. *Mokslas–Lietuvos ateitis/Science–Future of Lithuania, 1*(3), 17–20.

De Bruyn, A., Viswanathan, V., Beh, Y. S., Brock, J. K. U., & von Wangenheim, F. (2020). Artificial intelligence and marketing: Pitfalls and opportunities. *Journal of Interactive Marketing, 51,* 91–105.

Dobrowolski, P., Pochwatko, G., Skorko, M., & Bielecki, M. (2014). The effects of virtual experience on attitudes toward real brands. *Cyberpsychology, Behavior, and Social Networking, 17*(2), 125–128.

Eriksson, T., Bigi, A., & Bonera, M. (2020). Think with me, or think for me? On the future role of artificial intelligence in marketing strategy formulation. *The TQM Journal, 32,* 795–814.

Flavián, C., Ibáñez-Sánchez, S., & Orús, C. (2019). The impact of virtual, augmented and mixed reality technologies on the customer experience. *Journal of Business Research, 100*, 547–560.

Gursoy, D., Chi, O. H., Lu, L., & Nunkoo, R. (2019). Consumers acceptance of artificially intelligent (AI) device use in service delivery. *International Journal of Information Management, 49*, 157–169.

Hafez, M. (2019). Neuromarketing: A new avatar in branding and advertisement. *Pacific Business Review International, 12*, 58–64.

Ho, J. C., & Zhang, X. (2020). Strategies for marketing really new products to the mass market: A text mining-based case study of virtual reality games. *Journal of Open Innovation: Technology, Market, and Complexity, 6*(1), 1.

Hollebeek, L. D., Clark, M. K., Andreassen, T. W., Sigurdsson, V., & Smith, D. (2020). Virtual reality through the customer journey: Framework and propositions. *Journal of Retailing and Consumer Services, 55*, 102056.

Hsu, L., & Chen, Y. J. (2020). Neuromarketing, subliminal advertising, and hotel selection: An EEG study. *Australasian Marketing Journal (AMJ), 28*(4), 200–208.

Huang, M. H., & Rust, R. T. (2021). A strategic framework for artificial intelligence in marketing. *Journal of the Academy of Marketing Science, 49*(1), 30–50.

Hubert, M., Linzmajer, M., Riedl, R., & Kenning, P. (2018). Trust me if you can—neurophysiological insights on the influence of consumer impulsiveness on trustworthiness evaluations in online settings. *European Journal of Marketing.* https://doi.org/10.1108/EJM-12-2016-0870

Izhikevich, E. M. (2003). Simple model of spiking neurons. *IEEE Transactions on Neural Networks, 14*(6), 1569–1572.

Jarek, K., & Mazurek, G. (2019). Marketing and artificial intelligence. *Central European Business Review, 8*(2), 46–55.

Jin, S. A. A., & Bolebruch, J. (2009). Virtual commerce (V-Commerce) in second life: The roles of physical presence and brand-self connection. *Journal for Virtual Worlds Research, 2*, 1–12.

Jones, V. K. (2018). Voice-activated change: Marketing in the age of artificial intelligence and virtual assistants. *Journal of Brand Strategy, 7*(3), 233–245.

Juarez, D., Tur-Viñes, V., & Mengual, A. (2020). Neuromarketing applied to educational toy packaging. *Frontiers in Psychology, 11*, 2077.

Jung, T., tom Dieck, M. C., Lee, H., & Chung, N. (2016). Effects of virtual reality and augmented reality on visitor experiences in museum. In *Information and communication technologies in tourism 2016* (pp. 621–635). Springer.

Jung, T. H., & tom Dieck, M. C. (2017). Augmented reality, virtual reality and 3D printing for the co-creation of value for the visitor experience at cultural heritage places. *Journal of Place Management and Development, 10*, 140–151.

Kaplan, A. M., & Haenlein, M. (2009). The fairyland of Second Life: Virtual social worlds and how to use them. *Business Horizons, 52*, 563–572. https://doi.org/10.1016/j.bushor.2009.07.002

Kiron, D., & Schrage, M. (2019). Strategy for and with AI. *MIT Sloan Management Review, 60*(4), 30–35.

Kong, X., Liu, D., & Min, L. (2020). VR technology in marketing from the perspective of customer experience. *IEEE Access, 8*, 162581–162587.

Krampe, C., Strelow, E., Haas, A., & Kenning, P. (2018). The application of mobile fNIRS to shopper neuroscience – First insights from a merchandising communication study. *European Journal of Marketing*. https://doi.org/10.1108/EJM-12-2016-0727

Kroupi, E., Hanhart, P., Lee, J. S., Rerabek, M., & Ebrahimi, T. (2014). Predicting subjective sensation of reality during multimedia consumption based on EEG and peripheral physiological signals. In *2014 IEEE International Conference on Multimedia and Expo (ICME)* (pp. 1–6). IEEE.

Kumar, V., Rajan, B., Venkatesan, R., & Lecinski, J. (2019). Understanding the role of artificial intelligence in personalised engagement marketing. *California Management Review, 61*(4), 135–155.

Liu, X. (2020). Analysing the impact of user-generated content on B2B Firms' stock performance: Big data analysis with machine learning methods. *Industrial Marketing Management, 86*, 30–39.

Loureiro, S. M. C., Guerreiro, J., Eloy, S., Langaro, D., & Panchapakesan, P. (2019). Understanding the use of Virtual Reality in Marketing: A text mining-based review. *Journal of Business Research, 100*, 514–530.

Ma, L., & Sun, B. (2020). Machine learning and AI in marketing – Connecting computing power to human insights. *International Journal of Research in Marketing, 37*(3), 481–504.

Malhotra, N. K., & Dash, S. (2016). *Marketing research: An applied orientation*. Pearson.

Marinchak, C. M., Forrest, E., & Hoanca, B. (2018). Artificial intelligence: Redefining marketing management and the customer experience. *International Journal of E-Entrepreneurship and Innovation (IJEEI), 8*(2), 14–24.

Martínez-López, F. J., & Casillas, J. (2013). Artificial intelligence-based systems applied in industrial marketing: An historical overview, current and future insights. *Industrial Marketing Management, 42*(4), 489–495.

Martínez-Navarro, J., Bigné, E., Guixeres, J., Alcañiz, M., & Torrecilla, C. (2019). The influence of virtual reality in e-commerce. *Journal of Business Research, 100*, 475–482.

Mogaji, E., Soetan, T. O., & Kieu, T. A. (2020). The implications of artificial intelligence on the digital marketing of financial services to vulnerable customers. *Australasian Marketing Journal (AMJ)*.

Nilashi, M., Yadegaridehkordi, E., Samad, S., Mardani, A., Ahani, A., Aljojo, N., & Tajuddin, T. (2020). Decision to adopt neuromarketing techniques for sustainable product marketing: A fuzzy decision-making approach. *Symmetry, 12*(2), 305.

Overgoor, G., Chica, M., Rand, W., & Weishampel, A. (2019). Letting the computers take over: Using AI to solve marketing problems. *California Management Review, 61*(4), 156–185.

Rawnaque, F. S., Rahman, K. M., Anwar, S. F., Vaidyanathan, R., Chau, T., Sarker, F., & Al Mamun, K. A. (2020). Technological advancements and opportunities in Neuromarketing: A systematic review. *Brain Informatics, 7*(1), 1–19.

Redcay, E., & Schilbach, L. (2019). Using second-person neuroscience to elucidate the mechanisms of social interaction. *Nature Reviews Neuroscience, 20*(8), 495–505.

Rekha, A. G., Abdulla, M. S., & Asharaf, S. (2016). Artificial intelligence marketing: An application of a novel Lightly Trained Support Vector Data Description. *Journal of Information and Optimization Sciences, 37*(5), 681–691.

Roth, V. A. (2014). *The potential of neuromarketing as a marketing tool*. Bachelor's thesis, University of Twente.

Sebastian, V. (2014). New directions in understanding the decision-making process: Neuroeconomics and neuromarketing. *Procedia-Social and Behavioral Sciences, 127*, 758–762.

Shankar, V., Inman, J. J., Mantrala, M., Kelley, E., & Rizley, R. (2011). Innovations in shopper marketing: Current insights and future research issues. *Journal of Retailing, 87*, S29–S42.

Shen, F., & Morris, J. D. (2016). Decoding neural responses to emotion in television commercials: An integrative study of self-reporting and fMRI measures. *Journal of Advertising Research, 56*(2), 193–204.

Shen, Y., Shan, W., & Luan, J. (2018). Influence of aggregated ratings on purchase decisions: an event-related potential study. *European Journal of Marketing*. https://doi.org/10.1108/EJM-12-2016-0871

Stone, M., Aravopoulou, E., Ekinci, Y., Evans, G., Hobbs, M., Labib, A., & Machtynger, L. (2020). Artificial intelligence (AI) in strategic marketing decision-making: A research agenda. *The Bottom Line, 33*, 183–200.

Stone, M., Laughlin, P., Aravopoulou, E., Gerardi, G., Todeva, E., & Weinzierl, L. (2017). How platforms are transforming customer information management. *The Bottom Line, 30*(3), 216–235.

Subawa, N. S., Widhiasthini, N. W., Astawa, I. P., Dwiatmadja, C., & Permatasari, N. P. I. (2021). The practices of virtual reality marketing in the tourism sector, a case study of Bali, Indonesia. *Current Issues in Tourism*, 1–12.

Sung, B., Mergelsberg, E., Teah, M., D'Silva, B., & Phau, I. (2021). The effectiveness of a marketing virtual reality learning simulation: A quantitative survey with psychophysiological measures. *British Journal of Educational Technology, 52*(1), 196–213.

Tong, S., Luo, X., & Xu, B. (2020). Personalised mobile marketing strategies. *Journal of the Academy of Marketing Science, 48*(1), 64–78.

Tussyadiah, I. P., Wang, D., Jung, T. H., & tom Dieck, M. C. (2018). Virtual reality, presence, and attitude change: Empirical evidence from tourism. *Tourism Management, 66*, 140–154.

van Berlo, Z. M., van Reijmersdal, E. A., Smit, E. G., & van der Laan, L. N. (2021). Brands in virtual reality games: Affective processes within computer-mediated consumer experiences. *Journal of Business Research, 122*, 458–465.

Vecchiato, G., Astolfi, L., De Vico Fallani, F., Toppi, J., Aloise, F., Bez, F., & Babiloni, F. (2011). On the use of EEG or MEG brain imaging tools in neuromarketing research. *Computational Intelligence and Neuroscience, 2011*, 1–12.

Verhoef, P. C., Kannan, P. K., & Inman, J. J. (2015). From multi-channel retailing to omni-channel retailing: Introduction to the special issue on multichannel retailing. *Journal of Retailing, 91*, 174–181. https://doi.org/10.1016/j.jretai.2015.02.005

Verhulst, A., Normand, J. M., Lombard, C., & Moreau, G. (2017). A study on the use of an immersive virtual reality store to investigate consumer perceptions and purchase behavior toward non-standard fruits and vegetables. In *Proceedings of the 2017 IEEE Virtual Reality (VR)* (pp. 55–63). IEEE.

Vrechopoulos, A., Apostolou, K., & Koutsiouris, V. (2009). Virtual reality retailing on the web: Emerging consumer behavioural patterns. *The*

International Review of Retail, Distribution and Consumer Research, 19, 469–482. https://doi.org/10.1080/09593960903445194

Wang, Y., & Chen, H. (2019). The influence of dialogic engagement and prominence on visual product placement in virtual reality videos. *Journal of Business Research, 100*, 493–502.

Waterlander, W. E., Jiang, Y., Steenhuis, I. H., & Ni Mhurchu, C. (2015). Using a 3D virtual supermarket to measure food purchase behavior: A validation study. *Journal of Medical Internet Research, 17*, e107. https://doi.org/10.2196/jmir.3774

West, A., Clifford, J., & Atkinson, D. (2018). Alexa, "build me a brand" An Investigation into the impact of Artificial Intelligence on Branding. *The Business & Management Review, 9*(3), 321–330.

Wierenga, B. (2010). Marketing and artificial intelligence: Great opportunities, reluctant partners. In *Marketing intelligent systems using soft computing* (pp. 1-8). Springer, .

Wirth, N. (2018). Hello marketing, what can artificial intelligence help you with? *International Journal of Market Research, 60*(5), 435–438.

Xu, Y., Shieh, C. H., van Esch, P., & Ling, I. L. (2020). AI customer service: Task complexity, problem-solving ability, and usage intention. *Australasian Marketing Journal (AMJ), 28*(4), 189–199.

Zheng, X. (2021, February). Application of virtual reality technology in marketing training. *Journal of Physics: Conference Series, 1744*(4), 042199. IOP Publishing.

13

Leveraging Digital Marketing and Integrated Marketing Communications for Brand Building in Emerging Markets

Amrita Chakraborty and Varsha Jain

Introduction

The digital revolution has a prolific influence on markets, business, and organisations at micro and macro level. There is a surge in technological devices that has led to fast and unpredictable changes in individual cognition and our behaviour towards each other. Similarly, at the macro level, nations have embraced digitalisation into their economy and consider it a backbone for future development. Due to this, developing countries are quickly rising in status and capacity—for example, India, Africa, Thailand, Russia, Mexico, and Brazil.

Emerging markets, generally speaking, are "heterogeneous, have sociopolitical governance, a chronic shortage of resources exists, unbranded competition, and inadequate infrastructure" (Sheth, 2011). Emerging

A. Chakraborty (✉) • V. Jain
MICA, Ahmedabad, Gujarat, India
e-mail: amritachakraborty.fpm20@micamail.in; varsha.jain@micamail.in

markets influence consumers' decision-making process (Thongpapanl, Ashraf, Lapa, & Venkatesh, 2018). There is complete information about various products and services, brands, and offers available with heterogeneity in products and price discrimination. The process of decision-making creates issues of trust in the minds of consumers. Consumers do not trust online channels for buying products (Ventre & Kolbe, 2020).

Moreover, this obstacle is overcome by understanding the motivations of consumers for purchasing and not purchasing online. It also depends on the brands' relevance to promote and position their products in the emerging market. For example, Starbucks in India promotes local breakfast recipes by Indian chefs, such as Sanjeev Kapoor, in their outlets, along with coffee or any other drink (Starbucks, 2020). The brand has created relevance in its host country by considering the culture and psychological factors in an emerging market. Research also argued that brand prominence in luxury purchases plays an essential role in emerging markets (Pino, Amatulli, Peluso, Nataraajan, & Guido, 2019).

Along with the recommendations, word-of-mouth and reviews about the brand positively affect consumers' perceived usefulness (Sheth, 2011; Ventre & Kolbe, 2020). Along with websites, psychological and cultural aspects are essential for any brand to consider while framing strategies to understand and attract consumers online. Therefore, digital marketing and integrated marketing communication are the success pillars for brands in emerging markets. Thus, this chapter will discuss the role of digital marketing along with integrated marketing communication, using a new framework of marketing in emerging markets. We further explain in detail the process of branding in emerging marketing with digital marketing tools.

Digital Marketing Framework for Brands in Emerging Markets

The digital marketing framework for brands in emerging markets, which many global brands are adopting, encompasses digital marketing and integrated marketing communication tools. It has four phases, Collaborate, Positioning, Personalisation, and Purchase, which are further explained in this section.

Collaborate

Brands extensively use digital marketing for connecting with stakeholders such as allied forms, consumers, and society. When a global firm enters an emerging market, a collaborative approach is followed through joint ventures, strategic alliances, exporting, and franchising (Paul, 2019). For Example, Mahindra and Ford (a US-based automobile company) have agreed to a joint venture in India for long-term economic growth (Ford, 2020). Firms acknowledged that a collaborative relationship with the stakeholders enables a brand to develop (Dumont & Ots, 2020). For example, the Government of Rwanda worked with Silicon Valley robotic firms to be the first to deliver blood to local areas with drones (EY, 2020). The communication channels used by the brands to join are more through online mediums rather than offline. This communication has created enormous opportunities for brands to reach global consumers, as brands take initiatives to understand and interact with consumers to satisfy their needs and desires.

Similarly, it becomes necessary for consumers to understand various brands' perspectives and help them co-create strategies. The standpoint of a brand comprises the firm, consumers, and society (Swaminathan, Sorescu, Steenkamp, O'Guinn, & Schmitt, 2020). In this phase, their perspectives are essential and will be explained in detail in the following sections.

Firm Perspective

Strategic and financial approaches are the macro-level and structural development that form the brand's institutional framework. The guidelines explain the theories related to brands and the role of urbanisation, globalisation, and digitalisation in emerging countries. The views are strategic and financial. The strategic approach focuses on the structural features of the brand. The system includes developing and implementing brand identity, and positioning, targeting, launching, and growing brands, brand portfolio architecture, and brand monitoring across nations. It helps establish a context for the brand with digital marketing tools and creates a structure to target consumers. The financial approach explains the crucial element for a brand, which is finance. Digital transformation has enabled the emerging economy's domestic market to explore innovative digital potential (Rassool & Dissanayake, 2019). Whenever a brand wants to invest in digital marketing components for more revenue and increased sales, it also measures the return on investment (ROI). Generally, brands measure ROI concerning the brand effect, brand equity, and non-financial outcomes. Non-financial outcomes may include creating awareness, recommendations, and e-WOM. In an emerging market, community-driven marketing strategies emphasise extensively non-financial results.

Further, non-financial consequences are becoming popular because of the increasing role of communities in emerging markets. Studies have stated that emerging markets such as India and China provide many opportunities for global brands to expand due to the increase in economic growth and purchasing power (Paul, 2019). However, international brands also need to understand the consumers, helping them collaborate in successful ventures.

Consumer Perspective

Initially, the "top-down" approach produces goods and services for consumers based on their product-driven strategies (Alexander, Teller, & Wood, 2020). Later firms adopted the "bottom-up" approach for stakeholders such as consumers, which also plays an essential role in the co-creation of brand uniqueness (Jain, Shroff, Merchant, & Bezbaruah, 2021). If consumers can grasp the essence and differentiate the brand's unique value, this is considered the most significant brand victory. Outstanding value requires the brand to be relevant and meaningful to the right consumers (Keller, 2019). However, this is a challenging task for the brands in an emerging market. Consumers prioritise products or services that can be customised or personalised to fulfil their demand and provide a unique value proposition. If consumers are attracted and convinced, then they purchase the product. For example, in India, the luxury hotel chain The Taj has created advertising campaigns that communicate the "Feeling of Tajness" embedded with the culture, values, and hospitality that provide unique Indian meanings and symbols for tapping the international market (Tajness, 2021).

Moreover, digital marketing has provided an opportunity to enhance products' value by increasing their distribution globally on an unprecedented scale. For example, Nandos, a prominent South African food chain, launched a new online campaign, Tin for Tjips, using online platforms and their app (Nando's South Africa, 2021). Consumers' decision-making takes place considering the economic and psychological approach. The financial process explains that every brand has indulged in the production and manufacturing of multiple products. Therefore, organisations have details about the quality, quantity, and manufacturing process. Sometimes, consumers lack this detailed information about that exact product. The product leads to the creation of asymmetry of communication between the consumers and the brand. When consumers are introduced to a new brand for the first time in an emerging market, they must represent a positive image or identity. Also, there is heterogeneity in religion, history, and demography in an emerging market, which leads to differences in culture and traditions that become necessary for the new firms to consider for marketing (Sinha & Sheth, 2018). With the target consumers, digital marketing components are the medium that is used for the brands to communicate. Content marketing, blogging, and video marketing are practical measures explicitly used to share and transfer information about products, prices, ingredients, and directions to ensure a healthy relationship between consumers and brands.

The psychological approach aims at the consumer's decision to go for a brand and does not always lie in information transfer about a brand. Along with information, processing and intention for purchase of a product depend upon the psychology of consumers. Consumer psychology is displayed in the whole process of the consumer buying journey. Consumers gather brand knowledge (mental representation of awareness) to understand, which sometimes leads to recognition or recall based on the brand image built on unique features or emotional associations. Other psychological models, such as brand trust (Rajavi, Kushwaha, & Steenkamp, 2019) and emotional brand attachment (Thomson, MacInnis, & Whan Park, 2005), significantly affect digital marketing.

Digital marketing enhances these psychological constructs in consumers through dynamic and inspirational marketing and leads marketing on various online platforms to build connections with consumers.

Society Perspective

Society forms an important external factor that every brand needs to consider while deciding on marketing strategies. Brands launch a new product in a specific geographic area after acquiring knowledge about a place's culture, region, and traditions. Moreover, this is why it is observed that advertisements for the same brand are different in various areas because of the demography and culture associated with it. For example, Zara, a Spanish fashion retail chain, has aligned their fashion category with India's festivals, such as Happy Holi Collections, to create relevance and meaning in the market (Happy Holi-Collection-Woman | ZARA India, 2021). The societal perspective comprises sociological and cultural approaches. The sociological approach states that brands ensure that they communicate the right message when brands connect with the consumers. There is a meaning transfer that takes place in this process. Meaning transfer starts when the brand is perceived, produced, and delivered through the post-purchase stage (Swaminathan et al., 2020). To ensure that the proper meaning and value are transferred, it is essential for brands first to understand the consumer consciousness, regional rituals and traditions, and moral obligations of the society. Consumers perceive brands based on specific symbolic meanings. Brand communities in emerging market countries ensure the precise transfer of purposes. For instance, consumers form relationships with brands by imagining human characteristics, stereotyping brands as social entities (Wijnands & Gill, 2020). Referring to brands as social entities means they are evaluated based on the social dimension of personality and gender. One such example is Royal Enfield, which is considered a man's motorcycle.

Successful brands have aligned their marketing strategies with the underlying cultural philosophy in the consumption pattern. Brands curate data for inferences and product ideation from the online consumption pattern. Further, brands promote products and services in emerging markets for quick and easy acceptability in their culture. Standardisation of messages and building a picture for brands becomes tough in a different culture. Brands adopt this diverse culture and lack standardisation in their products and services. Globalisation's implications gave rise to the emergence of digitalisation, where brands can balance standardisation in diverse cultures by continually monitoring target consumers' digital footprints. Consumers trust brands related to the customs, associations, and heritage of that culture, lifestyle, and economic and cultural conditions.

Positioning

Digitalisation started in the twentieth century, and since then consumers, organisations, and various actors existing in the market have gone digital. Brands use digital platforms in an emerging market such as social media to position their products and services based on functional, symbolic, and experiential attributes among heterogeneous consumers to select their target audience. With digitalisation, experiential characteristics are more focused as they evoke the consumers' convergent and divergent cognitive processes (Ihtiyar, Barut, & Ihtiyar, 2019). This section will discuss digital marketing in branding to the emerging market for positioning products and services through various online channels.

The internet allows individuals to create online networks to exchange information and conversations (Hoffman & Novak, 2017). These interactions and information exchanges can be personal and also include brands and product recommendations and feedback. WhatsApp, YouTube, Facebook, Messenger, and Instagram accounted for more than 80% of South Africa's usage of social media platforms in 2020 (Statista, 2021). However, studies have stated that the increase in these online platforms' use subsequently enables users/consumers to construct brand meaning and significance (Fournier & Avery, 2011). The social media platforms create unique experiences for consumers in the pre-purchase, during purchase, and post-purchase phases. Consumers have adopted a circular bi-directional loop of purchase and consumption in the digital age where information is shared in the online space, empowering other consumers with product/brand information (Vieira, de Almeida, Agnihotri, da Silva, & Arunachalam, 2019). Building a brand in this dynamic marketing phenomenon is a very different format from the traditional one. Brands derive insights and generate new ideas for their products and services from the consumer. This process is known as the "bottom-up" approach (Jain et al., 2021).

Using the internet is ubiquitous, and technology is the most significant influencer in the twentieth century for consumers' changing preferences (Veloutsou & Guzman, 2017). In the presence of the internet and hyper-connectivity, it becomes vital to monitor brand identity and representation across channels on a broad range of technical devices as consumers access many devices (Swaminathan et al., 2020). Online platforms generate awareness, share information, cultivate relationships with stakeholders, and build a reputation (Mingione & Abratt, 2020). Consumers with shared interests and common understanding gather and form a community on the online platforms. Moreover, these communities share experiences and exchange information about social networking sites, creating brand communities. A brand community is defined "as a specialised, non-geographically bound community and based on a structured set of social relations among admirers of a brand" (Muñiz & O'Guinn, 2001, p. 412). The communities help connect with the members by developing active interactions and engagements. Brands listen to the community members, nurture adaptive identity using online feedback and insights, and learn about customers' perceptions to build brand strategy. This adaptability is through digitalisation, which forms the core to understanding the consumer's needs. Especially in emerging markets, communities play a vital role because communities' recommendations, updates, and reviews about national and international firms increase awareness and profit. For example, African Business communities provide updates and information worldwide about the African people's engagement and involvement, Government, and international firms (Communities, 2021). Communities actively interact and engage their members over various social media platforms, and generate new ideas. Brands position their products and services based on the latest ideas drawn from a brand's collaborators in an emerging market. To set the final products or services in the market through the "bottom-up approach", personalisation is considered one of the most demanding strategies in an emerging market like Asia (The Economist Intelligence Unit, 2016), which requires digital intervention.

Personalisation

Consumers are becoming tech-savvy and they want to explore the world within their palm, providing them convenience and saving time and effort (Bhattacherjee & Adhikari, 2018). To leverage this opportunity, brands are investing extensively in digital marketing tools and techniques. This section introduces digital marketing and explains its role and benefits for branding in an emerging market.

The internet has altered our everyday life. It has created numerous possibilities for market actors, such as consumers and producers, through digitalisation. The digital approach has bridged the distance and brought the actors of the markets closer for better understanding and prediction. Digitalisation is considered a crucial tool for every business for its easy accessibility and global reach. For global reach, emerging markets provide enormous opportunities because of their economic infrastructure and rapid technological adoption. Digital marketing can be defined "as activities, institutions, and processes facilitated by digital technologies for creating, communicating and delivering value for customers and other stakeholders" (Kannan & Li, 2017, p. 34). American Marketing Association has referred to digital marketing as "an adaptive and iterative, technology-enabled process by which firms collaborate with customers and partners to create, communicate, deliver, and sustain value for all stakeholders" (American Marketing Association, 2021). In simple terms, digital marketing is an adaptive process that is technology-enabled to create, communicate, and deliver values with consistency to retain the existing stakeholders, especially consumers, and reach new stakeholders within a short time. It is adaptive and communicates value to all stakeholders, especially consumers, meaning that this is a bilateral process where value is co-created between consumers and organisations. Value is created for consumers to develop awareness about new products, new brands, new information, services, or markets. This value creates brand awareness and new knowledge in an emerging market.

Purchase

Purchase is no longer considered the last consumer buying process, especially in emerging markets. Brands are redefining their strategies for providing consumers with experiences that are beyond transactions. Grönroos (1997) mentions that building a relational perspective is more important than offering goods and services. Brands need to encompass strategies that satisfy consumers by providing long-term values and connecting them emotionally. For example, Procter & Gamble promotes not a brand or product but a feeling, emotion, and value through its advertisements, which creates a connection with the consumers (Procter & Gamble, 2021). When marketers are successful in delivering value to consumers, consumers enter into a circular loop. Branding in an emerging market is an iterative process that needs to be changed as per the consumer's needs. At this juncture, marketers derive real-time insights from consumers through feedback and reviews. Based on the insights, marketers vary their positioning strategies for branding and this helps them to gain a competitive advantage.

Marketer's Benefit

Further, digital marketing is also designed for the organisation regarding the four benefits of expanding global reach and improved targeting. First, the internet has enabled fast connectivity and the right reachability, saving time and cost. A transaction can be carried out quickly with any target consumers worldwide, thus creating new consumer platforms. As stated earlier, digital marketing supports expanding the consumer's global reach for the business units. Second, there is low-cost entry and quick adaptability, as there is no cost or fees incurred for its implementation. Any startup can be established through a website involving negligible cost with minimum finance, providing many brands opportunities to enter with their ideas and creativity. Digital marketing encourages new ideas and creativity, quickly adapts its institutional structure in this fast environment, and provides the maximum benefit to consumers and the business. Third, there is measurable ROI, since every business procedure is an affiliate to the internet and technologies, accounts are easily maintained, and the exact ROI is also calculated. The technology helps the organisation create transparency in transactions and retains the employees' trust, morale, and loyalty. Fourth, relationship building is key. Traditionally, product-driven marketing strategies were developed. However, with time, the organisation realised the need of its stakeholders, especially consumers. Therefore, product-driven strategies were reframed into consumer-driven strategies to ensure more profit. Moreover, digital marketing tools can boost sales and gains, as well as expand the consumer base. The insights from digital marketing also communicate new value propositions with the brand and consumers and develop long-term relationships, which acts as the differentiating factor.

Consumer's Benefit

Digital marketing significantly influences communication methods about a brand and consumers' attitudes towards them. The five main advantages of digital marketing for consumers are explained in detail (Bala & Varma, 2018). First, there is no longer a time limit: the internet has increased the usage time and engagement time for every consumer as there is no time and cost involved. With digital marketing, consumers of emerging markets are curious and engage with the company's various events. This engagement allows consumers to assemble more relevant information about a brand through websites and aids them in the decision-making process. Second, know more and get more: through various websites, consumers have the opportunity to gather information about a product, compare it with other brands, and make a rational purchase decision. Digital marketing enables consumers to access new information about products or services based on reviews and searches anytime. This information has changed the shopping experience. Third, helping wise and easy purchase: brands are trying to endorse their products or services using digital marketing, providing consumers an avenue to compare products by different vendors/suppliers in terms of price and time. To get information, consumers do not have to visit retail outlets and spend time. This information enables quick purchase, as data is available within seconds. Fourth, making sharing easy: digital marketing bestows consumers the liberty to share their experiences, reviews, and feedback about brands online. Channels such as social media, blogging, or content marketing highlight the consumers' feedback and experience, making it easy for brands to know about their target consumers and making the purchase easy. Fifth, attractive pricing: one of the most significant advantages of the internet is that prices of products/services are available on the brands' websites, making it easy for consumers to decide. In addition, social media, mobile marketing, and online advertising also display the latest discounts and promotional offers made by the brands. These offerings attract more consumers as they are aware and well-informed, resulting in more sales. Therefore, digital marketing provides clear communication to its consumers to ensure proper decision-making.

Digital marketing is a boon for all types of business because of its comprehensive and versatile nature. Since digital marketing is broad and continually adapting to the dynamic marketing phenomena, an organisation needs to learn which particular feature is suitable and aligns with its objective. As the infrastructure is still developing, organisations can utilise these strategies as a foundation and make the first step to being recognised in the market through digital marketing. In this vein, the structure of digital marketing is briefly summarised below.

Structure of Digital Marketing

Inbound and Outbound Marketing

Digital marketing is an umbrella term, and its scope is far-reaching. Generally, digital marketing consists of two components: inbound marketing and outbound marketing.

Inbound marketing is concerned with creating content stored in the memory for a longer duration, such as content marketing, blogging, and social media marketing. At the same time, outbound marketing focuses on the increase in conversion rate by integrating traditional tools with digital spaces such as print ads, television ads, and newsletters (Bleoju, Capatina, Rancati, & Lesca, 2016, p. 5527). Further, the author explains that since outbound marketing is myopic, maintaining long-term relationships with the consumers becomes difficult. However, Jain et al. (2021) have mentioned the bottom-up approach. It has become necessary for brands to create brand value and engagement with the consumers in an emerging market. Inbound marketing techniques enable firms and brands to co-create value with potential consumers (Bleoju et al., 2016). Therefore, we will discuss inbound marketing techniques in detail and help to brand in an emerging market.

Inbound marketing techniques include the following:

- Website Marketing
- Social Media Marketing
- Video Marketing
- Mobile Marketing
- Bogging and Content Marketing

The website: One of the first unconscious consumer behaviours, when introduced to a new product or brand, is to gather information. With the rise of the internet, information is primarily collected from online sources such as direct brand websites or general search engines such as Google. Consumers, especially in emerging economies, rely on the internet for information and consider it an authentic source of information. As not all products or brands have independent websites, affiliate marketing websites such as Amazon, eBay, or Alibaba serve as a connector between brands and consumers and offer opportunities for direct sales. The process of online information hunting is aided by Search Engine Marketing, which comprises search engine optimisation, Pay-Per-Click, and Google AdWords. These tools under search engine marketing create brand awareness among consumers. Consequently, the internet has supported expanding the consumer to reach digitally and globally.

Social Media Marketing (SMM): The application of social media such as Facebook and Instagram has augmented seamless digital interface availability in emerging markets. Millennials use it, and Gen X and Gen Y use social media extensively as well. Therefore, brands can use this medium to increase consumer loyalty by connecting with diverse consumers, disseminating their message and values (Kaplan & Haenlein,

2010). For example, Airbnb has introduced online live experiences of the famous Brazil Carnival through extensive social media platforms to entice people to travel and use their house-sharing service (Online Experiences, 2021).

Video marketing: When a consumer sees a new product or service on the website or social media, he/she intends to play a video that can demonstrate its benefits or usage for clear understanding. Video marketing plays a crucial role in creating awareness of new products. It provides the correct visual information to the target consumers. The trend in video marketing is livestreaming adopted by Facebook, YouTube, and Google. Therefore, new brands can reach out to new consumers. The source is more important in visual online advertisements than the content.

Mobile marketing: One of the traditional yet popular ways for brands to reach consumers is through mobile features such as text messaging, multimedia messaging, and push notification. For example, in emerging markets such as India, with the increase in smartphone users' growth to 696.07 million (Statista, 2020a), mobile marketing is flourishing.

Blogging and content marketing: When there are seamless digital interfaces and information about global trends, blogging and content marketing add authenticity and value. Apart from buying a product, knowing its features, background, and multiple uses is equally essential. Brands communicate about the details of products in the form of content. Good content provides the necessary information the consumer is seeking and develops trust based on reality. Social campaigns related to sustainability or CSR engage in content marketing to build a relationship with the target consumers. Some examples are The Adventure Blog, Pinch Of Yum, Cookie & Kate Content marketing, Coke's "Share A Coke" campaign, Microsoft Stories, and McDonald's "Our Food, Your Questions". Content is also created to celebrate occasions that represent the brand's identity in the market. For example, Nubank, the world's largest online bank, made its first Brazilian March edition magazine by displaying a pregnant woman as a celebration of Women's Day (Mari, 2021). After understanding the advantages of digital marketing, it is imperative to know how digital marketing aligns with Branding and Integrated Marketing communication, discussed in the subsequent section.

Digital Marketing and Integrated Marketing Communication (IMC) for Brand Building

For a brand to achieve a competitive advantage in the dynamic marketing phenomena, IMC aligned with digital marketing is no longer just an option but a necessity. Brands and consumers are a separate entity that exists in the market. Both entities indulge in exchanging information and transaction so that a circular flow of money in the economy and benefit is distributed equally. A gap needs to be filled, connecting these entities to ensure the completion of circular flow. Brands require promotion, direct selling, advertising, or social media as a way to reach consumers. This process will connect them with the right consumers and create purchase intention based on content relevance and meaning. In simple terms, these tools will increase awareness about a brand and eventually accelerate sales in the firm. For appropriate promotional strategies, communication plays a vital role. Communication is a sensitive and crucial aspect as it deals with the brands and consumers simultaneously across various platforms online and offline globally. Therefore, Integrated Marketing Communication (IMC) can be defined as "an audience-driven business process of strategically managing stakeholders, content, channels, and results of brand communication programs" (Kliatchko, 2005, p. 19). As consumers are highly dependent on digital gadgets, especially phones, it becomes effortless for brands to communicate online. Therefore, the concept of digitally integrated marketing communication is developed. Brands can quickly achieve well-coordinated long-term competition. For example, McDonald's in the Middle East has renewed its purpose and marketing strategy to target consumers by implementing their 3Ds model of Digital, Delivery, and Drive-thru (Campaignme, 2021). As IMC tools enhance the curation of the right information to serve consumers' required demands digitally, brands can flourish in an emerging market. This process can prove to be a great success when a brand enters an emerging market.

The emerging market provides opportunities for brands to communicate with target consumers because this market is not rigid. There is a high level of adoption and acceptance of any brand's new product in these markets. In an emerging market, consumers need information about new brands and their products or services. The best medium to provide what is required by the consumers is through digital marketing components. For example, in India, 696 million people are internet users (Statista, 2021b), and they access the internet through mobile phones. In this case, mobile marketing or social media marketing can be implemented by brands to create awareness and promote their products and services through advertisements. Brazilian consumers are attracted to online videos, and thus video marketing or social marketing is well-suited for entry into the Brazilian market (Think with Google, 2021). Digital channels are used to develop marketing communication about a brand. Therefore, digital marketing tools aligned with IMC have been considered a successful measure to influence, interact with, and engage consumers with brands in emerging markets (Anabila, 2019). Besides, brands aligning with inbound marketing techniques also provide value to the consumers to retain long-term relationships through unique purchase experiences.

Purchase

Digital marketing is related to branding; similarly, branding builds a close relationship with its consumers, involving the dynamic process of value co-creation. Consumers prefer to buy branded products because there is an exchange of emotional feelings along with cognition. To construct this intimate relationship with the target consumers, brands need to understand consumers and serve a platter of real choices and preferences. Advertising provided a medium to connect consumers with the brands. Advertising offers a unique and desirable brand perception through an offline and online medium (Boyd, Kannan, & Slotegraaf, 2019). Conventionally, offline advertisements create appealing content to generate purchase intention. Since the internet's onset, online advertisements compete with the offline mediums as it is also a valuable tool to reach target consumers. Online mediums in advertising and branding provide an opportunity to be ubiquitous, communal, and interactive to engage the consumer to foster a warm and cordial brand image (Boyd et al., 2019). Digital marketing provides all the requisite tools and measures for the brands to understand, interact with, and predict the wants of the target consumers digitally in the emerging markets.

Social media is widely accepted by everyone, irrespective of demographics. Self-presentation is the means through which brands create their presence in the community or the crowd. Moreover, the advent of Web 3.0 technologies, where organisations depend on value-driven strategies, boosts digital marketing growth in any brand's emerging markets. It is not always that brands keep on reaching their consumers, but also that consumers connect and spread awareness about the brand. Consumers introduce a new brand in their community through online social networking sites (oSNSs) (Ozansoy Çadırcı & Sağkaya Güngör, 2016). To create an impression on the oSNSs, consumers upload photographs as selfies, share pictures, make videos, and comment. Selfies are cues that enhance personal branding and can also incorporate product promotion. Therefore, selfies are also considered as an effective medium for branding through oSNSs (Ozansoy Çadırcı & Sağkaya Güngör, 2016).

Platforms such as Facebook, Instagram, YouTube, Twitter, and LinkedIn have introduced innovative and engaging ways to connect with consumers and brands through selfies, videos, and pictures (Marketandmarkets, 2019). These are the most-used components of social media marketing in an emerging market. Various brands adopt social media marketing to build a strong brand image among consumers by offering opportunities. Consequently, this creates strong brand loyalty. Moreover, using social media, the brand creates an identity in the virtual space, also known as personal branding. Personal branding refers "to the process individuals use to develop and market themselves to others" (Jacobson, 2020). Social media curates the relevant information about the brand and presents it to the target consumers to create awareness and build a positive brand image. After making the image, brands strive to sustain it with the target consumers through interactions, providing promotional offers and endorsements through emails, campaign involvement, and blogging space.

Along with social media, the internet, from a broader perspective, serves as a robust instrument for increasing brand effect (Batton & Swoboda, 2020). Positive brand effect influences consumers and builds loyalty across nations, especially in emerging markets. The concept of brand effect is used by the fashion and beauty industry. Consumers incorporate various brands in their daily life that are guided by the motive of creating self-identity and inclusion in the communities, such as "cool girls", who "get it" on various social media platforms (Findlay, 2019). The consumer's aspiration to be identified in a social media community forces him/her to go for the brands and create a sense of confidence and belonging. Furthermore, in the case of luxury consumption, in emerging markets, other judgements, shared norms, collectivist values, and conformity play an essential role (Pino et al., 2019), which is transferred through digital spaces. Therefore digital marketing is considered the best form of marketing as it is a valuable tool to interact and connect with consumers. Digital marketing acts as a facilitator for connecting consumers with the business and also consumers to consumers. Sharing reviews, recommendations, and feedback in various digital spaces enables brands to understand consumer sentiments and preferences that enrich their positioning strategies for products and services in an emerging market.

Artificial intelligence (AI) is considered the next step towards digital marketing for brands and consumers. AI makes a significant contribution to digital marketing. It can help improve consumer experiences by curating data through tools such as sentiment analysis, big data analytics, and cloud computing (Marketandmarkets, 2019). For example, experiential marketing has resulted in positive post-purchase behaviour, ensuring customer satisfaction and creating a solid brand image in consumers' minds (Ihtiyar et al., 2019). Further, brands can convert dissatisfied consumers into loyal consumers by applying AI aligned with digital marketing strategies by reducing the environment's negative physical and psychological factors (Ihtiyar et al., 2019).

Consequently, brands will have more engaging consumers, and consumers will also be happy with the brands. Regarding the digital era, the scope of integrated marketing communication (IMC) is expanding. From direct selling, it has evolved to online selling through various components of digital tools. For example, Mini and Telsa in the automotive business focus on online selling (Ihtiyar et al., 2019). However, we can reframe it as a process of organisation, planning, and monitoring of marketing components and data digitally and influencing consumer associations and experiences. Digital marketing provides a valuable mix of marketing communication options to its consumers. A communication option becomes necessary as the local and international advertising competitions encourage innovations within this framework. Advertising strengthens client relationships, improves strategic marketing, attracts potential customers, and increases brand awareness (Zwerin, Clarke, & Clarke, 2019). Brands consistently work to maintain specific touchpoints with their target consumers (Belch & Belch, 2017). Moreover, IMC helps in keeping the consistency of the brand through various mediums and measures. As far as digitalisation is concerned, we can align the IMC tools with digital marketing; both serve as the pillar of any brand's success in the emerging market.

Implications

Digital marketing and integrated marketing communication are the solid pillars for brands to enter emerging markets. This chapter's contribution is to discuss and understand the role of digital marketing in IMC and branding in emerging markets based on the framework. Furthermore, there are four crucial implications: collaboration, positioning, personalisation, and purchase. First, in partnership, stakeholders play a pivotal role in the expansion of any business. As there is a lack of infrastructure and a shortage of resources (Sheth, 2011), global brands collaborate with local firms to enter these markets. Also, to minimise the investment risk, digital marketing tools and techniques have been incorporated in their marketing strategies to ensure financial safety and business expansion. Second, in positioning, the emerging market is characterised by market heterogeneity (Sheth, 2011). With marketing 4.0, apart from functional and symbolic, experiential attributes are demanded to provide unique value to the consumers.

Emerging market consumers have high purchasing power and desire to own products and services that provide exceptional value. Therefore, marketers need to focus on developing products and services that create new experiences for the consumers. Third, in personalisation, the "bottom-up" approach (Jain et al., 2021) emphasises consumer-driven marketing strategies that brands need to adapt to achieve a competitive

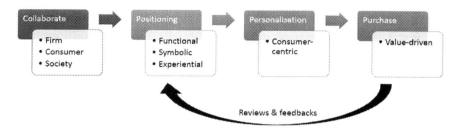

Fig. 13.1 Digital marketing framework for brands in emerging markets. Source: Authors

Fig. 13.2 Structure of digital marketing. Source: Adapted from Bleoju et al., 2016

advantage in an emerging market. The framework in Fig. 13.1 states that "personalisation" is the new approach of branding, incorporating digital marketing techniques and integrated marketing communication for an effective and positive customer purchase experience. Finally, for purchase, the framework in Fig. 13.2 depicts that investment takes place in various forms, such as positive word-of-mouth, loyalty, building long-term relationships, and satisfaction. Also, purchase and positioning are bi-directional and iterative. Reviews and recommendations are insights that brands curate and add into their positioning strategies to meet the consumers' demands and preferences in an emerging market.

However, managers will understand that it is necessary to implement strategies aligned with digital marketing and integrated marketing communication for branding their products and services in emerging markets. This chapter explains emergent digital marketing trends, consumers' attitudes towards the change, and branding elements in the digital era using the framework for academicians and practitioners. The chapter will also benefit society in understanding the new digital focus of brands in building relationships and accepting the recent evolution and unique identity of brands, especially in emerging markets. Finally, effective digital marketing approaches would be used by companies for developing brands in emerging markets through collaboration, positioning, and personalisation, leading to the final purchase.

References

Alexander, A., Teller, C., & Wood, S. (2020). Augmenting the urban place brand—On the relationship between markets and town and city centres. *Journal of Business Research, 116*, 642–654.
American Marketing Association. (2021). What is digital marketing? Retrieved January 24, 2021, from https://www.ama.org/pages/what-is-digital-marketing/.
Anabila, P. (2019). Integrated marketing communications, brand equity, and business performance in micro-finance institutions: An emerging market perspective. *Journal of Marketing Communications, 26*(3), 229–242.
Bala, M. B., & Varma, D. (2018). A critical review of digital marketing. *International Journal of Management, IT & Engineering, 8*(10), 321–339.
Batton, N., & Swoboda, B. (2020). Joint Roles of Digital Media Penetration and Communication Budgets for Corporate Brand Effects Across Nations. *Winter AMA Proceedings, 1*, 6–7.
Belch, G., & Belch, M. (2017). *Advertising and Promotion: An Integrated Marketing Communications Perspective (Irwin Marketing)* (11th ed.). McGraw-Hill Education.
Bhattacherjee, R., & Adhikari, A. (2018). Consumer Behaviour in Emerging Markets. *Strategic Marketing Issues in Emerging Markets, 1*, 19–30.
Bleoju, G., Capatina, A., Rancati, E., & Lesca, N. (2016). Exploring organizational propensity toward inbound–outbound marketing techniques adoption: The case of pure players and click and mortar companies. *Journal of Business Research, 69*(11), 5524–5528.
Boyd, D. E., Kannan, P. K., & Slotegraaf, R. J. (2019). Branded Apps and Their Impact on Firm Value: A Design Perspective. *Journal of Marketing Research, 56*(1), 76–88.
Communities, A. (2021). Home. Retrieved 30 March 2021, from https://africabusinesscommunities.com
Dumont, G., & Ots, M. (2020). Social dynamics and stakeholder relationships in personal branding. *Journal of Business Research, 106*, 118–128.

EY. (2020). https://www.ey.com/en_in/digital/how-collaboration-is-leading-to-new-innovation-in-emerging-market

Findlay, R. (2019). "Trust Us, We're You": Aspirational Realness in the Digital Communication of Contemporary Fashion and Beauty Brands. *Communication, Culture and Critique*, 553–569.

Ford. (2020). Media Centre Report

Fournier, S., & Avery, J. (2011). The uninvited brand. *Business Horizons, 54*(3), 193–207.

Grönroos, C. (1997). Value-driven relational marketing: From products to resources and competencies. *Journal of Marketing Management, 13*(5), 407–419.

Happy Holi-Collection-Woman | ZARA India. (2021). Retrieved 30 March 2021, from https://www.zara.com/in/en/woman-event-1-l1517.html?v1=1771762

Hoffman, D. L., & Novak, T. P. (2017). Consumer and object experience in the internet of things: An assemblage theory approach. *Journal of Consumer Research, 44*(6), 1178–1204.

Ihtiyar, A., Barut, M., & Ihtiyar, H. G. (2019). Experiential marketing, social judgements, and customer shopping experience in emerging markets. *Asia Pacific Journal of Marketing and Logistics, 31*(2), 499–515.

Jacobson, J. (2020). You are a brand: social media managers' personal branding and "the future audience.". *Journal of Product & Brand Management, 29*(6), 715–727.

Jain, V., Shroff, P., Merchant, A., & Bezbaruah, S. (2021). Introducing Bi-directional Participatory Place Branding: A Theoretical Model with Multi-Stakeholder Perspective. *Journal of Product and Brand Management*, 1–58.

Kannan, P. K., & Li, H. (2017). Digital marketing: A framework, review and research agenda. *International Journal of Research in Marketing, 34*(1), 22–45.

Kaplan, A. M., & Haenlein, M. (2010). Users of the world, unite! The challenges and opportunities of social media. *Business Horizons, 53*(1), 59–68.

Keller, K. L. (2019). Consumer Research Insights on Brands and Branding: A JCR Curation. *Journal of Consumer Research, 46*(5), 995–1001.

Kliatchko, J. (2005). Towards a new definition of Integrated Marketing Communications (IMC). *International Journal of Advertising, 24*(1), 7–34.

Mari, A. (2021). The Brazil Tech And Innovation Roundup—OLX Snaps Grupo Zap, Sage Finds A Buyer, 4-Day Week, Women's Day. Retrieved 30 March 2021, from https://www.forbes.com/sites/angelicamarideoliveira/2020/03/06/the-brazil-tech-and-innovation-roundupolx-buys-grupo-zap-sage-finds-a-buyer-4-day-week-womens-day/?sh=675ae4365330

Marketsandmarkets. (2019). Digital Marketing Software Market. Retrieved January 24, 2021, from https://www.marketsandmarkets.com/Market-Reports/digital-marketing-software-market-52158190.html.

Campaignme. (2021). McDonald's refreshes' intangible' brand purpose. Retrieved 1 April 2021, from https://campaignme.com/mcdonalds-refreshes-intangible-brand-purpose/

Mingione, M., & Abratt, R. (2020). Building a corporate brand in the digital age: Imperatives for transforming born-digital startups into successful corporate brands. *Journal of Marketing Management, 36*(11–12), 981–1008.

Muñiz, A. M., & O'Guinn, T. C. (2001). Brand community. *Journal of Consumer Research, 27*(4), 412–432.).

Nando's South Africa. (2021). Retrieved 30 March 2021, from https://www.nandos.co.za/explore/news/quarter-chicken-side-pilchards

Online Experiences. (2021). Retrieved 30 March 2021, from https://www.airbnb.co.in/s/Rio-de-Janeiro%2D%2DBrazil/experiences/online

Tajness. (2021). Our Philosophy. Retrieved 30 March 2021, from https://www.tajhotels.co.uk/tajness/

Ozansoy Çadırcı, T. Ğ., & Sağkaya Güngör, A. Ş. (2016). Love my selfie: Selfies in managing impressions on social networks. *Journal of Marketing Communications, 25*(3), 268–287.

Paul, J. (2019). Marketing in emerging markets: A review, theoretical synthesis and extension. *International Journal of Emerging Markets, 15*(3), 446–468.

Pino, G., Amatulli, C., Peluso, A. M., Nataraajan, R., & Guido, G. (2019). Brand prominence and social status in luxury consumption: A comparison of emerging and mature markets. *Journal of Retailing and Consumer Services, 46*, 163–172.

Procter & Gamble. (2021). Procter & Gamble India. https://in.pg.com/

Rajavi, K., Kushwaha, T., & Steenkamp, J.-B. E. M. (2019). In Brands, We Trust? A Multicategory, Multicountry Investigation of Sensitivity of Consumers' Trust in Brands to Marketing-Mix Activities. *Journal of Consumer Research, 46*(4), 651–670.

Rassool, R., & Dissanayake, R. (2019). Digital Transformation for Small & Medium Enterprises (SMES): With special focus on Sri Lankan context as an Emerging Economy. *International Journal Of Business And Management Review, 7*(4), 59–76.

Sheth, J. (2011). Impact of Emerging Markets on Marketing: Rethinking Existing Perspectives and Practices. *Journal Of Marketing, 75*(4), 166–182.

Sinha, M., & Sheth, J. (2018). Growing the pie in emerging markets: Marketing strategies for increasing the ratio of non-users to users. *Journal of Business Research, 86*, 217–224.

Starbucks. (2020). Starbucks Coffee Company. https://www.starbucks.in

Statista. (2021). The most popular social media in South Africa. Retrieved 30 March 2021, from https://www.statista.com/statistics/1189958/penetration-rate-of-social-media-in-southafrica/#:~:text=WhatsApp%20is%20the%20most%20popular,percent%20and%2087%20percent%2C%20respectively

Statista. (2021a). Total internet users in India. Retrieved January 24, 2021, from https://www.statista.com/statistics/255146/number-of-internet-users-in-india/

Statista. (2021b). Number of smartphone users in India 2015-2022. Retrieved January 24, 2021, from https://www.statista.com/statistics/467163/forecast-of-smartphone-users-in-india/

Swaminathan, V., Sorescu, A., Steenkamp, J.-B. E. M., O'Guinn, T. C. G., & Schmitt, B. (2020). Branding in a hyperconnected world: Refocusing theories and rethinking boundaries. *Journal of Marketing, 84*(2), 24–46.

The Economist Intelligence Unit. (2016). Made to order: Customisation advances in emerging markets. *The Economist*.

Thinkgoogle. (2021). Retrieved 30 March 2021, from https://www.thinkwithgoogle.com/consumer-insights/consumer-trends/branding-brazil/

Thomson, M., MacInnis, D. J., & Whan Park, C. (2005). The Ties That Bind: Measuring the Strength of Consumers' Emotional Attachments to Brands. *Journal of Consumer Psychology, 15*(1), 77–91.

Thongpapanl, N. T., Ashraf, A. R., Lapa, L., & Venkatesh, V. (2018). Differential Effects of Customers' Regulatory Fit on Trust, Perceived Value, and M-Commerce Use among Developing and Developed Countries. *Journal of International Marketing, 26*(3), 22–44.

Veloutsou, C., & Guzman, F. (2017). The evolution of brand management thinking over the last 25 years as recorded in the journal of product and brand management. *Journal of Product & Brand Management, 26*(1), 2–12.

Ventre, I., & Kolbe, D. (2020). The Impact of Perceived Usefulness of Online Reviews, Trust and Perceived Risk on Online Purchase Intention in Emerging Markets: A Mexican Perspective. *Journal of International Consumer Marketing, 32*(4), 287–299.

Vieira, V. A., de Almeida, M. I. S., Agnihotri, R., da Silva, N. S. D. A. C., & Arunachalam, S. (2019). In pursuit of an effective B2B digital marketing strategy in an emerging market. *Journal of the Academy of Marketing Science, 47*(6), 1085–1108.

Wijnands, F., & Gill, T. (2020). 'You're not perfect, but you're still my favourite.' Brand affective congruence as a new determinant of self-brand congruence. *Journal of Marketing Management, 36*(11–12), 1076–1103.

Zwerin, A., Clarke, T. B., & Clarke, I. (2019). Traditional and Emerging Integrated Marketing Communication Touchpoints Used in Effie Award-Winning Promotional Campaigns. *Journal of Promotion Management, 26*(2), 163–185.

Index

A
Advert brand avoidance, 65
Advertising, 232
African buying behaviour, 61
Age, 157
Artificial intelligence (AI), 254, 298
Association of National
 Advertisers, 86
Authenticity, 190

B
Banco Bilbao Vizcaya Argentaria
 (BBVA), 83
Beats Electronics, 94
Board of Control for Cricket in India
 (BCCI), 88
Bogging and Content
 Marketing, 293
Brand aversion, 62

Brand avoidance, 60
Brand awareness, 89, 121
Brand development, 4
Brand engagement, 121
Brand equity, 60
Brand fan pages, 122
Brand identity, 6
Brand image, 88
Branding tools, 4
Brand knowledge, 285
Brand love, 60
Brand loyalty, 60
Brand Personality Theory, 184
Brand trust, 285

C
Cognitive flexibility, 214–215
Collaborate, 283
Communicate health, 153

Communication technologies, 230
Connections, 192–193
Consistency, 190–191
Consumer behaviour, 210
Consumer-brand interactions, 60
Consumer-focused campaigns, 210
Consumer knowledge, 164–165
Consumer marketing strategies, 209
Consumer perspective, 284–286
Consumer's behaviour, 61
Consumers' decision-making process, 282
Consumers' emotions, 8
Conventional marketing tools, 256
Corporate bodies, 147
COVID-19, 137
  lockdown, 31
  pandemic era, 7

D

Demographic segmentation, 152
Destination marketers, 29
Destination planning, 19
Digital activation rights, 85
Digital innovation, 13
Digitally generating right-eye and left-eye images, 236
Digital marketing, 24, 282, 292
Digital revolution, 281
Dimensions of EF, 212–215
Domestic internal investors, 43

E

Education, 159
Electroencephalography, 217

Emerging economies, 148
Emerging technology, 24
Emirates Green Building Council, 49
Emotional brand attachment, 285
Entertaining content, 130
Entertainment sponsorships, 100
Event-Related Potential, 217
Executive function (EF), 210
Experiential brand avoidance, 63
Expertise, 192
Extended reality technologies, 230
Eye tracking, 238

F

Facebook, 297
Financial barriers, 62
Financial sustainability, 95
Firm perspective, 283–284
Foreign direct investment (FDI), 43, 46
Functional Magnetic Imaging, 217
Functional magnetic resonance (fMRI), 256
Functional near-infrared spectroscopy (fNIRS), 256

G

Gender, 158
Geographic segmentation, 152
Global community, 43, 51
Global consumption orientation, 163–164
Global economy, 60
"Green" movements, 156

Gross Domestic Product
  (GDP), 232

H

Health consciousness, 8, 161–162
Healthy and Indulgent Food
  Brands, 126–128
Healthy foods, 134
Healthy lifestyle branding, 147
Healthy lifestyle consumer, 151
The Hierarchy of Effects, 231

I

Identity brand avoidance, 63
Immersion, 238
Import-export trade, 42
Inbound and Outbound
  Marketing, 292–301
Income, 158
Indirect marketing approach, 87
Informational content, 129
Inhibitory control, 211–213
Instagram, 297
Integrated marketing
  communication, 20, 282
Intellectual capital, 42, 50, 52
Interactivity, 238
International capital, 42
International Olympic
  Committee, 94
Internet and social media, 230

L

LinkedIn, 297

M

Magnetoencephalography
  (MEG), 256
Marketing and Communication
  Working Group (MCWG), 22
Marketing communications, 4,
  5, 20, 229
Marketing communication tools, 5
Marketing mix, 187
Marketing practices, 4
Marketing tasks, 254
Mobile marketing, 293
Moral brand avoidance, 64

N

National Branding Model, 43
National treasure, 104
Nation brand elements, 44
Nation branding, 41–54
Natural stereoscopic viewing
  mechanism, 236
Need-based brand avoidance, 65
Negative word-of-mouth
  (WoM), 66
Neuromarketing, 210
Neuromarketing research are
  electroencephalography
  (EEG), 256
Neuropsychological tools, 8
Neuroscientific, 210

O

Olympic Games, 109
Online social networking sites
  (oSNSs), 297

P

Perceived behavioural control, 160–161
Personal brand elements, 190–193
Personal brand equity, 188–189
Personal branding, 181
Personal brand loyalty, 189–190
Personalisation, 289
Personal sponsorship, 93
Philanthropic, 84
Physical product brands, 60
Physical Tracking and Live Rendering, 238
Positioning, 287–289
Positron emission tomography (PET), 256
Product, Price, Placement, and Promotion, 187
Professional sport, 103
Professional tournaments, 105
Promotions mix, 5
Psychographic segmentation, 152
Psychological models, 285
Purchase, 290–292

R

Recapitalisation policy, 61
Relational content, 131
Remunerative content, 132
Risk factors, 150–151

S

Sales promotion tools, 21
Self-awareness, 181
Self-branding, 185
Self-efficacy and Perceived Behavioural Control, 160–161
Self-esteem, 181
Self-identity, 159–161
Social and economic growth, 3
Social and emotional values, 8
Social media, 121
Social Media Marketing (SMM), 293
Spanish fashion retail chain, 286
Spatial brand avoidance, 66
Sponsoring brand, 87
Sponsorship, 84
The Standard Bank Group's pan-African, 92
Story, 191
Strategic and financial approaches, 283
Sustainable development, 48, 54
Sustainable Development Goals, 24

T

Tangible and intangible components, 60
Technological advancements, 7
Tourism Malaysia's, 24
Tourism Marketing Strategy, 21
Tourists plan, 24
Traditional communications, 123
Traditional media, 230
Transcranial magnetic stimulator (TMS), 256
Tusker Project Fame, 85
Twitter, 297

U

Unhealthy lifestyle, 147, 150

V

Value proposition, 191
Video marketing, 293
Virtual reality (VR), 231, 255
Visibility, 186
VR In-Game Advertising (IGA), 239

W

Website Marketing, 293
Word-of-mouth, 282
Working memory, 210, 213–214
World Travel and Tourism Council (WTTC), 34

Y

YouTube, 297